Revised Edition

A THIRD GREAT DISAPPOINTMENT REMNANT?

A historical-theological exposition on the racial/ethnic divides of the Seventh-day Adventist Church

CANUTE BIRCH

20 Twenty
Literary Group

ISBN
978-1-962868-65-5 (Paperback)
978-1-962868-66-2 (eBook)
978-1-962868-64-8 (Hardcover)

TABLE OF CONTENTS

ACKNOWLEDGEMENTS

The upbringing that I had continues to shape my attitude toward life, peoples, and cultures. I am forever indebted to my godly parents, who raised me as a Seventh-day Adventist Christian, which gives me the perspective on life that is evident in this study. I deeply appreciate the dedication which they exhibited in raising my eight siblings and me in the best way they knew. To my father, the consummate disciplinarian, the late Isaac Robert Birch and my recently deceased mother, the ever-caring Minette Louise Birch, I say many thanks.

The McKee library served as an invaluable resource for information in this research. I am thankful to the library staff, which assisted me in locating numerous sources and accommodated my long hours on the computers. I appreciate the interest shown by my friends in this study and the insight gained from our dialogs on this topic. I am profoundly grateful to Greg Rumsey for his insightful pointers which helped me to strengthen this study. I found it very encouraging. My wife, Lorna; my three children, Alexa, Dorian, and Canute II, have been extremely patient with me during my long hours at the library and on the computer at home. I thank them profusely. And most importantly, to God, who teaches us all to love one another, who also assists us in our efforts to become **one**; I am thankful.

INTRODUCTION

No person, denomination, or movement originates or exists in a cultural or religious vacuum. The Seventh-day Adventist Church (hereinafter SDAC or Adventist Church) was birthed by the Millerite Movement in the social-religious context of Evangelical Protestantism. The Millerites were Evangelical Christians and the message of the Millerite Movement was essentially Evangelical. Thus the SDAC is Evangelical (Koranteng-Pipim, 1997).

Recent research shows that Evangelical Christians, by their domiciliary isolation in suburban neighborhoods, their 90 percent affiliation with homogeneous churches, and social interaction primarily with people of their own race/ethnicity, are helping to perpetuate racism and poverty in America even while desiring to end it (Emerson and Smith, 2000; Williams and Collins, 2004). The overwhelming majority of Evangelicals in the US are White. While the early SDAC did not adopt all the teachings of the Evangelicals or those of the Millerite movement in toto, its basic tenets are similar, with the exception of a few distinctive doctrines. And it appears that like other churches in Evangelicalism in the United States (US), more than 90 percent of SDAC congregations in the US are over 80 percent homogeneous. This happens as a result of the "cultural tool kit" which White Evangelicals bring to the marketplace of religion (Emerson and Smith, 2000).

This semblance of beliefs, coupled with the similarity in demographics, help to account for some of the SDAC's positions on social issues, although most Adventists would quickly retort that the SDAC acts independently of other Protestant denominations. They would point to its refusal to be a part of the National Association of

Evangelicals; its detachment from US politics, and its adherence to one creed only: the Bible. And that is factual, except that on the matter of slavery the Adventist Church was officially silent while abolitionist and anti-abolitionist Evangelicals were outspoken on either side of the issue and despite the fact that some of its pioneers were quite forthright in their stance against it. Yet in the area of Black-White relations, the nineteenth century SDAC acted just like the other Evangelicals and against the biblical position. Meanwhile it remains hesitant to move toward racial/ethnic reconciliation even though the other Evangelical denominations have been doing so. This study highlights the racial/ethnic divide in the Adventist Church, examines the SDAC in its social-religious context as an Evangelical movement, and presents some practical historical-theological arguments in hopes of assisting us in moving purposefully toward reconciliation.

Throughout its late medieval and modern history, the US was a republic of movements. "Reform movements sprung up nearly everywhere" (Land, 1998). This great nation which was conceived in liberty (Kyle, 2006) has several Rights that have always allowed for "movements" of all sorts: some popular, some not so popular; some political or apolitical, others religious, but each having its own following. One of these, the Millerites, was not to go unnoticed in the early 1900s as these religious enthusiasts held meetings all over the Midwest, New England, Northeast, and wherever else they could. With gripping exactness, unmistakable conviction, and fierce determination, they convened meetings in homes, rented halls, and under huge tents. Their message of the imminent return of Jesus resonated with so many who had escaped the religious persecution and spiritual apathy of Europe (Noll, 2003) and were now themselves getting spiritually lukewarm and jaded by the rampant spiritualism and the evolving modernism of the early nineteenth century.

Not unlike any notable movement, the Millerite Movement had a large following. It Began around 1839 (Schwarz, 1979; White, *Vol. 1*, 1948) and by the time of its Great Disappointment in 1844, the Millerite

Movement had attracted over 100,000 followers worldwide from all walks of life. After starting out as a small and insignificant prophetic movement, it grew to become a charismatic revivalist movement to reckon with, attracting members from mainline denominations such as the Baptist, Methodist, and Congregationalist churches. Crowds of up to 4,000 people were known to turn out to listen to the stunning prophetic messages of the pioneers of this advent Movement.

The pursuit of this study starts there. The question: "Do Adventists in the US have the spiritual infrastructure to handle the inescapable racial and ethnic dynamic which is at play in the church, which results in the perpetuation of the current structural divides at the local conference level in the NAD? This quest begins with a peek into the energizing, scintillating, stupendous evangelistic campaign of the Millerite Movement and the historical setting in which the Millerites prepared Western society for their Lord's return. It ends with the pitiful state of the remnant, who feel confident that their lifestyle reflects readiness to meet their Lord, but some of whom will probably hear him say upon his return—"Depart from me; you who did not reconcile with me" (Mt. 7: 23; *my paraphrase*).

I maintain that remnant believers are made of sterner stuff than is observable in the cowardice of American Adventists, who apparently shiver at the thought of seriously approaching the subject of our divides or engaging each other on it, due to their fragile if impotent faith.

This study is a bold, fiercely candid, and comprehensive examination of the elements that pertain to this issue. It is divided into three major parts. Each part is divided among several chapters. In the first part, which covers three chapters, the study examines the historical setting of the un-reconciled races in early America. It begins with a peek at the New World, just before the arrival of the Mayflower, and moves to the formation and early missionary activities of the Seventh-day Adventist Church (SDAC). Part 2 focuses on the un-reconcilable Christians in Christendom on the American landscape and their practice of racial segregation in the Evangelical movement in the US. History points to the culpability of the SDAC (Baker, 1996). Finally, Part 3 examines Jesus' prayer for unity among his disciples in Jn. 17:20-22, in light of the challenges facing the reconciled remnant.

In Chapter 1 the study offers a historical overview of the Millerite Movement in order to establish the historicity of the Great Disappointment and help the reader to understand it in its historical context. The Great Awakening was the period in which they sounded "The Midnight Cry;" a campaign message (Burchfield, 1996), which was significantly aided by the use of publications such as *The Midnight Cry* and the *Advent Herald*. The Great Disappointment occurred because these early Adventists erred. They erred in their interpretation of the event that would take place in 1844 based on the time prophecy of Dan. 8:14. They erred in setting dates for Jesus' return. The result of their errors was the embarrassing and bitter great disappointment. Chapter 2 examines how this disappointed Movement disintegrated and how one of its splinter groups ultimately gave rise to the Seventh-day Adventist Church. It also focuses on the scriptural basis for the concept of the remnant, on who comprise the remnant, and how the SDAC fits the description of the remnant.

Chapter 3 highlights the research which indicates that Evangelical Whites perceive Blacks in a similar light as the larger White population. It looks briefly at the Church's role in slavery and the schisms that resulted from their resoluteness to maintain the heinous system. Of interest here is the notion that Evangelical Whites generally think that Blacks should get over the notion that they were denigrated, debilitated, and dehumanized by slavery and Jim Crow laws, and should proverbially "pull themselves up by their bootstraps." It remains factual that Evangelical churches are still the most segregated places in America on Sunday mornings. And on Saturdays, the SDAC is the culprit. The chapter also deals with the fact that the Seventh-day Adventist Church is an Evangelical denomination with some distinct and unique doctrines, but just as probable, even more segregated than other mainline Evangelical denominations.

In times of crises, American Evangelicals abandon their faith for their race and its attendant privileges. The Evangelical movement in the US aided and abetted the civil authorities in institutionalizing racism since its inception in the US. Slavery was just one manifestation of their racist ideology that was baptized in an unbiblical theology and marketed to its victims as gospel. Even amid violent opposition, the Evangelical perpetrators of this evil system were adamant in maintaining it and fought tooth and nail to do so because it benefited them greatly. The Baptist Church rent asunder over slavery, as did several other denominations. Baptists, who were determined to continue owning slaves, together with their supporters, formed the Southern Baptist Convention in 1845 (Emerson and Smith, 2000). During Reconstruction and beyond, the Evangelical movement engaged in religious *Apartheid*. Until the present, the Southern Baptist Convention (SBC) is still the most segregated denomination and most resistant to integration of the Protestant denominations in America (Rosenberg, 1989). As benefactors of the resultant inequities, the White members of the evangelical movement, to this day, generally do not see any systemic injustice in the distribution of America's wealth and the prejudicial enforcement of its laws, and are more prone to label minorities as lazy, indolent people, just waiting for hand-outs from the government. Besides, how Christian are Christians who ignore the plight of their fellowmen "and say, 'if we had lived in the days of our fathers, we would not have been partakers with them in the blood of the prophets [slaves]'" (Mt. 23:30; NKJV)?

Throughout Chapter 4 the argument is laid out for the Second Great Disappointment of the SDAC. It deals with the facts of the second great disappointment: segregated governance, segregated worship; the nine regional conferences that were organized and the growth they have experienced since their organization. It also addresses the attrition that resulted from this segregation in the early 1900s and the attrition that is being caused presently. It is a view rooted in the observation that the Church had the opportunity to engage the prevailing culture of the twentieth century; that is, White racism and economic domination, but it failed; it disappointed God, our forebears, and those who have to live with the legacy of such oppression. In 1944 the Adventist Church in the US voted the segregated governance structure that remains to this day (Baker, 1996). And today, although the error of the decision to segregate into separate churches and all its ill effects can be clearly seen, as pointed out by Ellen White then, it remains unchanged. There is a reluctance to change it. There is reluctance on the part of Blacks and Whites, the two main factions. Consequently, this dampens our efforts to promote an atmosphere of genuine love and unity among the remnant. This is more disappointing.

In Chapter 5 the prayer of Jesus in Jn. 17:20-21 is carefully examined in its context. The study exposes what Jesus wants for his disciples and how he expects us as twenty-first century disciples to live among each other. Oneness does not suggest a change of who we are by race or ethnicity. Rather, it minimizes and relativizes that identity in the face of our transcendent identity in Christ, that is, we are Christians. As a remnant people we become a part of Christ's One New Humanity. We are, therefore, Christians first and every other identity after. Our identity in Christ becomes preeminent and transcendent. For this reason we should be able to get along: be governed by each other and worship and fellowship freely together. The chapter examines the reasons that are militating against our coming together as one. The study examines the historic challenges that surrounded the decision to adapt the segregated governance structure that now exists in the NAD. It focuses mainly on the ethnic challenges of the church going forward and issues a call for reconciliation among us irrespective of these challenges.

Chapter 6 posits that although Seventh-day Adventists have the right doctrines and do many good things, unless we learn to love one another and live as such, we may face a third great disappointment. This chapter presents a word of caution to the remnant Church regarding the Third Great Disappointment which many within it will face because of their unwillingness to reconcile with God and with fellow men. It then goes on to summarize all the main points of the study and makes a conclusion. Our lack of love and neighborliness may cause many among us to miss the opportunity to be among the saints who will be translated at Jesus' coming or be resurrected to meet him; for Christ will say to those who fail to love--"I never knew you..." Like the first Great Disappointment, this final Great Disappointment will be bitter. The disappointed will weep and wail, much more than those in the first Disappointment.

Chapter 7 looks at the biblical use of reconciliation as a Christian moral imperative. Arguments are advanced for reconciliation as the theme of the Bible and the need for it to be the primary occupation of believers. The "ministry of reconciliation" is the only ministry that was explicitly enjoined on all the disciples of Christ (2 Cor. 5:18, NIV).

The study further seeks to establish a biblical theology of reconciliation. That the need for reconciliation is urgent is a point that is missed by many well-meaning Adventists, who typically shove the subject aside, saying that "The Lord will fix it in His own good time." It is argued in this chapter that reconciliation is the essence of Christianity and that it is warranted that we find a way to get along. The ministry of reconciliation is the sum total of the gospel message and the Great Commission. The very call to become a disciple of Christ is a call to reconcile with God and the Great Commission must be understood as a charge to believers to reconcile with fellow believers and a charge to call others to be reconciled with God and each other. Acceptance of this call enjoins on each disciple of Christ the need to reconcile with his neighbor.

Reconciliation entails bridge-building and that is the focus of Chapter 8. Christ made it clear to his disciples that their neighbor was that person, any person, who needed their help. Things happen in the daily operation of life to cause rifts and schisms, but just as Christ built a bridge between us and God, he provides the means to bridge the chasm between races and ethnic groups. This may be done by practicalizing some of the simple things that Christ did in his life and ministry: love, forgive, interact, and so on. In chapter 8 the study makes some recommendations to the Church for serious consideration as we prepare for the coming of Christ. The recommendations include a call for a resolution by the world church at its next General Conference (GC) session in 2015. This study in its entirety presents the rationale for the proposed resolution.

Chapter 9 presents a new paradigm of governance. It is a united governance structure for conferences based on the Southern Africa Union Conference model and a local church model that is modeled after the New Testament church of Antioch. This will require a total reconfiguration of the present White (state) and Black (regional) conferences in the NAD.

The study concludes in chapter 10 by summarizing all the major points of the preceding chapters and by synthesizing them to accentuate the need for urgent action by the leaders of the SDAC. The NAD did not act alone in creating this behemoth in the church; it was the official decision of the General Conference (GC). The current leadership, therefore, cannot like others before, justifiably push the problem aside and say it is the responsibility of the NAD alone. The two organizations should work together in fixing it as they did in creating it!

Presently, the palpable presence of systemic racism in every facet of the American society is as it was throughout its formation and history, only in more covert forms. It is no less evident in the wider Christian church and very noticeable in the SDAC. Richard Rothstein, in his seminal title The Color of Law, has unearthed a plethora of evidence to this end as it pertains to the former. Perhaps Rothstein's single most disturbing and discomforting finding is the extent to which the Christian clergy was involved in perpetrating the dastardly practice of de jure segregation (Rothstein, 2017). And sadly, it continues in more subtle ways presently.

It has been approximately one hundred and fifty years since the SDAC was formed. The number of Adventist minority members was insignificant in 1863. Presently in the US, however, we have approximately 250,000 minorities as members of the regional conferences (NAD statistics, 2010), not including another huge number who hold membership in state conferences. Yet we still do not get along. Local churches are essentially segregated, local conferences are segregated, our educational and health institutions are essentially homogeneous with only token minorities and we seem complacent in maintaining this segregation. We still find that whenever a White congregation is infiltrated by minorities and the percentage of minorities gets to a certain percentage of the congregation, we still experience "White flight." Yet we all plan to go to the same heaven. But "why can't we all just get along?"

The racial/ethnic segregation in the North American Division (NAD) of the SDAC is not unique to this denomination. During slavery, the Methodists, the Episcopalians, the Baptists and other mainline Protestant denominations divided over the issue and though some have moved toward reconciliation, many have still not reconciled. The impact of slavery was not lost on the SDAC and while we did not take any official position in support of the heinous institution, we allowed ourselves to be molded into the socio-cultural mores of racial segregation. The perpetuation of this segregation for decades has done and continues to do much damage to the image of the denomination and to countless people, members and non-members, who correctly view it as diabolical. As a consequence and in addition to other factors, the NAD is experiencing stunted growth.

US attorney General, Eric Holder, in a recent televised speech in honor of Black History Month, referred to Americans as "essentially a nation of cowards." He noted that though we proudly think of this nation as an ethnic melting pot, we are afraid to talk to each other about the race problem that troubles us (Thomas and Ryan, 2009). The purpose of this study is to challenge all of us as Seventh-day Adventists in the US to live according to the creed which we hold. Our (SDAC) only creed is the Word of God. God's Word exhorts us to love one another as Christ has loved us. And when we do each other wrong, the Spirit of God woos us to reconcile. For too long the racial tension between Blacks and Whites has plagued the church, yet neither Black nor White Adventist officials in the US are publicly calling for reconciliation among the members of the races/ethnicities in its membership. This has resulted in significant attrition and may be one of the underlying factors for well over fifty percent of our adolescents and young adults leaving the church nationwide before age twenty five. Could it be that they are seeing through our hypocrisy?

Meanwhile, we operate an organization of segregated governance that oversees local churches which are over 90 percent homogeneous. "White flight" from previously White congregations in which the percentage of African Americans is approaching thirty percent and "Black flight" from church-owned educational and health institutions which are traditionally White due to a sense of being merely tolerated, are the present reality. This is unbecoming of the church which bears the testimony of Jesus and professes to keep the commandments of God. Love, the essence of these commandments, is sadly lacking. Racial and ethnic reconciliation is the current and arguably the most urgent need of the remnant church in the US.

Over the last decade, the US has experienced significant racial tensions. As if to make sure that this never happens again, since the end of the presidency of the US's first non-White president, Barack Obama, a vociferous, if militant populist movement, apparently founded and funded by Evangelicals, has all but upended the nation. Resulting from the overt pandering of the reality star turned political figure and, at the time of this writing, past president of the United States, President Donald Trump, many apparently once closeted Jesus-professing, US flag-bearing, White Evangelical supremacists, have been emboldened to put their bigotry on full display before the nation and the world. Swaths of social media and a plethora of private websites have flooded the internet with racist rhetoric, intent on furthering their agenda to "Make America Great Again" by marginalizing minorities and maligning members of the immigrant communities, and self-confessedly all in the name of Jesus.

Upon the election of Barack Obama as US President, many Americans began to voice the notion of a post-race era in the US. Pundits and academics (Hollinger, 2011; Russinello, 2016; Tosolt, 2010) alike posited that we were approaching the beginning of a colorless society, as Obama received overwhelming support from White Americans, particularly educated White female suburbanites, which accounted for 76.3% (Pew Research Center, 2009). To the surprise and chagrin of many, however, race relations in the US have worsened since President Obama took office in January 2009. This according to a CNN poll that showed 54%supportiing this position (Agiesta, 2016). And his election resulted in a political backlash during the Trump presidency and its aftermath.

In a June 2023 Public Agenda USA Today poll, Audrey C. Price reports that the common belief among Americans is that racial issues divide Americans, but people of faith can help unite us. She contends further,

> As a public theologian and cultural critic who identifies as a Black woman, I glean hope from this data. Americans of every faith tradition can confront structural racism and its historical and ongoing harm to our society. They need a lens allowing them to see the problems clearly and the power to resolve them (Price, 2023).

This finding gives a glimmer of hope to those who desire to change the status quo. Yet it will take much effort to realize this goal. Meanwhile from Sunday to Sunday and Sabbath to Sabbath, Evangelicals nationwide turn out to church in mostly segregated congregations.

Most Americans identify as Evangelical Protestants. Among them, Whites make up the majority at 76%, Latinos 11%, blacks 6%, and Asians 2%, according to the latest report by the Pew Research Center (Pew Research Center, 2023).

Based on a 2014 finding, the population of the US is growing more ethnically diverse. The Seventh-day Adventist Church remains the most ethnically diverse religious group with Muslim in second place (LIPKA, 2023). This racial diversity was further reflected in local congregations between 1998 and 2019. Dougherty, et al affirms—

> There are more congregations in which no one racial or ethnic group comprises more than 80 percent of the people, congregations' average diversity level has increased, and the percentage of all-White congregations has declined (Kevin D. Dougherty, 2020).

PART 1

We Did Not Get Along

The Unreconciled

The Black/White racial divide has characterized the US since the introduction of Africans as indentured servants in 1619.

"But now in Christ Jesus ye who sometimes were far off are made nigh by the blood of Christ"—Eph. 2:13 (NIV)

1

The Millerite Movement and the First Great Disappointment of the Remnant in 1844

The Backdrop: ABrief Overview of American History from the 17th to the 19th Century

At the time of its inception, the Millerite Movement was not homogenous. While it was predominantly White, and there is no extant account of anyone among them who identified as Native Indian, there were Blacks in the Movement. In fact, we know of the presence of several Black ministers of the Movement. In addition to the famous William Foy and Frederick Douglas, other Millerite Black ministers were William Watkins, John W. Lewis, and Charles W. Bowles (Baker, 2018), and William Still (Baker, blacksdahistory.org, 2)

> Despite the reality that the vast majority of African Americans were enslaved during the entire Millerite Movement (1831-1844), and there was only a paucity of blacks in New England where the movement was the largest, there was a sizable contingent of black Millerites (Baker, 2018).

The segregation that existed in the US during the early years of the Millerite Movement, as well as other historical factors, provide the backdrop to the time in which the Movement developed. Of necessity, this study warrants the setting forth of that backdrop in order to provide a clearer picture of what shaped the new Movement and later the SDAC. Pursuant to this study, this author will show how the prevailing culture of modern America influenced the SDAC, as it did the Evangelical movement and is therefore culpable for the current racial/ethnic divides. Of note also is the fact that the same "midnight cry" of the Millerites as depicted in Jesus' parable (Mt. 25:1-18) will be actuated just before the second advent of the Christ.

The SDA Church did not evolve out of a religious-cultural vacuum. Frankly, it was steeped in its contemporary religious culture. Several marks of its religious-cultural milieu are evident in its origin, doctrines, mission, message, and polity. Yet it must be understood that religious, cultural, or social norms and mores do not justify systemic evil or absolve organizations, religious or other, of wrongdoing. One wonders to what extent this legacy impacts the current disposition of the Church. The facts will speak for themselves in the pages below.

In the 1700s America began to develop its reputation as the land of religious freedom. Occupied by Europeans of Anglo-Saxon origin, they had an extraordinary crave for freedom.

> "Both the English and the Americans believed that their ancestors had devised free political institutions over a thousand years before in England, and that even earlier a spirit of freedom had existed in the woods of Germany among the peoples from whom the Anglo-Saxons descended" (Horsman, 1981).

Thomas Jefferson and his contemporaries explained this phenomenon as coming out of the "Enlightenment view of a general human capacity for progress" (Horsman, 1981). This freedom entailed free thinking and a generally free lifestyle or individualism (Tocqueville, 2009; Noll, 2003). In their minds, this freedom was apparently a mandate to oppress and annihilate, as is evidenced by the destruction wrought on the Native Indians first and later the Africans.

The nineteenth century Anglo-Saxon freedom-thinkers (Noll, 2003; Kyle, 2006) thought of themselves as the superior race. They theorized that they could make the world a better place by shaping it according to their desires. Horsman affirms, "There was a firm and increasing belief that what was good for the Anglo-Saxons was good for the world" (Horsman, 1981). Thus the British sought to regenerate the world. This intent was observable as they continued along the lines of the early march of Aryan tribesmen at the dawn of history. Pursuant to this philosophy, Benjamin Disraeli reflects—

> "A Saxon race, protected by an insular position, has stamped its diligent and methodic character on the century. And when a superior race, with a superior idea to work and order, advances, its state will be progressive... All is race; there is no other truth" (Horsman, 1981).

The US became fertile ground for this new Teutonism (belief in the supposed racial superiority of the Teutons, especially of the Germans) as this ideology of continental, hemispheric, and world destiny for the chosen people of this race melded with a variety of other European themes (Horsman, 1981). They believed in hierarchy of the races. Nineteenth century anthropologists, Georges Cuvier, Samuel Morton, and Josiah Nott (also a physician), were the chief proponents of the view and contributed greatly to the hatred of Negroes by their shaping of the intellectual thinking on the hierarchy of the races (Pollard, 2000).

Leslie Pollard notes that the prevailing view among ethnologists was that in this hierarchy, the Caucasians were permanently at the top of a pyramid of intelligence and capability and Negroes at the bottom (2000). They and others provided science to offer confident explanations for the enslavement of Africans, while other theories explained the extermination of Native Indians (Horsman, 1981). Pollard posits that scientific racism joined in unholy matrimony with legal codification in an 1857 High Court ruling to render Negroes inferior without any protection under the law. This prevailing view became socially acceptable especially in light of the economic pressures and growing demand for cheap labor. The Negroes, because of their perceived inferior intellect, were identified as being particularly suited for the menial labor (2000).

The early nineteenth century Frenchman, Tocqueville, while touring America for the French government observed—

> Considering what happens in the world, it seems that Europeans are to men of other races what human beings are to animals. They use them to serve themselves, and when they do not submit, destroy them" (Tocqueville, 2009).

The Blacks, who were brought to America for slave labor, were concentrated in the South. Three quarters of Blacks lived south of the Mason-Dixon Line (along the Pennsylvania-Maryland border) until after World War II (Thernstrom and Thernstrom, 1997). Tocqueville observed that those who were in the North were merely tolerated by the northerners, who preferred freed slaves to remain in the South. Even the dedicated White abolitionists loved the Negroes only at a distance. There were over four million Blacks in the South while only 250,000 were in the North. The plantation owners in the South depended on them for labor (Dattel, 2009).

The importation of Africans as slaves began in 1619 when the first indentured servants were delivered in Jamestown, Virginia by a Dutch ship. They continued to import Africans as slaves until it was outlawed in 1808. But the Emancipation Proclamation was not to occur until the 1860s (Horsman, 1981).

After slavery, came Reconstruction, which did little to alleviate the plight of Blacks. With the advent of Reconstruction, the Yankees of the North celebrated the equality of Blacks and the inalienable rights of all humans, but the South remained unmoved by this development.

Southerners kept Blacks in check and harnessed every means to extract from them maximum labor for minimum compensation, as they sought to retain control of every aspect of their lives (Tocqueville, 2009). Reconstruction ended in 1877, but the agony of Blacks continued. "Breaking bread with Whites was another 'ordinary symbol of respect' denied to Blacks," in addition to the denigrating pejoratives that White folk used as "badges of inferiority" for Blacks (Thernstrom and Thernstrom, 1997).

Essentially, Blacks were treated with indignity and regarded just as animals of a lower species. Besides the sheer reality of man's inhumanity to man, it is more startling to think that all this was done under the guise of religion by Evangelical Christians. This negative history remains a sore spot in the relations of Blacks and Whites in the US.

Religious Climate in the US- Rejecting the dogmas of established churches in Europe, religious dissidents flocked the shores of the US, spawning numerous sects all over the country (Horsman, 1981). The German Community of the Woman in the Wilderness, The Pilgrim Fathers, the Rapites, the Separatists of Zoar, and the Amana Society were among them. Later on during the early 1900s several revivalists traversed the religious landscape of the US. Most notable among them were Jemima Wilkinson, later the self-styled "Universal Friend," "Mother" Ann Lee Stanley (British-American founder of "the Shakers"), Joseph Smith (founder of the Mormons), and others, most of whom dabbled to one degree or another in spiritualism (Gaustad, 1974; Horowitz, 2009; Schwarz, 1979). This renaissance in Western society served as a call to action for Baptists, Congregationalist, Methodists, and other established denominations (Dick, 1994). From among the Baptists a dynamic leader, William Miller arose and would gain much attention for his interpretation of the prophecies and his proclamation of the imminent return of Jesus.

William Miller- Gaustad observes that much like today, in the nineteenth century, Miller (Grand Master), and other members of the Christian churches were active in Masonic lodges and other secret societies that had begun taking root in the US by the late 1700s (Kah, 1996; Horowitz, 2009). William Miller, born February 15, 1782 in Pittsfield, Massachusetts, the eldest of sixteen children, was taught to read by his mother, then as a young man, developed a strong intellect and read widely. By using the libraries of numerous men of stature in his town, Miller got his exposure to the works of Voltaire, Hume, Paine, and other deistic philosophers. He soon became a Deist adherent (White, 1875; Wellcome, 1915; Knight, 1994).

In 1816 Miller converted from Deism to the Baptist Church (White, 1875; Wellcome, 1915) while still maintaining membership at a local Masonic lodge (Land, 1998; Burchfield, 1996). Following much criticism from his church for his involvement with the Masons, in a conciliatory move after fifteen years of membership with the Masons, Miller resigned from the local lodge in 1831 (Rowe, 2008).

The Great Awakening

"Awakening" suggests a "lull," "laze," or "sleep" had been occurring and from which some needed to be awakened. This was precisely the spiritual status quo in America which necessitated the Great Awakening. In this case, however, it was a spiritual sleep, which warranted a spiritual awakening. Yet it was not one continuous event; it had several episodes. The Puritan and Anglican Parish system of England had proven difficult to transplant in the New World. Consequently, with the few inhabitants spread over the vast territory in the US, many second and third generation Anglo-Saxons were un-churched. Those on the religious landscape lulled into spiritual decline from Northampton, Massachusetts to Jamestown, Virginia, only to be ignited by the spark of religious fervor from fired-up Christians, though not without opposition (Noll, 2003; Matthew, 1995).

Historians concur that there were two Great Awakenings at a minimum (Noll, 2003). By some accounts, the First Great Awakening was between the years 1730 and 1755 (Marsden, 2003; Noll, 2003; *Wikipedia*, 2010). One historian places its beginning in the 1730s and its end about 1770s (Heyrman, 2008). Other historians hold that it began earlier, in the 1720s (Emerson and Smith, 2000). Meanwhile, still others purport that it could be as early as early as 1679 when the sermons of Solomon Stoddart, caused a revival in New England (Matthews, 1995).

The timing of the second Great Awakening is also regularly misconstrued with local Congregational revivals in New England in the 1790s or the revival under Charles Grandison Finney in upstate New York in the 1820s, Noll argues. Noll contends further that it occurred in the 1780s in the South and rural New England (Noll, 2003). Kyle insists it ran from about 1800 to the 1830s (Kyle, 2006). For our purposes the precise period of these Great Awakenings is not critical, but that they occurred before Miller's movement suffices. They all preceded Millerism (1840s), or from all accounts the latter ran up until the time of the Millerite Movement in the early 1900s. Notwithstanding, it seems reasonable to conclude that both the first and second awakenings occurred in the late eighteenth to the early twentieth century. But unfortunately, none was interested in the plight of the Negro slaves or marginalized Native Indians and were negligible with respect to the scourge of racism in the US.

American religion was dominated by the Anglican Church in the 1800s. In some Southern states it was illegal for any worship or marriage services to be officiated over by anyone other than an Anglican clergy. The First Great Awakening which began in the 1720s and continued into the 1740s (Emerson and Smith, 2000) had only minimal impact on the South, the bedrock of racial hatred. It was concentrated mainly in New Jersey, Pennsylvania, and the New England colonies. Despite its failure to seriously impact the South, however, the Great Awakening was "one of the most influential religious movements in American history" (Boles, 1994). Evangelical Christians were on fire for their Lord, proclaiming his message of salvation with much fervor. It was this fervor (albeit devoid of any concern for the oppression of Blacks) that later propelled William Miller and the Millerite lecturers into action.

Sensing the urgency of their task, in the early 1840s, the Millerites set out to spread the Word of God like wild fire wherever they could convene their meetings. It was urgent! Both Miller (1826) and later, Ellen White (1844), saw in vision a path illuminated by light (Burchfield, 1996).

The gospel of Matthew chapter 25 records Jesus' parable of the ten virgins who were waiting for the Bridegroom. On this scriptural ground the Millerites found consolation that when the Lord's coming was announced as being near, there was a "tarrying time" connected with it (Mt. 25:5, 6; Hab. 2;1-3) The "tarrying time" of the Great Awakening was likened to the waiting period before the bridegroom of the parable came (Loughborough, 1905).

After the first disappointment in the spring of that year, *The Midnight Cry* carried an article on May 9, 1844 in which the Millerites contended, "We believe that we are occupying that period spoken of by our Savior, when the bridegroom tarries (Mt. 25:5). J. N. Loughborough affirms that the "tarrying time is likened to that period in which the evil servant said in his heart, 'My Lord delayeth his coming...'" While the parable states that the servants were abused by a fellow servant, this did not ignite a spirit of compassion for the Black slaves who were being beaten and oppressed before his very eyes. He further suggests, "The tarrying of the bridegroom must represent some disappointment on the part of those going forth expecting to meet their Lord" (1905). Hence the "tarrying time" was the time between the two disappointments (spring and autumn) of 1844. That is a period of six months: "the whole length of the 'tarrying time'" (Loughborough, 1905; Knight, 1993).

The Midnight Cry- The Midnight Cry was both a historic event and a religious publication. The periodical was first published in November 1842 by J. V. Himes. It was published in twenty-four numbers (Knight, 1994).

For two years, William Miller, engaging in systematic theology, painstakingly combed through the prophecy of Daniel 8:14, using a rationalistic approach to the text of Scripture. Miller developed fourteen principles for interpreting prophecy (White, 1875). Between 1816 and 1822 (Burchfield, 1996; Howell, 1935), Miller observed a link between the seventy weeks of Daniel 9 and the 2300 days/years of Daniel 8:14. He understood 457 B.C to be the starting point of both these prophecies (White, 1875). Consequently, he concluded that in twenty-five years Jesus would return to Earth. In 1833, without Miller's knowledge, his local Baptist church, voted him a preaching license (White, 1875; Schwarz, 1979).

Beginning around late 1831 (White, 1875), the farmer-turned-sensational preacher, William Miller, began preaching and printing his lectures. His first lecture was in his brother-in-law's (Hiram S. Guilford's) log house in August 1831 (Land, 1998). His spell-binding preaching persuaded thousands to surrender to Christ. It was a great awakening "such as had not been witnessed since the Reformation of the sixteenth century" (Branson, 1933). A little Methodist girl, Ellen Goulde Harmon was convicted also and later baptized (White, *Vol. 1*, 1948).

In Maine, people continued to crowd into homes and halls to hear the prophetic truths expounded. Joshua Himes joined Miller and went throughout the Midwest preaching this urgent message. Himes used his influence and printing press to assist Miller in covering a wider field. Himes reported 4,000 people gathering to hear Miller with "almost breathless attention" in Cincinnati (Hewitt, 1983). After word of her baptism reached her Methodist church, she and several others were disfellowshipped (White, *Vol. 1*, 1948; Knight, 1993; Land; 1998). Much of the Millerite preaching centered on "the midnight cry" in the parable of the bridegroom in Matthew 25 (Loughborough, 1905).

As the seventh day of the tenth month drew near many Millerites disposed of their earthly possessions. In New Hampshire, a follower referred to only by the name Hastings, left his potato field undug. When his anxious neighbors offered help to dig them, he replied, "No! I am going to let that field of potatoes preach my faith in the Lord's soon appearing." It was almost a total loss of the potato crop in New Hampshire that year as reported by the newspapers (Loughborough, 1905). One testimony claimed that some followers of Miller laid out thousands of dollars at the *Voice of Truth* publisher's desk on October 22, 1844 and begged in anguish for him to accept and use it in the work of advancing the proclamation of Christ's coming. But he refused it saying, "You are too late! We don't want your money now! We can't use it" (Loughborough, 1905)! Distressed and frustrated, the men took their money and declared that God had frowned upon them for their lack of faith (Dick, 1994). The "midnight cry" was an urgent call by Millerite lecturers as thousands sought to reconcile with God before it was too late to do so.

In August 1844, S.S. Snow preached a sermon in Exeter, Massachusetts, which was later published in *The True Midnight Cry*, Reading 14. That catapulted him into prominence in the Millerite Movement. In his sermon, Snow challenged the Millerite position of a spring 1844 fulfillment of the 2300 day/year prophecy but soon after concluded that Christ would come on the tenth day of the seventh month of 1844. He propounded that the sacrifices of the Old Testament were types and that Christ was the Antitype. Furthermore, "'those types which were to be observed in the seventh month have never yet had their fulfillment in the antitype.'" His conclusion was later corroborated by George Storrs (White, 1875; Knight, 1993; Dick, 1994).

William Miller's Interpretation of the Prophecies

Miller based his reasoning on the year-day principle of Num. 14:34 and Ezek. 4:6, in early 1843 and reached the conclusion that Christ would return during the Jewish year of March 21, 1843 to March 21, 1844. Miller's lectures were read and reviewed by eminent preachers and scholars of the day in New England, Dr. Josiah Litch (Methodist preacher) and Charles Fitch (Congregationalist preacher) and Joshua V. Himes (a New England Antislavery Society organizer) being among them. But most noteworthy is what Fitch wrote in a letter to Miller—"'I find nothing on which to rest a single doubt respecting the correctness of your views'" (Schwarz, 1979; Numbers and Butler, 1993; Dick, 1994).

Miller read where the prophet Daniel declares in Daniel 8:14—"He said to me, 'it will take 2,300 evenings and mornings; then the sanctuary will be re-consecrated'" (NIV). Miller observed also that the decree uttered by the king of Persia in 457 B.C. and recorded in Ezra 7, marked the beginning of the 2300 days/years prophecy. Since that period ended in either 1843 or 1844 (White, 1875), depending on what time of the year that decree went forth, the cleansing of the sanctuary would then be realized. It was later ascertained that the decree was given in the latter part of 457 B.C. (White, Vol. 1, 1948; Maxwell, 1994; Numbers and Butler, 1993). Obviously, Christ did not return in 1843, but the prophetic window spanned parts of the years 1843 and 1844.

When Christ did not return in 1843, the early Adventists took it as a test and kept on preaching the third angel's message of Revelation 14 (Howell, 1935). Scholars did not dispute it, scoffers would not disprove it, deists and infidels were convicted by it (Dick, 1994), the orthodox churches could not prevent it, but alas, October 22, 1844 passed and nothing happened. Jesus did not come. This was a great disappointment (White, *Vol. 1*, 1948).

The company of Adventists, many of whom had resigned their jobs, left crops un-harvested, ground provisions un-dug (Loughborough, 1905; Howell, 1935), and closed shops, were disappointed though not disoriented (*Daily Argus*, 1844). Devastated, they wept uncontrollably (Loughborough, 1933; Schwarz, 1984). The remnant had suffered its first Great Disappointment. People from various racial and ethnic backgrounds were a part of the Millerite Movement and some minorities made distinct contributions to it. We will now examine how the collaborative efforts of Whites and Blacks and benefited the mission of the Movement.

The Racial Composition of the Millerite Movement

By the time William Miller came on the scene, the Europeans and their descendants had overrun and marginalized the Indians as nonentities, sequestered the Africans on plantations, and created for themselves a land they could freely traverse. They had no sense of cultural relativism, thus they saw no value in the culture of those who occupied the region when they entered it. This attitude prevailed with their assumption that the transplanted European culture was superior (Horsman, 1967; Okholm, 1997). Miller and the overwhelming majority of his followers were of European descent, but not all.

The membership of the Millerite Movement was hardly a diverse racial group; it was predominantly White. Nevertheless, despite the racism in America during the early 1800s, the Spirit of God which captivated Miller and his followers appears to have neutralized their racial identity and brought their transcendent faith identity into focus. Thus many Blacks, moved by this message of an eschatological deliverance, came together with Whites all over New England and crowded into churches to hear the gospel of Jesus Christ. Before long the Millerites were collaborating across racial lines to call others to Christ.

Reynolds contends that while members of other denominations separated in disagreement over the question of slavery, the Adventist Church offered "a haven for those who had been objects of continual bigotry and discrimination." Besides, even predominantly White Seventh-day Adventist churches included people of color when they were organized (1984).

People of Anglo-Saxon Descent

Pilgrims from Europe came by the boatloads to America between 1700s to 1900s seeking religious freedom and economic prosperity in the New World. In 1607 the first group of 100 English men and boys landed in Jamestown, Virginia, with the hope of striking it rich.

Another group, having abandoned the Church of England, which they thought had come to resemble the Catholic Church too much and lived in Holland for twelve years, came on a different mission. These self-styled Pilgrims, sailed through much difficulty for 65 days on the Mayflower and arrived in Plymouth, Massachusetts on September 6, 1620 (Canada, 2001). Miller and his followers would later preach to their descendants during the 1830s and beyond. Hazen Foss, a gentleman of European descent, with "good education and a good speaker," was among them and received visions of the Holy City, similar to Foy's and White's, but did not relate them (Spalding, 1922; Baker, 1987).

People of African Descent

The importation of Negro Africans by White Americans throughout the seventeen hundreds was not the first time that Africans came to the continent. They came before Columbus. Two extant accounts of West African Maritime expeditions to the Americas in the 1300s show that the Mali emperor, Abubakari II attempted to discover the limits of the Atlantic. The first was in 1307 in which he sent 400 ships; the second was in 1312 on which he sent 2000. The *Journals* of Christopher Columbus is the only other known account of these voyages. In addition to the writings, linguistic, philological connections (similar-sounding words), evidence in the material culture (as in gold alloyed with copper), can be identified between the Mandinga language and that of the Americas. Countries such as Hispaniola, Panama, and parts of South America (Van Sertima, 1992) are among them. Dutch sailors dropped off Africans in 1444. By the time Columbus came, Africans were living in the US with the Indians and were called African-Indians (Bennett, 1987; Dudley, 1997).

In *We Have Tomorrow...* Louis B. Reynolds delineates the involvement of Blacks in the great awakening that transformed America in the 1830s. Many of those who heard the preaching of William Miller and became a part of the Millerite Movement were African descendants. Negroes flocked to camp meetings and other meeting places to hear his stirring messages, which brought to them hope for better times ahead amid the racial discrimination of their day (Reynolds, 1984; Knight, 1993). In a 1932 historical account of the Negro work in the US, Harold D. Singleton expressed uncertainty whether the "colored people," who converted to Adventism during the Great Awakening, continued with the Movement after the first Great Disappointment. Nevertheless, he affirmed that many were won through efforts held for whites and through the literature ministry (Baker, 1996).

African American Millerite Preachers- At least three men of African descent were among the Millerite preachers: John W. Lewis, of Providence; Charles Bowles, of Boston; and William Ellis Foy, of Portland, Maine. Also, Black females such as Phoebe Palmer, Lucy Maria Hersey, Olive Maria Rice, among several others, converted to Adventism and joined the ranks of preachers in the 1840s (Reynolds, 1984; Knight, 1993). Bowles preached effectively throughout the White congregations and by 1843 he had established several churches. Foy is the most renowned of the Millerite preachers of African descent.

William E. Foy- While believers were still grappling with the disappointment, Foy, a mulatto, or mixed-race Black man, received visions intended to stabilize them (Baker, 1987). Foy was convicted by the Advent message in 1835 and was received into the Freewill Baptist Church. After two disturbing visions in 1842, he joined the Millerites and became the first of three persons in the Advent Awakening to receive visions to strengthen the believers after the first Great Disappointment (Reynolds, 1984). Foy, dressed in robes of the Episcopal clergy, traveled widely, sharing the messages of his visions to congregations of various denominations, urging them to turn to God. But lacking sustenance he was forced to withdraw and resorted to manual labor in order to provide for his family. After three months, however, he felt compelled to continue at all odds and he resumed preaching the soon return of Jesus (Reynolds, 1984).

By the time of his death in 1893, Foy had received a total of three visions. Ellen White, in a 1912 interview, subsequent to her own vision which she related, indicated that upon speaking with Foy he told her that her account was a revelation of just what he had also seen (Reynolds, 1984). During this period, many Blacks were breaking ranks with their White churches in disgust with the prejudice they were facing. They began forming their own churches to cater to their spiritual needs. Foy's visions made it clear that God did not discriminate and served to generate faith that the Adventist Church, *"unlike other communions that were split over questions of slavery and segregation, offered a haven for those who had been objects of continual bigotry and discrimination"* (Reynolds, 1984).

Although Foy was initially opposed to the doctrine of Jesus' soon return, after the visions he joined the Millerites and preached it with a sense of great urgency. Foy initially sensed the need to declare his first vision to others but became unwilling to do so, citing he had not been instructed to relate them. But unable to rest peacefully, he committed it to print. Upon hearing this and in fear of publicity, the Millerites quickly fired criticisms at him and once again Foy became hesitant to relate his visions (Reynolds, 1984; Baker, 1987; Knight, 1993).

Foy's fear of criticism coupled with the existing prejudice toward people of color, caused him to become more hesitant, but only until he was invited by a local pastor to describe the visions to his congregation on February 6, 1842. While he spoke, the fear disappeared and he related the vision with confidence. Foy then began traveling widely, relating his visions as he preached the return of Jesus in 1844. Ellen Harmon recounted occasions on which she rode with her family on Foy's sled to his lectures in Portland, Maine, while she was still a little girl (Reynolds, 1984; Baker, *Unknown Prophet,* 1987; Dudley, *Vol. 1,* 1997).

Later, Ellen Harmon, who apparently had Colored roots (Dudley, 1995), and Hazen Foss, received similar visions to Foy's. Upon hearing her relate the first vision, he remarked that she had been given the revelations which he had earlier received in vision. Both John Loughborough and Ellen Harmon gave testimony that the Spirit of God had given revelations to Foy. It appears that up to the time of his death, Foy did not understand his third vision in which he was shown the developments in the Advent movement beyond 1844. Foy died in 1893 (Reynolds, 1984; Baker, 1996).

The Native Americans

No extant evidence suggests the involvement of Native Indians in the Millerite movement. Their rejection of the Anglo-Saxons who took their land, raped their women, deprived them of economic development, and marginalized them, was too great to allow them to heed "the Midnight Cry." They totally rejected the White culture and religion (Horsman, 1981).

The Native American Indian population was concentrated mainly in Arizona and New Mexico, which accounted for 54 percent of the Indian population in the early 1900s. As a group, the Native Indians were discriminated against, while, ironically, they were romanticized as "noble savages" (Land, 1987). Feeling terribly wronged and obviously robbed and neglected by the White ruling class, the aborigines crowded unto reservations in these parts, rejecting the White culture and religion and returning to their traditional heritage and traditions (Horsman, 1981).

One account suggests that Adventists "lumped the original Americans with foreigners" (Baker, 1995). An unnamed Chippewa couple was the first Native Indian convert to Adventism in the 1890s, while the first local church was organized among the Native Indians in 1897. For a while no inroads were made into Native Indian territory. It was not until about 1916 that Ono Follet, a White missionary, settled among the Navajos, acquiring their language, learning their culture, but after fourteen years in the highlands, he had to relocate to lower grounds for health reasons. Mr. and Mrs. Stahl picked up the work among the Navajos and later established a school for them at Holbrook. After several decades of work among them, some accepted the advent message, were baptized, and churches were raised up in Ontario, Michigan, Wisconsin, and elsewhere (Schwarz, 1979; Land, 1987).

The Disappointed Millerites

In the paragraphs below, careful note should be given to the nature of this disappointment and the way it was received by the expectant Millerites, as a portrait of the possible disappointment that many among the remnant will face at the second coming of Christ. Yet while the first disappointment and its effects were ephemeral, the third will be fatal and its effects eternal.

After the Great Disappointment, the Millerite Adventists were disappointed but not discouraged, heartbroken but not disheartened. An earlier account suggests that William Foy failed to give the message of his vision which would have helped the Adventist people during their time of disappointment (Spalding, 1922). Contrary to this account, however, Reynolds presents coercive evidence, as cited earlier, that Foy related his visions to several audiences with the exception of the last, which he could not recall (Reynolds, 1985). The Millerites remained confident that their understanding and calculation of the prophecy was correct and resumed their search of the Scriptures for an answer to their disappointment. After setting several subsequent dates in 1845, 1846, and 1847 (Schwarz, 1979), Miller and his followers soon received light from God that instead of the prophecy of Daniel 8:14 referring to the purifying of the earth, it was now plain that the prophecy pointed to the closing work of our High Priest in heaven, the finishing of the atonement, and the preparing of the people to abide the day of His coming (White, Vol. 1, 1948; Knight, 1993).

The newspapers in the Fall of 1844 reported the disappointment in several articles. The *Daily Argus* in the New England city of Portland, Maine, reported in an article entitled "The Miller Epoch," that October 22, 1844 was the day on which "Father Miller and Elder Hymes" expected the great catastrophe to come. In a "P. S." to that article, it read--"Millerites Rejoice!" It went on to note that the New York Evening Post of that day had reported that an old Jewish gentleman, an "unexceptionable authority," had informed them that the Jewish festival was ended according to Jewish computation; it being on the 22nd of September earlier that same year. It reported further,

> We trust that this statement will allay the apprehensions of those who have been driven to the verge of madness, by the audacious, not to say impious prognostications of Father Miller, Mr. Storrs and their co-adjutators.

> A custom house officer in New York has resigned his office in consequence of his belief that the world is to end tomorrow, the 22nd. There is no doubt but this man is sincere' "(NENA, *Daily Argus*, 1844).

The *New Hampshire Patriot* reported that in a letter to the Secretary of State in the week prior to October 22, 1844, Justice of the Peace, Wm. S. Hershey stated, "'I believe the Lord will come on this seventh month of this sacred year; therefore I do not wish to remain Justice of the Peace any longer.'" In another note sent to the Secretary of State in New Hampshire on Sep. 11th 1844, E. G. Colby wrote—

> 'Dear Sir - Enclosed is my commission as Justice of the Peace, which I have no further use for, believing as I do beyond a doubt that the Lord is coming on the 10th day of the seventh Jewish sacred month 1844' (*Daily Argus*, October 25, 1844).

In the days immediately following October 22, 1844, other articles continued to appear in the local newspapers. Some reported that insanity had set in and that Millerites were committing suicide (*Daily Argus*, October 25, 1844). The *Daily Argus* further carried an article from the *Boston Post* alluding to what it characterized as "public indignation" toward the leaders of the Movement, in particular, "Brother Hymes," for whom they thought it would be risky to make his whereabouts known. It reported that many followers of Miller had given up their livelihood as "contributions" to the Movement (*Daily Argus*, 1844). Thus it has been reliably established that the first great disappointment of the remnant occurred in 1844 as evidenced by newspaper articles of the day, by Miller and some of his followers, and by the pioneers of the SDAC.

Following the bitter disappointment, the tear-drenched, disappointed Millerites would not dare to leave their homes, but avoided the jeer and mockery of their neighbors by remaining inside. While they stayed indoors and wept, they also spent much time searching the Scriptures carefully as they sought to find out where they had erred (Arthur L. White, 1985). They soon ventured outside and began comforting and encouraging each other. Within days Himes resumed publication of the *Advent Herald* and *The Midnight Cry* through which he reassured fellow believers—"We have found the grace of God sufficient to sustain us, even at such a time." Miller himself offered a statement of encouragement in which he affirmed, "Although… twice disappointed, I am not yet cast down or discouraged." He declared further, "surrounded with enemies and scoffers, yet my mind is perfectly calm, and my hope in the coming of Christ is as strong as ever" (Schwarz, 1979).

Hiram Edson was, a Millerite follower received light on the morning following October 22, 1844, that the Sanctuary of the 2300 day/year prophecy was the heavenly one and that the High Priest had entered there for the first time to minister before he would return to Earth. A meeting was speedily called at Edson's home. After relating the revelation to them they left encouraged and renewed their efforts to search the Scriptures some more (Howell, 1935). By studying the book of Hebrews they later discovered that the "cleansing of the sanctuary" referred to the Christ's ministry in the Holy Place prior to 1844, but now he had moved into the Most Holy Place to continue His ministry there (Howell, 1935).

Shortly after the disappointment, Picklands and Enoch Jacobs resorted to fanaticism and started to promote "spiritual wifery." Miller and Himes countered the new beliefs and practices and purge them from among the followers of the Movement. The Albany Conference voted to reaffirm the traditional Millerite teachings with the omission of fixed dates (Knight, 1993; Schwarz, 1948). Arthur L. White affirms that in the latter years of Miller's life, no coherence remained among the fifty to one hundred thousand (1985) disenchanted members of his Movement. The Millerite movement disintegrated into several splinter groups.

Summary- The evangelistic fervor of William Miller and his followers undoubtedly caused a great awakening in the Northeast and Midwest but had little effect elsewhere. God raised up the Movement at a time when early America was in a state of spiritual decline, a lull. The movement had minimal diversity but was open to all who heard the message and responded positively to its call. A few African Americans participated in delivering messages while many others who were enjoying their newly-found freedom, were welcomed into the fellowship of the Movement, which, based on the evidence, had no hint of segregation.

Miller's calculations were correct, but both he and his followers erred in thinking that they could predict when Jesus will return to Earth. While Jesus was still with his disciples he informed them and us that "no one knows about that day or the hour, not even the angels..." when Jesus will return (Mt. 24:36, NIV). The Millerites were wrong to overlook that important instruction. Consequently they were bitterly disappointed when Jesus did not return on the dates they set. But they later realized their error, however, and refrained from further date-setting.

The remnant SDAC, conceived in heaven, was birthed by the Millerite Movement in the aftermath of the Great Disappointment. The Millerite lecturers of this era subsequently became pioneers of the remnant church. God raised up a special messenger (Ellen Goulde Harmon) to his last-day church from among the disappointed saints. Her messages helped to guide the church to its organization into a denomination, during its fledgling years, and will guide the remnant until Jesus returns. Both Ellen White and the pioneers of the SDAC denounced slavery as an evil system. Ellen White went as far as to aver that God used the Civil War to punish the US for the "high crime of slavery." She was totally against racism and although she supported segregated worship during her time, she did so in order to avoid endangering both Black and White since it would stir up the prejudice of the Whites. Her counsel was contingent on the prevailing conditions and has to be juxtaposed with her position that it was to be practiced only "until the Lord shows us a better way." She expressed remorse at the decision to segregate and affirmed that it was a mistake (White, *The Southern Work*, 1966). While she received no revelation regarding the first Great Disappointment prior to the event, if her counsel were heeded, the second Great Disappointment would have been avoided. Nevertheless this Great Disappointment was just the first, others were to follow. Besides the disappointments caused by date-setting the SDAC would later make a very disappointing decision that I will examine in a subsequent chapter as the second Great Disappointment of the remnant.

Throughout the Scriptures there are numerous references to the concept of a remnant. In perhaps all occurrences of the reference to the concept, those referred to are identified by God or God's messengers as such and God is the one who chose them. The idea of self-identifying as the remnant is a modern development. Strong's Exhaustive Concordance (keyed to the King James Version of the Bible) has sixty-two occurrences of this word in the Hebrew Old Testament Scriptures. Far fewer references occur in the New Testament. The next chapter explores how this concept has been interpreted by the Adventist Church and generally used by Adventists to self-identify as the remnant almost exclusively and typically to the exclusion of other Christians.

2

Formation of the Remnant Church: 1844-1944

The Christian Church has endured much since its birth in 1st century AD. Amid the persecution of that era it grew to become a worldwide religion, but was greatly traumatized during the severe onslaught of persecution by the Roman Catholic Church of the Dark Ages (White, *The Great Controversy*, 1971). Yet it endured and the Reformation was born out of this period of great tribulation. The French Revolution served as a startling reminder that an apostate church will not go unopposed for too long or last as the only representative of God, but God will rise up a people for himself from the ashes of apostasy.

The Pilgrims fled Europe to escape the persecution there and came with a determination to establish a new approach to the institution of the church. The freedom and individualism that characterized their approach to doing church led to emergence of the Evangelical movement, the Great Awakening, and the formation of many denominations. Among them, the Seventh-day Adventist Church stands out as one that continues to hold to the doctrine of the biblical Sabbath and other unique doctrines, which set it apart as the genuinely Protestant church of the Protestant churches that resulted from the Reformation.

The Concept of the Remnant

The concept of remnant is biblical. It is embedded in the Jewish religion. The Hebrew language renders it with the word *sar*, which is translated "remnant" in the English Bible. The Hebrew *sar*, means "what remains," "residue." The Septuagint translates it with *leipo*, "to leave behind;" *loipos*, "other," "the rest;" *leimma*, ""remnant;" also, *sozo*, "to save," "to preserve" (Rodriquez, 2009). Hasel contends that this word denotes "what is left after a catastrophe" (1972). He argues further that in the *eschaton* (last days) God's people is not national Israel or even a specific denomination, but those who trust and obey God (1972).

From the early years of the Millerite Movement, Adventists have appropriated the designation of the "remnant" as referenced in Rev. 12:17. Adventist apologists affirm—"When a person looks for…identifying marks of God's true people, he finds that there is only one Christian movement in all the world that fits…and that is the Seventh-day Adventist people" (Shuler, May 8, 1958; Teel, 1995). William Miller saw this movement as the last of the commandment-keeping people who have the testimony of Jesus (Numbers and Butler, 1987). Further, in reference to the SDA Church, while commenting on Rev. 14:6-12, J. L. Shuler averred--"God's threefold message is eventually to reach people everywhere and gather them into His remnant church" (May 15, 1958). Thus the early Adventists were not exclusivists, but a reconciled and reconciling body. They understood the remnant to be open to all who would keep God's commandments while possessing the testimony of Jesus.

The term "remnant" came into use among SDAs to designate the SDAC during its earliest years. It is not found in the Church's doctrines, but is discussed in the preparation of candidates for membership. The president of the worldwide SDAC, Elder Ted Wilson, recently reminded us of this fact in a recent article in the Adventist Review (2010). Remnant has the following attributes: it is ethical, prophetic, ecclesiastical, missiological, and eschatological. Yet none of these can take credit for the salvation of the remnant. Angel Rodriquez asserts that in Revelation as elsewhere in Scripture, the remnant is saved by the grace of God only, through the blood of the sacrificial Lamb (2009). Hence the Adventist use of the terminology does not preclude the admittance of people from other denominations in the remnant. Rodriquez posits further, "Adventists believe that the church is not essentially visible, but rather that it is a reality represented worldwide and inclusive of all nations, peoples, and tongues" (2009).

It is pointed out elsewhere that Rom. 11:5 alludes to an invisible remnant and Rev. 12:17 a visible remnant. The former (invisible) is represented by all of God's true children regardless of religious affiliation; the latter (visible) remnant did not become visible until after 1798. It was in the aftermath of the French Revolution that the church became recognizable as the 1) those who keep the commandments and 2) as those having the testimony of Jesus. Furthermore, Robert W. Olson propounds that while only the SDA Church meets this requirements of Rev. 12:17, "not all members of the visible remnant church will be saved" (1986).

Rev. 12:17 references the "remnant" of the seed of the woman (Church) against the dragon (Devil) was wrath. The early Adventist pioneers took this to refer to the commandment-keeping people who have "the testimony of Jesus Christ." In Rev. 19:10--"The testimony of Jesus Christ is the Spirit of Prophecy." They understood Paul to corroborate this understanding in 1 Cor. 1:5-7—"...even as the testimony of Christ was confirmed in you: so that ye come behind in no gift; waiting for the coming of our Lord Jesus Christ." SDAs have held since the earliest years of the Church's existence that this gift of the Spirit of Prophecy was manifested in Ellen White's work and writings (Branson, 1933). Ellen White also applies Rev. 12:17 to the "'remnant people of God,'" "'a remnant,'" and "'the true children of God.'" These designations pertain to those who are reconciled to God and are engaged in reconciling with each other. Ultimately they are keeping the commandments of God and espousing the testimony of Jesus (Rodriquez, 2009).

LaRondelle posits that the mission of the Christian Church was the mission of Israel, which it failed to carry out. God's covenant with Israel continued through the remnant even when he cursed and punished them (Deut. 27-28; Lev. 26). Thus the fulfillment of this mission in the Church rests on 1) the survival of a faithful remnant; 2) the fulfillment of the covenant promise in Jeremiah 31; 3) the promises of the life-giving Spirit of Ezek. 36-37. In the New Testament the apostolic Church saw itself as the replacement of ancient Israel (Mt. 21:43) and the recipient its promises (Rom. 9-11). Hence the territorial promises of Israel are universalized in the New Testament through the Spirit of Christ and on account of his sacrifice (1983). And the judgment of Jerusalem now becomes the distress and tribulation of the Church, his elect, all through the Christian era and until the time of the end. Faithfulness to God is possible only after reconciliation with God. The covenant and life-giving promises are given only to those who have reconciled to God.

The Bible's focus has never been on Israel as a historical nation, but on Israel as a covenant-keeping people, believing in and worshiping God. It must be understood further, that the blessings of the old covenant cannot be correctly applied unconditionally to the modern State of Israel; rather, these are transferred to the faithful remnant of God—the covenant-keeping people. Therefore, when salvation history climaxes and culminates in the *Parousia* (second coming of Christ), it does so not with Christ's rule confined to the State of Israel, but with Christ as Lord of the united (reconciled) universal Church (Rev. 1:7; Is. 40:5). The Church becomes Christ's messianic Israel, the domain of his rulership in the present world (Mt. 16:18; 13:41; Larondelle, 1983). In this state the remnant is one, united and unified in its mission: Jn. 17:20, 21—"...that all of them may be one..."

The founding of the remnant SDAC during the period of the 1860s did much to shape its doctrines and polity. The socio-cultural and socio-religious milieu of the era seriously impacted the church's decision on critically important social issues. Of the splinter groups of the Millerite Movement, the one that evolved into the SDAC was not by accident, but by divine arrangement. The SDAC is in essence Evangelical (Bloesch, 1978; Lake, 2003; 2010). Yet it does not subscribe to the Evangelical movement's practice of "engaged orthodoxy" (Emerson and Smith, 2000) among other approaches of the Evangelical movement to its larger society. It does not subscribe to several other common tenets of Evangelicals.

Gary Land asserts that since its formation the SDAC has wholly avoided all political discussions and social issues that would normally be classified as the "social gospel" (1998). In few instances only has the SDAC taken a public stance on social or political issues. During the Civil War it took a noncombatant position on the War and issued a statement of this position in a pamphlet (Schwarz, 1978). On the account of Roy Branson, Joseph Bates, James White and other sided with the abolitionists during slavery (1970). The evidence seems to suggest that all three abandoned the abolitionist movement shortly after becoming Adventists. Besides, their individual involvement does not suggest the official participation of the SDAC in social reform (Baker, 1996). Understand, however, John Wesley Taylor advances, that this social or political disengagement is not biblically enjoined on the chosen of God (2008).

As a remnant body we are admonished by biblical authors and characters to behave like salt. Just as salt is not a passive agent in that whenever it is added to a substance it alters the taste or changes the flavor. Christians are mobilized into social, even political activism by Christ's declaration--"you are the salt of the earth" (Mt. 5:13, KJV)… Salt is no good that is just left to lay around all by itself without making contact with any substance. S. S. Baker insists that for salt to be useful, effective, and impacting, it must be "sprinkled over or mingled with, or made to interpenetrate the substance it is to flavor or preserve" (1991). If the remnant would fulfill its divine calling, we must engage the culture. There must be cries from within our ranks against the evils of society. Jeremiah's prophetic diatribes are rife with this sort of proactive socially engaging agitation (Jer. 14). In the New Testament, Jesus serves as a prime exemplar (Mt. 23:13-29). It becomes the more urgent for the remnant to engage the culture when the purveyors of un-Christ like behavior or perpetrators of evil are within its ranks. How can they sit quietly under these circumstances?

The remnant Church has generally assumed a reactive rather than proactive posture in its response to social ills and spiritual deformity with a social dimension, while remaining aggressive in its evangelism. It is hoped, however, that despite the remnant's refusal to initiate the move toward reconciliation in the American society, now that the society has taken the lead toward racial/ethnic equality and in most of the country people seem amenable to racial/ethnic reconciliation, that we will advance deliberately toward realizing reconciliation within the remnant church in the very near future.

Splinter Groups of the Millerite Movement: 1844-1863

After the first Great Disappointment the Millerites lost momentum. Splintered and scattered by this trauma, the Millerite Movement disintegrated and fragmented and ceased to exist beyond 1844 to early 1845. Nevertheless the message of the movement remained intact. George Knight observes three distinct orientations resulting from this fragmentation (2005) each based on what position they held regarding the fulfillment of prophecy in October 1844.

Knight identifies the first orientation among two groups: the "shut door" Adventists, who believed that prophecy had been fulfilled in October 1844 and the "open door" Adventists, who denied a fulfillment and believed that the door of probation was still open as the first. The second were the "spiritualizers," a group which "offered a spiritual interpretation of the event of October 22" (2005). For the latter, the Millerite interpretation of both time and event of the prophecy was correct. Hence Christ had returned spiritually. The third orientation was that they were correct on the time but wrong on the event that occurred on October 22, 1844 (Schwarz, 1979).

The "Sabbath and Shut-Door" believers developed a series of doctrines that explained their disappointment in 1844. These were a group of laymen and minor advent lecturers, who were scattered across Maine, New Hampshire, Massachusetts, and western New York. Joseph Bates was the only one among them who had prominence in the Millerite Movement (Schwarz, 1979). Bates, a retired sea captain and a man of "remarkable faith," wrote the first Sabbath tract that was printed by Seventh-day Adventists (Howell, 1935). Although they had no coherence and only little interpersonal contact, yet through prayer, extensive Bible study, and, as they affirm-- divine encouragement, this group grew to become the largest body of the Adventists.

Ellen White said later on Sabbath, March 24, 1849... ,

> I was shown that the commandments of God and the testimony of Jesus Christ relating to the shut door could not be separated, and that the time for the commandments of God to shine out with all their importance, and for Gods people to be tried on the Sabbath truth, was when the door opened in the most holy place in the heavenly sanctuary, where the ark is, in which are contained the ten commandments. This door was not opened until the mediation of Jesus was finished in the holy place of the sanctuary in 1844. Then Jesus rose up and shut the door of the holy place, and opened the door into the most holy, and passed within the second veil, where He now stands by the ark and where the faith of Israel now reaches (*Early Writings*, 1882).

Sabbatarian Adventists- During the 1840s, the Sabbatarian Adventists, continued to meet regularly and developed fundamental beliefs based on biblical doctrines. They were not invited to the 1845 Albany Conference, but the group would later become organized as the Seventh-day Adventists in 1863 (Knight, 2005). They were initially opposed to organization, but later acquiesced in order to avoid sectarianism. Of the three others that continued to meet until 1852, one, the Evangelical Adventists, was in favor of developing a strong organizational church structure and by 1853 had organized into sectional conferences (Land, 1998). Joshua Himes, Sylvester Bliss, Josiah Litch, I. C. Wellcome, and Hales provided leadership for this group which was based in Boston

(Schwarz, 1979). While no Blacks were in the leadership during this period, evidence of any efforts to deny them participation in leadership is nonexistent.

From the inception of the first indigenous Christian religion to the US, the Christians agitated against slavery. "Sabbatarian Adventists inherited a strong antislavery perspective from the Christian Connection movement." Branson contends in a 1970 article in the *Review* that "Adventists were abolitionists at a time when most opponents of slavery were advocating other solutions" (April 9) James White, Joseph Bates and the Farnsworth family collaborated with other Christians with whom they had strong ties in fighting the injustices being done to the Black race. Joseph Bates worked with the abolitionists until the 1840s when he decided to dedicate all his time to the proclamation of Christ's soon return. Joshua Himes supported the abolitionist and lifelong friend, William Lloyd Garrison in the antislavery cause because he saw it as a way to advance the kingdom of God (Haloviak, 1999). Uriah Smith related the prophecy of Rev. 13:11 to the "White washed villain of many of the pulpits" supporting slavery in America (Branson, April 16, 1970).

William Kinkade, "a major theologian," and David McGahe, also a Christian minister, worked to keep slavery out of the constitution of Illinois. They served lengthy period in the Illinois legislature. Kinkade affirmed--"The 'Christian' reading of this prophecy stressed an activist position. Make the world better by abolishing slavery." Kinkade and others studied Rev. 18 and saw in it an argument against slavery. Although Sabbatarian Adventists read the same prophecy, they came to different conclusions (Haloviak, 1999). After the Emancipation Proclamation on January 1, 1863, all twelve issues of the 1863 *Review* carried front page articles which showed that the Bible condemned slavery (Branson, April 16, 1970). Finally, it is noteworthy that these pioneers of the SDAC were implicitly supportive of racial reconciliation as indicated by their denunciation of slavery.

Advent Christian Church- Based in the Hartford, Connecticut-New York City area, this group looked to Joseph Turner and W. S. Campbell, co-editors of the *Second Advent Watchman* for leadership. They held to a post-millennial doctrine, which taught that man will sleep in death until the final destruction of the wicked. They were joined by Himes in 1862 (Schwarz, 1979).

Age-to Come Adventists A- third group advanced a pre-millennial position, which advocated that the millennium was still future. The group was led by Joseph Marsh and his *Advent Harbinger and* Bible *Advocate.* They fiercely opposed formal organization and for this reason were unable to become strong and united.

The Formation of State Conferences- The first conferences formed in the NAD were organized by geographic regions, not by race or ethnic group. Ellen White opposed the proposal to form ethnic conferences toward the end of the nineteenth century (*9T*, 1948). The first eight state conferences were formed as follows: Michigan Conference, 1861; Ohio, 1863; Wisconsin, 1871; Minnesota, 1862; New York, 1862; Iowa, 1863; Texas Conference, 1878; Florida, 1893. The New Jersey Conference (1901), Greater New York (1902) and other local conferences were formed later (SDA Online Yearbook, 2010). All the leadership positions of all the state conferences were held by Whites only.

Membership and Contributions- As the church progressed, the membership and financial contributions from every state and regional conference increased. By 1870 the SDAC membership in the US stood at 5,390 (Land, 1998). In 1899 it grew to 53,206; in 1912 membership grew to 98,044; by the end of fourth quarter 1944, it was a total membership of 206,908 (GC Archives, 1899; Adventist Archives, 1944). In 2000, membership was at 933,935 (GC Archives, 2000); in 2002 there were 974,271 with 303,066 African Americans (London, 2009); at the end of fourth quarter 2007 it was 1,054,788; in 2008, 1,084,838 Adventists in the NAD membership; accessions were a mere 3.4% of the world church's total accessions for the year (GC Archives, 2008). NAD Executive Secretary, G. Alexander

Bryant reported that as of September 30, 2009, the NAD had 1, 097,217 members; an increase of 7,353 over the 2008 total of 1,084,838 (Kellner, 2009). Membership in the NAD grew to 1,108,158 by the end of the fourth quarter 2009 (Adventist Archives, 2009).

The tithe intake in the NAD in 1944 was $3,503,002.01 (Adventist Archives, 1944)); by end of fourth quarter 2007 it was $632,610,275.00 by the fourth quarter of 2008 it was $1,929,768,053 and the total of tithe and offerings was $2,627,027,513 (Adventist Archives, NAD, 2007; GC Archives, 2008). Much of the church's wealth has been concentrated in the White community. More and often, better health and educational institutions were built, but unfortunately Blacks and other ethnic Adventists have often been refused employment and admission at some institutions and are simply tolerated until they resign from employment at others for that reason.

The Early SDA Evangelists/Pioneers (1863-1915)

One of the legacies of the Millerite Movement was mission. Mission suggests evangelism. Evangelism requires evangelists, much like those who proclaimed the "midnight cry." As the group became organized as the Seventh-day Adventists, they had one mantra—mission. Their mission-mindedness resulted in evangelistic tent meetings being conducted wherever they could. Their goal was to call as many people into a reconciling relationship and ministry with Jesus. They were reconcilers who practiced Christian reconciliation. This led them to agitate against slavery as a part of their Christian duty. In fact, in a 1970 article in the *Review and Herald* Roy Branson stated that the early Adventists were "kissing cousins" of the radical abolitionists. He further averred—

> If anyone had told the founding fathers of our denomination that their attitudes toward race had nothing to do with their theology, they would have shaken their heads in disbelief.

By utilizing the print pages and oral proclamation, the early evangelists of the remnant church labored assiduously to make the movement a world endeavor. They published the first Sabbath-keeping tract in 1846 and in 1849 a periodical called *The Present Truth*. They held their first general meeting in 1848 in Rock Hill, Connecticut and organized their first local congregation in 1861. By 1874 they began sending missionaries abroad with the intent to establish the work on every continent and island. The work was buttressed by publishing houses, health and educational institutions, set up to educate the mind and heal the body as they prepare others for service in the cause of God. By the end of 1931 there were 10,850 evangelistic workers, 71 union conferences, 154 state or provincial conferences and 278 organized mission fields were in service in 455 languages (Branson, 1933).

Some of the more renowned pioneers were Joseph Bates, George Storrs, James White, and Ellen White, Uriah Smith, J. N. Andrews, Merritt E. Cornell, Charles Fitch, Sylvester Bliss, O. R. L. Crosier, Joseph Harvey Waggoner, and John Loughborough. In our next section I examine the work of a few of these pioneers.

Joseph Bates- Joseph Bates, a former sea captain of New Bedford, Massachusetts, helped found the abolitionist society in his home town (Branson, Apr. 9, 1970). Bates, in a conversation with Judge Hopper on one of his evangelistic outreaches in Maryland, remarked, "I am an abolitionist, and have come to get your slaves, and you too! We teach that Christ is coming to take His people home; and we want you to come with us, and bring all your servants (Spalding, 1961). Bates, baptized in the Christian Church in 1826 and a preacher of little renown in the Millerite Movement, concluded soon after the disappointment that keeping the Sabbath was necessary for salvation. This was after reading an article by Thomas M. Preble in 1844.

Bates became a member of the Sabbatarian Adventists and along with James and Ellen White, became a strong force for good in the early years of the church (Land, 1998). While Branson alludes to the involvement of church pioneers Bates, Byington, and Kellogg in the abolitionist movement, a position that was liberal for the time, the research indicates that Bates and company cut ties with the abolitionist movement shortly after becoming an Adventist (Baker, 1996). His evangelistic outreaches took him throughout the states of the Midwest, North Eastern U. S., and Canada. As James White noted, after he departed from some of his short evangelistic missions his "deference and genuine affection" (reconciling evangelism) led many to tears when they had to part his company (Spalding, 1961).

John Loughborough- John Loughborough and Cornell purchased the first tent in Rochester, New York and pitched it in Battle Creek, Michigan. The use of tents for evangelistic meetings started with John Loughborough and Cornell in Battle Creek and later in Grand Rapids. The first meeting was held in June 10 and it was reported in the July 4, 1954 *Review and Herald* that one thousand people attended the first meeting and many interests were aroused. Thus began this new approach to evangelism by the pioneers (Arthur White, 1985). They began as two-day meetings and interests were garnered through these means. Loughborough stood for unity among all members of the church. His statement on the matter reflects his stance—

> It is a source of encouragement to know that these different organizations in various countries and nationalities are all united in the promulgation of the one great cause of truth, and the salvation of men. Not in the mere formal machinery of organization do we trust, but in God, the author of order and organization. With his blessing upon the united and harmonious action of his workers we may realize how good and pleasant it is for brethren to be united, to dwell together in unity, and to have" all things done decently and in order (Loughbourough, Folio Views, 0159).

Uriah Smith- It was James White, Uriah Smith and J. H. Waggoner who were first to move the SDAC in the direction of ethnic diversity. This was done with their publication of the first German language tract for the German immigrants. Uriah Smith served as editor of the *Review and Herald* during the time before President Lincoln's Emancipation Proclamation. When the sitting president announced that he engaged the Union troops in the Civil War only because he wanted to save the Union and not to free the slaves, Smith used the printed pages of the church's official paper to denounce him for his negligence in not immediately freeing the slaves.

James White- James White is described as being of a sanguine and ardent temperament (Spalding, 961). James White was a school teacher before he became a preacher in the Millerite Movement. He met Ellen on one of her trips to give assurance and guidance. After he heard her relate her visions he accepted her visions as divinely sent and began accompanying her and others on her mission trips (Land, 1998). Along with his wife, Ellen, James White became a pioneer of the SDA Church. They labored together for many years in the US and overseas.

On one occasion as James served as a substitute teacher at Burnham, used the opportunity to hold evening lectures. Sixty interests stood for prayer. Later when invited to Kennebec in January 1843 by a hearer, he preached at a country schoolhouse. Being the hotbed of the Universalists, they were outraged and plotted to mob him. He learned of the plot but proceeded to the place anyhow. The mob interspersed throughout the crown and used every attack (they made catcalls, howls, and threw snowballs) to disrupt him, but he, turning to the terror of the judgment, called them to "'Repent and call on God for mercy and pardon, Turn to Christ…'" Before long the audience were in tears and James called for all who desired prayer; nearly a hundred got up. He prayed and departed with the help of a noble gentleman, who locked arms with him and escorted him through the menacing mob. When James turned to thank the gentleman, he had disappeared from sight (Spalding, 1961).

On the issue of slavery, James White was very forthright in his denunciation of the institution. He viewed the oppression of slaves in America as evidence that the beast (that looks like a lamb and speaks like a dragon) in Rev. 13 was the United States (Baker, 1996).

Ellen White- Ellen White, born Ellen Gould Harmon in Gorham, Maine on November 26, 1827, became one of the pioneers of the SDA Church. After receiving conviction on the Sabbath doctrine, Joseph Bates published a tract in 1846, which convinced James and Ellen White of the necessity of keeping the Sabbath (Land, 1998). Ellen White went on to become a special messenger of God to the church, but made no claim to being a prophet (Spalding, 1961). Ellen White places her first vision around December 1844 although she could not recall the exact date. As reported to the *Day Star* on January 24, 1846 (Arthur L. White, 1985), it was a vision of God's people traveling together in a cloud for seven days to the Holy City (Spalding, 1922).

Ellen White was called by God to be a special messenger to the remnant. This has been challenged on numerous occasions by Adventists as well as others outside of Adventism. She has also been accused of plagiarism by others. All the challenges and charges have been coercively disputed by Adventist apologists and historians (Jemison, 1955; Nichol, 1951; Brand, 2005; Lake, 2010). A few months (December 1844) after the first Great Disappointment Ellen White received two visions. The first showed that God "had led his people" (Arthur White, 2000). She saw that the light behind them that illumined their path was the Midnight Cry and that they were only at the beginning of the path rather than the end. God instructed her in the second vision to go out and declare the things he had shown her. At the time she was in poor health, her family was impoverished, and she was timid hence she felt incapable of assuming this duty. She prayed for several days and until late at night asking God to "remove the burden from her and place it on someone more capable of bearing it" (Arthur White, 2000). In vision with an angel she pleaded with god that if she must relate what she was shown that she would be preserved from "undue exaltation." She received assurance that her prayer was answered and thus committed herself to do whatever he asked at whatever cost (Arthur White, 2000).

Ellen White did much to assist in reconciliation among the races in the remnant during her time. She denounced the prejudice that was shown toward the Blacks and often reminded the White members of the church that all races are going to the same heaven. This being the case, they were to learn to worship together in peace. This does appear contradictory to other statements she made regarding seeking equality between the races. Each statement, however, must be carefully examined in its context (Graybill, 1970). C. E. Dudley traced the genealogy of Ellen White back to her mulatto roots, the daughter of an African American woman by the name of Eunice Gould (1999).

Ellen White encouraged civil disobedience in the matter of slavery. She urged Adventists "we are not to obey" the Fugitive Slave Act, a law passed in 1850 "requiring us to deliver a slave to his master." She once admonished a member whom she learned had defended slavery by affirming—"You must yield your views or the truth… We must let it be known that we have no such ones in our fellowship that we will not walk with them in church capacity" (Baker, 1996). She affirmed, Baker argues, the equality of Blacks and Whites, of all humans, because of their common creation and ancestry and redemption (1996).

A Mission-focused Remnant

Since its birth, mission has been the central focus of the remnant church of God. The goal of mission was to call others to reconcile with God and prepare for his coming. We saw earlier in this study that the Seventh-day Adventist Church was spawned by a great awakening of God-consciousness and energized by the spiritual fervor of the pioneers. The great commission is the mission of the remnant. The remnant *kerygma* (preaching) is nicely summed up in Jesus' invitation in Mt. 3:28-30—"Come unto me all you that labor and are heavy laden and I will give you rest…Take my yoke…" The yolk (burden) of God is our service to Him. It is a "yoke" to give hope to and reconcile the oppressed, the imprisoned, and the helpless. Thus reconciliation becomes the mission of the Church.

As if to help us understand this better, the apostle affirms that the Church's mission is the ministry of reconciliation (2 Cor. 5:18, 19). There is no ministry in turning; the ministry is in reaching out to others after we have turned to God. Hence God calls us urgently to turn to him in faith. God challenges us to reconcile with each other. Then he sends us on the mission to call others to be reconciled to God. We can teach only what we know. The reconcilers, therefore, must first be reconciled.

Who Comprise the Remnant?

What does the Bible say about the remnant? In ancient Israel, the remnant of the Hebrews after the flood was Noah and his extended family. They were the faithful few remaining of the nation of Israel. Lot and his extended family were the remnant of Sodom and Gomorrah after God destroyed the twin cities by fire (Gen. 19:27-29). The remnant in the book of Revelation is those who have entered into the new covenant relationship with God. It is not national Israel, but "spiritual" Israel, those who are connected as one by the Spirit of God. Yet the remnant is not to be considered to be merely an exclusive "club" of saints in a specific denomination, in which no other can enter unless they sign up. Rather, it may best be understood to be a core group of saints, who have chosen to obey God's commandments and who bear the testimony of Jesus Christ (Rev. 12:17). There is no implication of a "once saved, always saved" remnant, however.

On the contrary, the late Kenneth Mulzac propounds that in the book of Jeremiah there is indication that the remnant can "degenerate into a universal curse or taunt." Persistence in evil, such as idolatry amounts to covenant unfaithfulness and may result in a "cutting off" or "destruction" of the entire community. The consequence of this reality is that no remnant remains as denoted by the preposition of negation in Jer. 44:2-6. The possibility of a "remnantless" community is present in the pericope of Jer. 39:9-10 also, which occurs because of the persistence of the covenant community in idolatrous practices (2008). Idolatry is not the only sin that could lead to a cutting off of the remnant. Neither is idolatry to be understood only as the physical erection of a material statue to which one offers worship. Persistence in any sin amounts to a rebellion against the true God and that constitutes idolatry in that the sin displaces God and become a god to us.

As Seventh-day Adventists we have traditionally referred to ourselves as the remnant Church on the basis of the Scriptures (1 Cor. 1:5-7; Rev. 12:17; 19:10) noted above. Yet God will not save Adventists as a church. You see, "not all Israel is Israel." In fact, in the May 9, 1996 *Adventist Review*, Jon Dybdahl, director of the Institute of World Mission at Andrews University averred, "There are tithe-paying, Sabbath-keeping, Ellen White-studying Seventh-day Adventists who are not part of the remnant" (Dybdahl, 1996). Each person will appear individually in God's judgment. When the eschatological "midnight cry" of Mt. 25:31ff goes out and the Bridegroom appears, all will be asked the same question, essentially—"What did you do with your life?" The sin of omission is in focus in Mt. 25:42-43 ("you gave me *nothing*...you *did not* invite me in... you *did not* clothe me...," NIV) as the reason for Christ's rejection and exclusion of some by God. To bear the testimony of Jesus is to minister to those around us in love. That is, to personally personally communicate the love of Jesus to them by our acts of love.

It is regarding the sin of omission that Ellen White remarked a century ago—

> The Lord is grieved at the indifference manifested
> by His professed followers toward the ignorant and
> oppressed colored people. If our people had taken up
> this work at the close of the Civil War, their faithful

labor would have done much to prevent the present condition of suffering and sin (Graybill, 1970).

God had chosen Israel to be his people millennia before Jesus came as the Messiah. He offered to make them his treasured possession, a royal priesthood, a holy nation (Exod. 19:5, 6, NIV). The Hebrew people seem to have cherished an aura of entitlement because of their privileged position as the chosen ones. They flaunted it and began adding their own laws to God's law. And instead of being priests to the nations around, calling them to reconcile with God, they became pompous and legalistic. But when Jesus came as a baby in Bethlehem, they did not recognize him as the Messiah for whom they had been waiting.

Jesus denounced their pharisaical, legalistic practices--"Their worship is a farce, for they teach man-made ideas as commands from God" (Mt. 15:9, NLV). Using the imagery of their culture, He referred to them as whitened sepulchers, looking beautiful on the outside, but which are full of dead men's bones on the inside (Mt. 23:27). Despite their identification with the chosen body (the Hebrews, Abraham's descendants) and their possession of many of the right doctrines, they were a misguided and lost people.

Prompted by their ignorance and arrogance, and alarmed by the cognitive dissonance as they heard the teachings of Jesus, in desperation the Jews conspired with the Romans to kill Jesus (Mt. 26-27). For millennia they had been waiting for him, only to be disappointed that he did not come as a king to overthrow the Roman Empire and return the Promised Land to them (Acts 1:6). But he came, despised and rejected by men. He came as a lamb to the slaughter and a humble sheep before its shearer (Isa. 53). He came to his own and they did not welcome him. And though he was crucified, yet he was resurrected and he will come again. He promises to come and receive his own to himself and take them to the place he is gone to prepare for them (Jn. 14:1-3). Until then, they must remain true, faithful, and reconciled.

Who comprise the remnant? Dybdahl correctly asserts that ultimately "it's God's call." Dybdahl pinpoints that there are at least three historical occasions on which the emergence of a remnant was necessitated: 1) when the ancient Israel apostatized, 2) when the remnant of Israel strayed and the Christian Church emerged, 3) when the Christian church fell into apostasy and a remnant church was foretold in Rev. 12:17. In the light of this progression, Dybdahl notes that some believe that the process could be repeated again (Dybdahl, 1996).

Summary- It was with the knowledge of the nearness of Jesus' return and the urgency of the need for humans to reconcile with God that The Great Awakening began. In the 1700s, the US was mired in spiritualism which lulled them into a spiritual slumber from New York to New Mexico. The Anglo-Saxon descendants of the Pilgrims to the New World and their captive African slaves were spiritually famished. God wanted to awake them to their need to be reconciled to their God. Thus began the First Great Awakening by the Evangelical Christians on the Western shores of the Atlantic. Yet the need for reconciliation was not just vertical (with God), it was also horizontal (human with human).

The concept of the remnant is biblical. It usually denotes a covenant residue which remains true to God throughout disastrous times. They endure much trauma, but still remain faithful to their covenant. The persecution of the Dark Ages resulted in the Reformation. The Reformation gave rise to the Great Awakening. Out of the Great Awakening emerged the SDAC. Seventh-day Adventists have traditionally applied the designation "remnant" to the Adventist Church. Yet the remnant is not an exclusivist club that precludes other Christians who are not members of this denomination; neither is it the sovereign Israel or the Jewish people in Israel and the diaspora. The concept of remnantlessness is biblical. Thus there is no reason to think that being a part of any church guarantees anyone a place among the remnant. The remnant is comprised of those "who keep the commandments of God and have the testimony of Jesus Christ (Rev. 17:12). As Adventists, we must constantly evaluate our conduct against this standard.

The remnant is not a passive entity that sits quietly by in apparent oblivion and apathy. The remnant, rather, is like salt that alters the substance by mingling and proactively engaging the culture, which could be society or even the Christian church; wherever evil, is present. The Adventist Church pioneers engaged the culture of their day by taking unpopular positions as individuals, though not as official positions of the church. Even while being mission-focused, the remnant should be socially, even politically engaged.

The remnant Church should exemplify the unity that is becoming of a reconciled body. Where we have erred in patterning the errors of the "world" or the rest of Christendom, we ought to correct our error and allow the Lord to lead us to reconciliation. The Evangelical movement became prey to the racial prejudices of the US in the centuries before and without variation, the SDAC similarly did also. Meanwhile, it behooves current Adventists to disentangle God's church from the shackles of racist history and live righteously in the present. But will we?

Throughout the history of the religion of Christianity, the followers of God have shown a tendency to pattern and indulge practices of the larger society. Hence presently in the Adventist Church, cultural norms and mores have largely been practiced by the people of faith, albeit typically without official prescription or endorsement. This obtains in the US currently. Evangelicals, Catholics, as well as other Christians generally practice the status quo, albeit with variations. The call to be countercultural goes largely unheeded as adherents of the faith take the comfortable and easy path of least resistance. Such is the case in the matter of race relations.

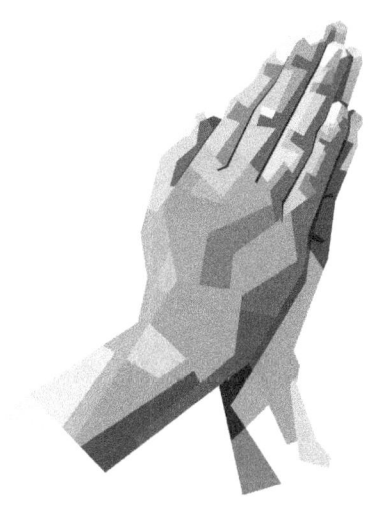

PART 2

We Could not Get Along

The Irreconcilable

"Remember that at that time you were separate from Christ, excluded from citizenship in Israel and foreigners to the covenants of the promise, without hope and without God in the world" (Eph. 2:12, NIV).

3

Evangelical Apartheid and the Remnant Church

Evangelicalism played a significant role in the formation of the American republic and in the Great Awakening, as I showed earlier. Much of its tenets were expressed in the formation of public policies and enactment of civil laws. Denominations that grew out of the movement were greatly influenced by it and developed doctrines and assumed social and political postures based on its legacy and akin to its hallmarks. The general disposition of the movement impacted the way many denominations approached slavery, Jim Crow laws, and the subsequent racialization. Current trends in Evangelicalism are apparent in churches that identify with it and are generally espoused by its individual adherents. At this juncture I will examine the impact of Evangelicalism on the SDAC and the latter's attitude toward the issue of racial and ethnic reconciliation.

Apartheid: Definition The English word apartheid means "racial segregation." It is a compound Afrikaans noun from *apart*, which means "apart" and *heid*, which means "hood" (Mirriam-Webster, 2003). As a compound word *Apartheid* denotes "separation based on race." It bears the negative connotation of the idea of a system that legalizes and promotes the segregation of different races of people in a community or society, religious or otherwise. Is the Evangelical movement guilty of practicing apartheid? The section below will consider this question.

The Origin of Evangelicalism Evangelicalism had its origin in England in the 1730's and was popularized in the US during the Great Awakening by Jonathan Edwards and George Whitefield. Evangelicalism was introduced to America alongside Democracy. Its ideals helped to shape Evangelical Christianity, which in turn helped to forge a democratic society. Both Democracy and Christianity are closely and intricately intertwined to the point of confusion (Kyle, 2006). Evangelicals offer practical and theological reasons why they should engage in politics (Sider, 2008). The pioneer of American Evangelicalism was English evangelist and revivalist, George Whitefield, who immigrated to America in the 1730s and became the voice of the Evangelical movement. His spell-binding eloquence and tear-evoking passion and emotionalism, had a mesmerizing effect on his audience (Kyle, 2006; Noll, 2003; Belden, 1930). Whitefield was responsible for adding the social dimension as well as its consumer appeal to Evangelicalism. It has been estimated by sociologists and political scientists that Evangelicals comprise 25 to 30 percent of the US population. Galbreath avers that this does not include African American Protestants, who hold typical Evangelical theological positions with the exception of a few distinctive doctrines (2006). Demographers Barry A. Kosmin and Ariela Keysar of Trinity College in Hartford, Connecticut, surveyed 54,461 adults in the US in February to November of 2008. They discovered in their 2008 survey of religious identification in the US that of the seventy six percent of American adults who identified themselves as Christians, thirty four percent claimed to be "Born Again" or Evangelicals (2009).

Donald G. Bloesch proposes that Evangelicalism has been impelled to uphold and defend certain tenets of the historic faith such as:

> "absolute sovereignty and transcendence of God; the divine authority and inspiration of Scripture; the radical sinfulness of man; the deity of Jesus Christ; His vicarious substitutionary atonement; the eschatological and superhistorical character of the kingdom of God; a final judgment at the end of history; the realities of hell and heaven; and evangelization as the primary dimension of the Christian mission" (1982).

Evangelical Slaveholders In a letter to W. E. Bailey dated December 18, 1848, James C. Furman indicated, "We who own slave, honor God." This was not written in defiance of the abolitionist rhetoric or to support the divine origins of slavery, rather it was from one slaveholder to another, intended to decry his mistreatment of his male slave. Furman's exposition on slavery epitomized the Evangelical ethic on slavery. Their ideological platform was birthed by the Southern ideology that "Negroes were 'destined by providence' for slavery and that this was made evident not only by the color of their skin but also by 'the intellectual inferiority and natural improvidence of this race'" (Fredrickson, 1971).

Governor George McDuffy, a Presbyterian, in an address to the South Carolina General Assembly in 1835 argued that Negroes were unfit for any kind of self-government and were physically, morally, politically, and in all respects inferior to millions of the human race (Fredrickson, 1971). This was the typical position of the slavery apologists, who were primarily Evangelicals. The revivalist Charles G. Finney and other abolitionists introduced an ideological shift that no longer considered Blacks as brutes and slavery as salvation from a barbaric African existence, but a new evangelicalism that decried intemperance and denounced war, slavery, and racial discrimination as evil. But not all would be persuaded to accept this. The apologists instead developed a "scientific" theory of slavery and other facades to mask their evil (Pollard, 2000). This was published in a pamphlet in 1833 in New York entitled *Evidence Against the Views of the Abolitionists, Consisting of Physical and Moral Proofs of the Natural Inferiority of the Negroes.* This pamphlet affirmed the racist theory of the Negro character, which bore no resemblance of true science (Fredrickson, 1971).

Essentially, Evangelicals thought that by converting slaves to Christianity, they could regain the respect, trust, and leadership of Southerners that had been diminished by the arguments of the abolitionist movement (Matthews, 1977). In response to this, the Evangelical movement developed a Mission to Slaves. The purpose of the Mission was to "convince slaves that Whites had the slaves' best interests at heart." Through this Mission they hoped also to evangelize Blacks (Matthews, 1977).

Billy Graham, inarguably the most prominent Evangelical evangelist of the twentieth and twenty-first century America stated that "racial and ethnic hostility is the foremost social problem facing our world today" (Emerson and Smith, 2000). Galbreath alludes to what he designates as a "Black flight" by Evangelical Blacks from Evangelical ministry organizations. Some of those who take flight from such ministry organizations concluded that they were not embraced as equals, but were merely tolerated in these entities (2006). I have observed as have others (Blacks and Whites) to whom I have spoken, that the same is true of some of our White SDA educational and health institutions. Of the few Black (and Hispanic) employees of our educational and health institutions, many have voiced the same frustrations. One Black Evangelical minister affirms, "There can never be unity or reconciliation between the Blacks and Whites until we see each other as *equal*. This equality is found in the image of God" (Edwards, 1996)... Note also an insightful assertion by Rosenberg—

> "In few places would Blacks actually be turned away from the door of a church today, but there are, of course, many other ways of making them feel alien and unwelcome. In some areas there has been re-segregation. Southern Baptists *need* a few Blacks in order to counter allegations of discrimination. If there start to be more than a few, help will be forthcoming to start a new Black SB church" (Rosenberg, 1989).

Evangelicalism and the American Race Dilemma

What I refer to as the American race dilemma was identified over fifty years ago by Swedish Social scientist, Gunnar Myrdal, as "the American dilemma," in a two-volume work by that title. While Evangelicals (ninety percent of which is White), espouse freedom, independence, privacy, individualism, and equal opportunity, and advocate "engaged orthodoxy," the concept that as a religion their faith must engage the larger culture and society, seeking solutions to social problems such as race relations. Notwithstanding their practice of "engaged orthodoxy," Ronald C. Potter pinpoints that White Evangelicals scholars (Carl Henry, E. J. Carnell, Paul Jewett, Bernard Ramm) failed to engage the best contemporary scholarly literature on race relations (Okholm, 1997). They successfully utilized this during the era of slavery, but they were wholly misguided in their theological and scientific reasoning, which declared Whites as the superior race and Blacks as inferior and less than human.

Appealing to the text in Gen. 9:24 regarding Ham, they reasoned that Ham was cursed and that Africans were the descendants of Ham. Further,

> "It is a Christian responsibility to protect and provide for them. In light of their inferiority and inability to control themselves, slavery allows for social order, and limits crime and vice that would otherwise occur…Christians should obey the law, which permitted and protected slavery, and not get involved in merely temporal matters such as slavery abolition" (Emerson and Smith, 2000).

The Evangelical movement was deeply involved in the shaping of American democracy. The Pilgrims and their descendants espoused the Evangelical faith and followed its practices. The principle of homogeneous units was introduced to Western Christianity and popularized by them (Rosenburg, 1989). It is a principle which stresses homogeneity, which in turn creates separateness, which Ralph Elliott affirms goes "hand in hand with a lack of concern, if not a prejudice against, those outside our own milieu" (1982). He further sees Hitler's demonic championing of a superior race and the heinous atrocities of the enslavement of Blacks in America as the perverse extension of this principle (Elliott, 1982).

That this was at the core of their polity is evidenced in their general lack of integration and apparently in their widely-practiced HUP. In 1958 there were only 14 Black members in the entire SBC. By 1983 only those of their approximately 4,000 churches near a military base (10% of location) had Black members (Rosenberg, 1989). This reality is not peculiar to the SBC as most Protestant denominations in the US remain homogeneous, though more integrated than the SBC, and most generally shy away from "racial" issues (Rosenberg, 1989). Meanwhile, the membership of all mainline denominations is decreasing.

> "That problem is the weakening of the spiritual conviction required to generate the enthusiasm and energy needed to sustain a vigorous communal life. Somehow, in the course of the past century, these churches lost the **will** (emphasis mine) or the ability to teach the Christian faith and what it requires to a succession of younger cohorts in such a way as to command their allegiance. Admittedly, doing so has become increasingly difficult for churches as close to the very center of American culture and institutional life as the mainline denominations are" (Johnson, et al, 1993).

The Millerite Movement grew out of the Evangelical movement. Methodists, Baptists, Presbyterians, Congregationalist comprised the earliest followers of the Millerite Movement (Schwarz, 1979; Numbers and Butler, 1987). As the Movement grew, they were blamed for a dwindling membership in the denominations listed above and for "a general malaise in the late 1840s" (Numbers and Butler, 1987). This assertion, however, does not stand up under closer scrutiny.

The Frenchman Alexis de Tocqueville toured the US on a mission for the French government in the 1700s in order to closely observe the penal system and get an experiential understanding of the American democratic system of government. After touring for some time, Tocqueville's outlook on the racial divide between Blacks and Whites became very pessimistic. Upon observing the treatment of Blacks by Whites he concluded that these two races will never live together as equals anywhere, even more so in America. His argument was based on his hypothesis that an entire people group does not have the ability to rise, as a people, above itself. This is further complicated by the American democracy which provides significant freedoms to the White population. He noted that the Whites in turn utilize their freedom to isolate themselves from the Blacks (Tocqueville, 1835). That is, by abandoning the cities and relocating in the suburbs.

The core values and assumptions of the American society as well as its reliance on market principles contribute significantly to the racial divide. Evangelical Protestant Christianity is the biggest proponent of these values and assumptions—freedom, individualism, independence, equality of opportunity, privacy, and so on, which they have come to value in the New World to which they escaped from the religious tyranny of Europe. Evangelicalism became the mainstream religion for the first century and a quarter of American history (Emerson and Smith, 2000) and significantly influenced the nation during the first half of the nineteenth century (Kyle, 2006). To the present they are well integrated in American society. Their religious philosophical position is "engaged orthodoxy." This essentially has to do with using their religion to engage the larger culture of society (Emerson and Smith, 2000). The Evangelical involvement in American politics at present is not subtle but blatant and it often appears that they would like to make of the US a theocracy rather than a democracy.

Recent research has shown a remarkable similarity in the thinking of Evangelical Whites and the White mass culture (Emerson and Smith, 2000). This is not surprising to many, however, in light of the fact that "Evangelicals have to a large extent been assimilated into American culture…they have thoroughly adapted to American popular culture" (Kyle, 2006). The American society is racialized. The authors of *Divided By Faith* advance the concept that in the aftermath of the Civil Rights Movement, "the racialized society is one in which intermarriage rates are low, residential separation and socioeconomic inequality are the norm, our definitions of personal identity and our choices of intimate associations reveal racial distinctiveness, and where 'we are never unaware of the race of a person with whom we interact'" (Emerson and Smith, 2000). Research data suggest there are no noticeable differences between the attitude and thinking of White non-evangelicals and Evangelical Whites in the US Furthermore, Blacks are as likely as Whites to attend churches that are 80 percent homogeneous.

The nature of racialization is such that it could go undetected for significant periods in any entity by the unsuspecting. Racialization is insidious and covert. It occurs in the normal operations of institutions; it avoids racial terminology and it is invisible to most Whites. In the Evangelical movement as in the US generally, however, it is responsible for the misuse of power and diminished opportunities in life for members of other racial groups than White (Emerson and Smith, 2000). We shall examine later on in this study how it has impacted the work in the Seventh-day Adventist Church and has contributed to our present divided governance structure, a polity that has characterized the entire movement for centuries. This may be more appropriately characterized as Evangelical *Apartheid*.

Evangelical *Apartheid*

Apartheid is used in this study as a foreign word for "systemic separation." The polity of the Evangelical movement includes a rationale for segregation. That Anglo-Saxonism was "no benign expansionism is inarguable in light of the fact that Evangelical *Apartheid* flourished under the notion that one race was destined to lead, others to serve, one race to flourish, many to die" (Horsman, 1981). This nefarious philosophy was clothed with and dispensed under the garb and guise of religion. Evangelicals developed fallacious theological and contrived "scientific" support for racism (Emerson and Smith, 2000; Putnam, 1962). This included manufactured evidence to suggest the inferiority of the Negro race. And though evangelicalism used the rhetoric of redemption in its theology of slavery, the diabolic nature of the latter did not go unnoticed by the slaves, at least not for long. In time they began to realize that their masters did not mean them any earthly or heavenly good and soon they began to refuse to sing his songs. Instead, in groans they mumbled the pains of their oppression in cryptic lyrics, melodious strains, and cadences unknown to the masters—"Swing low, sweet chariot…" and "Nobody knows the trouble I see, nobody knows but Jesus…"

Rothstein highlights the extent to which the church, in numerous instances, participated in and spearheaded efforts to discriminate against Blacks through segregation. The clergy and their churches as well as synagogues, frequently led efforts to foster restrictive covenants through lawsuits to evict Blacks from all White neighborhoods. A case in point is that of the Waggoner Place Methodist Episcopal Church co-sponsoring the *Shelley v. Kraemer* lawsuit in St. Louis, alongside the Cote Brilliante Presbyterian Church. The 1948 case involved evicting a "distinguished" Black attorney, Scovel Richardson, who purchased a house in the White neighborhood where Louis and Fern Kraemer lived. Richardson went on to later become one of the first Black attorneys nationwide to be appointed to the federal judiciary. Also, in 1942, a priest led the campaign to prevent Blacks from living in a neighborhood in North Philadelphia. Such involvement by the clergy and their churches and synagogues were not uncommon (Rothstein, 2017).

Indigenous Church Principle- The Evangelical rationale is rooted in its Church Growth Movement (CGM). The CGM was founded by Donald McGavran, a former Disciples of Christ missionary to the Kerala people of India's Southwest coast. While on mission assignment in this region, McGravan, being faced with its complex caste system, became convinced that the most effective way to evangelize them was to be sensitive to their endogamous restrictions. Upon realizing that converts were outcasted when they converted to Christianity individually, and that it became impossible for single converts to Christianity to marry, he adopted the practice of all the other religious groups in Kerala and began to convert entire groups (extended families, members of subcastes, tribe lets, and so on, to avoid cutting off the new converts from their community (McGravan, 1970; Rosenberg, 1989). Yet it has been reported by UCA News that Christians have been denied benefits under the Indian Constitution because Christianity does not recognize the caste system (Britto, 2006).

In a recent booklet "Christians and Dalit Liberation," V. T. Rajshekar, paints a picture that Christianity is the best thing that ever happened to the "Untouchables" of India. Rajshekar contends that Hinduism is based on hatred with an ethos of division and disintegration. This hatred created India's *Apartheid*, which is the most destructive to humans of all forms of *Apartheid* including South Africa's and the slavery of the West. It is so because it destroys the mind of the person; it is anti-human. Contrarily, Christianity provides liberation for the Untouchables. Rajshekar postulates "The Untouchables are kicked, killed, burnt, raped and their little property destroyed not because they are poor… They became poor because the Hindus robbed their human rights" (2009). Thus he denounces leaders like Ghandi and others as insincere. The mistake that the Christian leaders made, however, is that they allowed the converted Hindus to bring their caste system into Christianity in order to gain more members (2009). He affirms,

> "To repeat, the sickness of Hinduism is so contagious that it has not spared any other religion. Those who went over to Christianity carried their caste with them and we have evidence that to gain more members, the Church leaders allowed the converts to keep their caste identity. There are even today separate churches and graveyards in the church for Untouchable converts" (Rajshekar, 2009).

Homogeneous Unit Principle- The Homogeneous Unit Principle was introduced in the US by Donald McGravan. McGravan began publishing his theories in the 1930s but only after his retirement did it find wide acceptance. He established his Institute of Church Growth at Fuller Theological Seminary in 1965 and made his services accessible to Evangelical denominations. Among Evangelical denominations the Southern Baptists have used the method most successfully. The Homogenous Unit Principle of the Southern Baptist Convention (SBC) has been used to maintain this endogamy and shape the nature of local congregations, particularly in the South. To avoid the appearance of racism they use it to blur the "language," "race," and "ethnicity" distinctions. Southern Baptists have rejected the "melting pot" theory of America, which they allege is not working. One executive of their Home Mission Board affirmed that America is being re-tribalized (Rosenberg, 1989).

It is with much candor that the Southern Baptist's HUP has been compared with South African apartheid. A former member of the SBC asks pointedly, "'can it be that the church simply cannot minister and succeed in a community of diversity?'" Rosenberg contends that the SBC has forged coalitions with American Jewish groups for this very reason also: to keep the Jews over there, in Israel. In that way the members of the SBC who have anti-Semitic inclinations can still be pro-Zionist and become harder to detect (1989).

The evidence for the practice of *Apartheid* by the Evangelicals is compelling. Rather than allowing the unity ethos of biblical Christianity to prevail, evangelicals have succumbed to the countervailing winds of earthly prosperity to drive their sail. The paternalism of centuries of slavery has not lost its impact even on the twenty-first century evangelical movement, which is centuries closer to the second coming of Christ. Support of this position is advocated by some of the leading church growth experts of the Evangelical movement (Elliott, 1982). Richard Kyle, professor of history and religion at Tabor College observes— "For all their 'cultural bogeys,' they 'have chosen to adapt more to the main lines of American life than most other groups'" (2006). What have been the views of mainline America? History points to the racist philosophies masquerading in religious garb. Could the Seventh-day Adventist Church be guilty of this practice also by its perpetuation of a segregated structure of governance?

In India McGravan utilized the indigenous church principle, which is the mother of the HUP and commonly used by missionaries there (1970). Rosenberg avers—

> "Southern Baptists, and other Southerners, are thus using the HUD to rationalize the maintenance of Black-White segregation because they feel that these two groups, in a very powerful and special way because of the long weight of Southern history, should be endogamous castes, just as if they lived in Kerala, India" (1989).

The SBC's use of the HUP is factual, but not biblical. Christ's commission--"Go ye" does not suggest making disciples who are kept to their ethnic/racial group, but disciples who become a part of the cosmic *koinonia* ("fellowship") inaugurated by Jesus. At Pentecost and beyond, the apostles evangelized and baptized peoples of all ethnicities into the Christian church. Rather than segregating them, the apostles denounced segregation and urged them to integrate (Eph. 2:14ff). There are numerous racially integrated Protestant churches that defy the HUP (Marti, 2005).

American Evangelicals

Evangelicalism is the preeminent religious persuasion in American Protestantism. With Roman Catholicism facing "staggering problems" and mainline Protestantism on the decline, one quarter to one third of the US population currently identify themselves as Evangelicals (Kyle, 2006; Kosmin and Keysar, 2009). Evangelicals believe in personal salvation, the death, burial, and resurrection of Jesus Christ, the inerrancy of Scripture, and baptism, among other doctrinal positions which vary from conservative Evangelicals to liberal Evangelicals (Bloesch, 1978). Adventists are among the conservative Evangelicals. John C. Green, a senior Fellow at the Pew Forum on Religion and Family Life used polling to divide current Evangelicals into three camps: traditionalists, centrists, and modernists.

- "The *traditionalists,* characterized by high affinity for certain Protestant beliefs, (especially penal substitutionary atonement, justification by faith, the authority of scripture, priesthood of all believers, etc.) which…
- *Centrist Evangelicals* are described as socially conservative, mostly avoiding politics who still support much of traditional Christian theology.
- *Modernist Evangelicals* are a small minority in the movement, have low levels of church attendance, and "have much more diversity in their beliefs." (Luo, 2006; *Wikipedia,* 2010).

A 2004 survey of religion and politics put the number of Evangelicals in America at 26.4 percent of the population, Catholics at 22 percent and mainline Protestants at 16 percent. The statistical Abstract of the U. S. reports that in 2007 the population was divided into 28.6 percent (Evangelicals), 24.5 (Roman Catholic), 13.9 (mainline Protestant) (Kosmen, 2001). Based on the fundamental beliefs of the SDAC, they would seem to fall under the category of *traditionalists.*

The Evangelical Movement from Slavery to the 1960s

In a recent study by sociology of religion theorists, Emerson and Smith, they argue that "Evangelicals desire to end racial division and inequality, and attempt to think and act accordingly. But, in the process, they likely do more to perpetuate the racial divide than they do to tear it down" (2000). The period (Reconstruction) in which they had hoped to make progress on equality of the races was to become arguably the worst period for Blacks in America. Reynolds maintains,

> "In the turbulent period after Reconstruction, practically all political rights given the Negro following the conflict between South and North were retracted…Before the Civil War the question was how to free the Negroes in the South from the violence of the slaveholders. Following Reconstruction the question became how

to free Negroes from the violence of all the Whites, in the North as well as the South. Some of the worst conditions facing Blacks now prevailed over the entire nation. In fact, this was the darkest period in the history of the Negro in America" (Reynolds, 1984).

Slavery and Its Aftermath During slavery in the US, most White Southern lay Evangelicals owned slaves. This was true of the clergy also. The prominent Evangelical clergyman, George Whitefield, made an outspoken plea to the Georgia legislation for the legalization of slavery and was also a slave owner himself. At his death, Whitefield bequeathed his slaves to Countess Huntington (Stout, 1991; Emerson and Smith, 2000). Billy Graham, who was an outspoken anti-communism advocate (Kyle, 2006) acquiesced to segregation at his meetings and desisted only after the *Brown vs. Board of Education* in 1954 (Emerson and Smith, 2000). This was the norm among evangelists of the Evangelical movement at the time. The prominent Presbyterian pastor and professor at Union Theological Seminary averred—

> While we believe that 'God made of one blood all nations of men to dwell under the whole heavens,' ... "we know that the African has become ... a different, fixed *species* of the race, separated from the White man by traits bodily, mental and moral, almost as rigid and permanent as those of *genus* (Snoke, 2010).

Despite the rhetoric of racism and hatred in the South, several Southern clergymen joined the ranks of the North and agitated for the abolition of slavery. The famed revivalist Charles Finney became a part of the new abolitionists and prevented slave owners from taking communion. He dismissed them as child-sellers, women-whippers, and thieves, and referred to America as "a disgrace to humanity." Yet while Finney denounced slavery, he did not speak against racial prejudice and segregation. This was observed also among other Evangelicals in general, who saw slavery as sinful, but because they viewed African Americans as inferior, they were, nonetheless, prejudiced against them (Emerson and Smith, 2000; Horsman, 1981). Emerson and Smith postulate that this attitude set the stage for the Jim Crow laws after slavery was abolished (2000). Thus rather than denouncing the evil practice and coming to the aid of the oppressed, the Evangelical movement became the oppressor. To whom could slaves turn in such a situation when these religious officials so strongly influenced the government? Only God provided solace.

In their adamancy at keeping their slaves, Southern Christians developed a theology of slavery (Matthews, 1977). By their theology they justified their actions and assuaged their guilt, all the while ignoring the plight of the oppressed Negroes. They cunningly divided this misguided theology under four reasons: 1) biblical; 2) charitable and evangelistic; 3) social; 4) political. Finney's church segregated Blacks and Whites. For this reason a leading abolitionist and member of Finney's church in the 1830s, Lewis Tappen, had sharp disagreement with Finney on this issue and ultimately left his New York City church because of it (Emerson and Smith, 2000).

Historical records indicate that 25,000 members of Evangelical churches owned 208,000 slaves and 1200 clergy were slave owners. Between 1846 and the Civil War slaves were owned by ever bishop in the Methodist Episcopal Church, South. They were not dissimilar to all the other Southern denominations (Emerson and Smith, 2000). The abolition of slavery and outlawing of Jim Crow laws have not resulted in equality between Blacks and Whites. To this day the Evangelical movement continues to practice with great subtlety in some areas of its operation, the discrimination that it cannot do overtly under the law (Galbreath, 2003). Presbyterian Clergyman and professor, Robert L. Dabney articulated the philosophical argument for slavery well and labored to maintain the institution. Through speeches and books he defended the institution and offered support for slaveholders.

Overt racism of the earlier centuries has morphed into an insidious ethnocentrism in the late twentieth and twenty-first centuries. Hence

Billy Graham's assessment noted above holds true: America's biggest problem remains the problem of race. It appears also to be the biggest problem of the Evangelical movement. Undeniably the remnant church remains its prey.

How else do we account for the lack of growth by evangelism in America? It appears that Adventist churches face generational attrition as they can hardly retain membership of those beyond eighteen years of age. Could it be that the youth can see through our hypocrisy? The membership of the NAD has experienced minimal growth recently because of immigration. Left to biological growth and growth by evangelism, we would be declining. That is the reason the US SDAC is an aging church with the biggest percentage of its members over 63 years old, the next largest is Baby Boomers (ages 48-63).

The American Civil War- The Civil War in the US began when South Carolina and the states of the Deep South seceded from the Union. Lincoln and other Northern congressional officials viewed this move as illegal and resolved to save the Union. Although the secession resulted from the Southern states' reluctance to end slavery, nationwide emancipation was **not** the goal of the War as attested by historians (Horsman, 1981; Bennett, 1987; Reynolds, 1984). Seventy five thousand troops enlisted in the president's first call for troops (Schwarz, 1979). Three regiments of Negroes joined the ranks of the South after the government refused their offer to join the Union army (Reynolds, 1984).

Reconstruction appears to have had very admirable objectives. It promised equality under the law for Blacks. Historian Leon Litwack noted that Reconstruction failed because "the challenge of racial equality overwhelmed the American imagination." In the early stages of Reconstruction, Union General William T. Sherman met with twenty Black men and the Reverend Garrison Frazier to discuss how to deal with tens of thousands of freed Blacks who had abandoned inland plantations and followed his forces to the sea of Savannah. In 1865, asked what needed to be done for the Blacks, Frazier retorted that each should be given forty acres and a mule for each freed slave. An outgrowth of this was the experiment on St. Catherines Island with four hundred Blacks having their own constitution, Supreme Court, Congress and armed militia. By June 1865 some 10,000 former slaves occupied over 400,000 acres of land in South Carolina and Georgia (Alexander, 2004).

This experiment ended after the assassination of Abraham Lincoln when Lynden Johnson took office and ordered that confiscated lands be returned to their original owners. With no land and no means of subsistence for Blacks, the system of sharecropping began. Under this system a farmer would work twenty acres of cotton or rice for a White owner and earn an opportunity to plant his own crops (Alexander, 2004; See also, *Wikipedia*, "40 Acres and a Mule").

Seventh-day Adventists and the Civil War- Unlike some of the outstanding pioneers of the SDAC, Seventh-day Adventists have generally practiced social disengagement throughout the church's history. SDAs were reluctant to enlist in the Civil War and this caused suspicion among the neighbors of many members of the Church. Ellen White received a vision from the Lord regarding the War. After the battle of Bull Run, she saw that the Lord prevented the North from disaster as a means of prolonging the War (Schwarz, 1979; Reynolds, 1984). She also published a statement indicating that the War came as God's judgment on America for the "'high crime of slavery'" (Reynolds, 1984).

Three groups developed among Adventists in response to the War:

- The warhawks: those who were ready to fight;
- the pacifists: those who were non-compliant even in the face of imprisonment or death;
- the non-combatants: those who would serve without bearing arms.

The latter position reflects the church's stance on war during that time (Wilcox, 1936) and continues to be the SDAC's position presently.

Later on, membership was withdrawn from several members who enlisted voluntarily during the final months of the War. The reason for their dismissal appeared to have been in order to prevent the government officials from questioning the majority of the memberships' noncombatant stance, as articulated in a pamphlet entitled "The Draft." This pamphlet was presented to Provost Marshall General James B. Fry by J. N. Andrews of the GC Committee on August 30, 1864 as the Church's official position. Meanwhile the leaders called on the membership of the Church to engage the Lord in prayer and fast from March 1-4, 1865. The War ended in six weeks with General Lee's surrender (Schwarz, 1979; Reynolds, 1984).

The Adventist Church as a denomination did not align itself with a political party during the Civil War era (1860-1865) or at any other time throughout its history. Founded in a turbulent time when the nation's long debate over slavery was climaxing, the SDAC wanted to keep its mission focus. But several in its ranks were reform-minded. Joshua Himes and Joseph Bates and others in the Millerite movement were instrumental in organizing units of the Antislavery Society and articulated the Church's position in the *Review*. They averred-- "'slavery is pointed out in the prophetic word as the darkest and most damning sin upon the nation" (Reynolds, 1984). That resulted in the publication being banned from the slave states. The issue did not become a major concern for the newly organized Church. During the Civil War, the pioneers were too preoccupied with preparing for the second coming of Christ to be distracted by the political controversy over slavery at the time. Adventists were generally uninvolved in the calls for the abolition of slavery and other social reforms (Reynolds, 1984).

Neo-evangelical Theologians and Social Injustice

The neo-evangelical theological thinkers have willfully ignored Gunnar Myrdal's indictment of the US and by extension the evangelical movement, in his statement that a nation conceived in liberty and justice was also conceived in the sin of slavery. Esteemed neo-evangelical fathers such as Henry, Carnell, Jewett, and Ramm, along with famed preachers like Billy Graham and others are guilty of the sin of omission, Potter argues, because they did not address the racial crisis in America in any meaningful fashion. In Carnell's attempt at a cop-out he stated that if too much stress is placed on racial injustice, it will rob us of the opportunity to point sinners to their need to repent of a life of self-centeredness. Carnell self-inflicted his greatest wound on this matter with much candor, however. He admitted that his own racial pride remains undefeated and it is difficult for a man to preach against his own sin. For this reason he has not devoted an entire sermon to the sins of the White man. Even among contemporary mature White neo-evangelical scholars, literature on this dilemma is nonexistent, except Paul Jewett's posthumous work—*Who We Are: Our Dignity As Human—A Neo-evangelical Theology* (Okholm, 1997).

The SDAC and Social Injustice While abolition was clearly advocated by some of the pioneers, it remains unclear to this author that the Adventist Church supported the position. Published statements by Church pioneers in the Church's official paper do not necessarily constitute denominational sanction of their position. There is no extant record of any voted actions by the church officials on the matter of slavery. The Adventist Church typically allows editors and contributors to the paper to make statements that have not been considered or voted upon by the official body.

Ellen White stood out from among other Adventists, however as she referred to slavery as a sin and affirmed that the Lord used the Civil War to punish America for the "sin of slavery" (White, *The Southern Work*, 1966). In the 1960s the church had to revisit its treatment of Blacks in the wake of the Civil Rights Movement's initiatives for social change.

> "Theologically, Adventism adhered to the position of the conservative Evangelicals that rejected the 'social gospel,' arguing instead that social improvement would come about only as the result of individual conversion" (Land, 1998).

A 1965 General Conference committee made a ruling on the racial discrimination that disallowed any denominational institution from continuing their patterning of prevailing local customs on race relations. The church voted a resolution the following year at its General conference session stipulating that the Adventist Church should have "'No Wall of Partition'" between members of different races. Continued dissatisfaction among Blacks led to another challenge of the status quo when they charged the church with displaying a "'callous and racist attitude'" at the 1970 GC session. This resulted in a statement being added to the baptismal vows which rejected the consideration of color in matters of church membership (Land, 1998).

Historically the remnant church has assumed a similar position to Evangelicals regarding the social ills of postmodern America. A few years ago on October 10, 1997, at the Symposium on Mission and Social Action, Monte Salin admonished the church that if we are to be taken seriously as Christians, we cannot live in a state of spiritual isolationism. He alluded to the famed Evangelical theologian, John Stott's assertion that there are two attitudes to the world: "escapism" or "engagement" as he went on to emphasize the need for Adventist Christians to be involved not just in vertical evangelism, but also social engagement (Wilcox, 1997). The traditional and current attitude of the SDAC to the racial/ethnic divide in Adventism and the US at large has not been and is not an attitude with any admirable or redeeming quality, but one of apathy. With the exception of two Black Adventists, Harriet Tubman and Frederick Douglass, none other became prominent in the anti-slavery movements (Reynolds, 1984; Baker, 1996). We had the opportunity to take a public position of slavery just as we did on The Draft, but we did not. Our silence and dispiritedness during that time elicits this question even now: Why?

This attitude of the remnant irks the victims of systemic injustice and societal neglect or marginalization. It is not surprising therefore, that African Americans and Native Americans are usually neither attracted to our message nor mobilized by our mission. Their perception seems to be that our God wants their "soul" but is unconcerned about their body. Contrast the Nation of Islam with their attempts at reforming prisoners and cleaning up drug dealers among other social programs they run; this has resulted in huge successes for them among the African Americans. According to the 2009 Gallup poll, African Americans comprise 28% of the Muslim population in America, Hispanics, 35%, and Asians, 18% making the Muslims currently the most racially diverse religion in the US (Younis, 2009).

Following the Emancipation Proclamation, Blacks were landless and penniless. They had their freedom but nothing to do with it. Reconstruction followed, but proved futile for the African descendants in the US. The promises made to them did not materialize into meaningful sustenance let alone economic prosperity. This was a frustrating period for them: forty acres with no mule (Bennett, 1987) was the height of madness. Consequently, more than a hundred years passed after the Civil War and the end of slavery and the freeman still did not have access to much of America's wealth. For this reason Blacks decided to agitate for their rights. Thus began the Civil Rights Movement in the 1960s.

SDAs in the Civil Rights Movement The Adventist Church did not have any significant involvement in the Civil Rights Movement as an organization. Samuel C. London, Jr. affirms, however, in his recent study, *Seventh-day Adventists and the Civil Rights Movement,* that numerous African American Seventh-day Adventists played significant roles in the Civil Rights Movement (London, Jr., 2009). Segregation in the Evangelical movement is suffocating. Not only does it choke the oxygen of spirituality and sap the energy of its evangelism and mission, but it also stunts the growth of the Church (Holmes, 2000).

SDAs in the Rwandan Genocide The occurrence of the Rwandan genocide paints a pitiful picture of the Christian Church, particularly the Evangelical Protestants. Additionally it casts a huge shadow over the SDAC and other religious movements, considering that the state is predominantly Christian and the Adventist Church has the largest or second largest membership of the Protestant denominations there (Salin, 2009). It has been reliably reported that among the perpetrators of the atrocities of this genocide were Christian clergymen. Several Catholic priests have been identified and indicted by the Rwanda courts. An Adventist pastor, Elizaphan Ntakirutimana and his son, Gerard, were also indicted in 1996, after fleeing to Texas in the US in 1994. The father-son co-conspirators appealed to the US Supreme Court to avoid extradition. The pastor was then extradited when the US Supreme Court refused to hear his extradition case in January 2000, tried and sentenced (*Philadelphia Enquirer,* 1996; *ANN,* September 1996; http:// news. adventist.org/2003/02/rwaa-pastor-fou-guilty-by-u-tribual.html).

Evangelical Splinter Groups

Many slaves became weary of their White-dominated churches and branched off the form their own organizations. The American Methodist Episcopal Church was organized in Philadelphia in 1787 as they sought to avoid racially prejudiced harassment for worshiping at the established church. In some situations while worshiping they were removed from the normal congregational seats and placed in the gallery or "around the wall" (Dudley, 1997). The American Methodist Episcopal Zion Church later came out of the Methodist Church in 1796 for similar reasons.

Another splinter organization that came out of the Baptists was the American Baptist Home Missionary Society, which was organized on April 27, 1832 in New York City (Dudley, 1997). Through this organization, Blacks were trained to be pastors, to do home visitations, establish Sunday schools and rebuilt churches (Wojcikowski, 2010). In the decades leading up to Emancipation, many Northern Evangelicals joined the abolitionists and wanted an end to slavery. Meanwhile the Southerners of the Evangelical movement were determined to keep their slaves. After the Emancipation Proclamation in 1862, freedmen were allowed to freely choose their places of worship. Subsequently there was a split in several denominations over the issue of slavery.

Separation and Reconciliation: Presbyterians, Methodists, Southern Baptists

Presbyterians- The Presbyterian Church in the U. S. was the first to split over the issue of slavery. The North was anti-slavery and interested in social reform, while the South was pro-slavery and conservative. The clergyman Robert L. Dabney was one of the principal proponents of slavery in the Evangelical Presbyterian Church. He and others held to Enlightenment evolutionism, which taught that Blacks were like babies and White were to be a parent to them. Their paternalist racism was thus justifiable. The view advocated that Negroes should be subjected to a "permanent subservience based on innate inferiority" (Snoke, 2010). The Southern members of the organization became increasingly worried over the notion that the Church was becoming an "Abolition Society." As they jostled for control of the Church, they began to pull apart, so that by 1838 there were Presbyterian Churches (Boles, 1994). Recently the Presbyterians have decided to work toward reconciliation.

Since 1977 the Presbyterian Church in the US has been making strides toward racial reconciliation, firstly by participating in discussions of the issue and later by position statements. The thirtieth General Assembly of Presbyterians developed position papers in 2002 to declare their resolve. The church confessed both its personal and corporate sins. To show some seriousness, Presbyterians also admonished each member to take individual stance on reconciliation and each local church to engage in bridge-building activities to integrate the church (See Excursus II).

Methodists- Next of the three to split apart over slavery was the Methodist Church. At the dawn of the nineteenth century its British-born leaders were adamantly against slavery, but later retreated from the stance as it reprioritized. In this position it reasoned that its first priority was to preach the gospel rather than preaching against political and civil evils at the expense of its freedom to preach. They revised the *Methodist Book of Discipline* in 1808 to give permission for members to own slaves. In the South, the Methodists could freely own slaves while in the North they continued in their opposition to slaveholding as it stated in the original *Methodist Book of Discipline*. But the Church grew to become dominated nationally by the Southerners in the 1840s. With this development many Northerners left the fellowship of the national organization and formed splinter organizations. Among them was the Wesleyan Methodist Church. The Northerners regained control of the national body in 1844 and the Southerners continued to hold their ground on the issue of slavery. The tension reached breaking point when Bishop James O. Andrew of Georgia, given the option of freeing his slaves or give up his office, refused to free the slaves he had inherited through his wife. This precipitated a Plan of Separation which would become reality at its General Conference convention on May 1, 1845 (Boles, 1994). Ultimately, three African American groups came out of the Methodist Church due to the racial problem. In addition to the A. M. E. and A. M. E. Zion churches, there is the Christian Methodist Episcopal Church, a combined 5 million plus members (Schuman, 2010).

At their General Conference in 2000, there was a call for racial reconciliation in the Methodist Church in the US. Members were asked to repent of past racially prejudiced acts and attitudes (Schuman, 2010). There is a constant struggle to avert the segregation in the Methodist Church. Jim Shaw, an Indiana Annual Conference lay leader in the Methodist Church affirmed--"There is a need for racial healing between the African American group that stayed (in the Methodist Church) and the Caucasians.'" Racial reconciliation has still not happened on a universal scale in the Methodist Church but many within its ranks are taking intentional steps in that direction.

The Methodists have developed a historical video and study guide for members of the church entitled "Steps Toward Wholeness: Learning and Repentance." Meanwhile various conferences in the denomination are holding racial reconciliation and repentance discussions. More recently a group (Black Methodists for Church Renewal) was started to eradicate racism within the United Methodist Church (Schuman, 2010). Several of its local churches have been making valiant attempts to foster reconciliation. Among them is the Reconciliation United Methodist Church in Durham, NC, which began with the initiative of two pastors, one Black and one White (http://www.trianglegivesback. org/organizations/reconciliation-united-methodist-church/e).

Southern Baptists- The Baptist Church has put down strong roots in the US since the pilgrims came aboard the Mayflower in the 1770's. Many Southern Baptists owned slaves before Emancipation. In 1844, at its national Triennial Convention, the body voted to deny the appointment of a slaveholding minister, James E. Reeves as a missionary. This event precipitated the South's secession from the Convention. Exactly one week after the Methodist separation, on May 8, 1845, three hundred seventy seven (377) delegates from eight Southern states and the District of Columbia, met in Augusta, Georgia and voted to form the Southern Baptist Convention. Since then it has become the largest Protestant denomination in the U. S.

DeYoung suggests that the trauma of the persecution of the Anglo-Saxons in Europe, which caused them to flee for liberty in the New World, may have contributed to the abuse that they inflicted on the Indians and Blacks in America (1997). In contrast, it appears more plausible, however, that these Europeans sought to decimate the Indians, Blacks, and their culture, because they felt that they were superior to them. Numerous accounts indicate that the ideology that served as the driving force behind their conquests and atrocities was their racist ideology that the Anglo-Saxons were a superior people (Horsman, 1981).

While DeYoung's assessment is in concert with the psychological theory that the abused victim is prone to abuse others, it should be made clear that such unfortunate reality must not serve to condone the resultant wrong. Rather, the appropriate steps should be taken to obtain therapy and bring healing in order to head off a cycle of abuse. In this instance, corporate therapy may be in order. Any mass therapy that could potentially cure such heinous disposition would be well-nigh useless, I submit, unless it is divine. Unfortunately, if therapy is currently being administered, the Anglo-Saxon racism must be an extremely resistant strain of the racist gene, since after decades, hardly any rehabilitation is noticeable. Indians still live primarily on Reservations with minimal facilities and abundant alcohol. More than 15% of Blacks still live below the poverty line and have a greater rate of incarceration than the percentage of high school education. Hispanics are tethering on the brink of the precipice of economic disaster. Meanwhile, in 2007, one percent of predominantly White Americans owned more than 34 percent of the country's wealth with the bottom 80 percent of the population owning a mere seven percent of the financial wealth. Wealth of the top one percent has become more concentrated and has remained consistently above 30 percent since 1922, except 1945, 1949 and between 1976 and 1981. This wealth translates into economic power; this power is used to influence government in their favor (Domhoff, 2010; Rosenberg, 2007).

> The Census report showed increases in poverty for Whites, Blacks and Hispanic Americans, with historic disparities continuing. The poverty rate for non-Hispanic Whites was 9.4 percent, for Blacks 25.8 percent and for Hispanics 25.3 percent. The rate for Asians was unchanged at 12.5 percent (Eckholm, 2010).

It is noteworthy that the SBC, which segregated over slavery, at its 150 year anniversary, voted a resolution on race reconciliation at its general session in 1995. On the occasion of its Convention in Atlanta, Georgia, in 1995, grassroots members of the SBC brought a motion to the floor to adopt a resolution on race reconciliation in the denomination. This was quickly passed after little discussion. Representatives of both the White and Black membership of the Convention exchanged apology and forgiveness for the corporate sins of racial discrimination in the church (See Excursus II).

Over the last decade, Adventist tertiary educational institutions (Walla Walla University, Andrews University (2017), Pacific Union College, Union College Southern Adventist University, La Sierra University, Advent Health, and Loma Linda University), have all appointed Chief Diversity Officers, to address matters regarding diversity and report to their respective university president on matters of diversity, equity, and inclusion. This is a welcome and significant development to move us toward the diversity, inclusiveness, and equity we seek.

Summary- The Evangelical movement in the US was founded during a time when Europeans (Portuguese, Dutch, British, French, Spanish) were engaged in enslaving people around the world. The intellectual climate in the US had accepted as an established fact that Blacks and Indians were inferior and Whites were superior. In an attempt to justify their oppression of Blacks and Indians, Whites developed biblical arguments and "scientific" reasons why this had to be so. Nevertheless with the help of abolitionists of the North and the Divine hand, slavery was outlawed then abolished.

Reconstruction followed, but this was also a horrific time for Blacks and Indians. Forty acres and a mule proved futile for the freedmen. Jim Crow laws segregated Blacks and Whites, while Indians were marginalized and forced unto reservations with little or no civilization. The Evangelical movement condoned and promoted slavery because many within its ranks were slave owners and were profiting personally. While the remnant Church did not advocate the perpetuation of slavery (Ellen White denounced it as an "evil system"), the SDAC was guilty of practicing racial segregation and still is, presently, as are the other Christian denominations, several of which had split over the institution.

The Adventist Church was not segregated when it was first organized; everyone worshiped together. The local conferences were organized geographically; Blacks and Whites were in the same conferences and worshiped together in the same local churches. Ellen White stated in MS 114, in 1904 that Whites were not to worship by themselves and Blacks by themselves, but realizing that prejudice was so strong in some places, she counseled as a concession, "neither are we to say that they are to worship together" (Baker, 2007). This was her recommendation when any specific area had such strong racial prejudice that Whites would not attend evangelistic meetings if Blacks were present, for fear of endangering themselves and the Blacks.

The SDAC traditionally has not been a socially engaging movement. While the church issued a statement on the Civil War, that appears to have been its only explicit reference to any social issue of the US. It has generally remained disengaged from discussions on social injustice. It followed the lead of many of its American counterparts and voted to divide by race.

One research indicates that while White Evangelicals and Whites in the larger society in the US are interested in integrating, doing so would go against their market principle and the core values and assumptions that they hold. Among these core values are freedom, individualism, independence, equality of opportunity, and privacy. They do not want to have to sacrifice any of these in order to facilitate racial reconciliation. . In contemporary parlance that position is often classified as "White privilege." Consequently, we remain divided by the very faith, which teaches us to unite (Emerson and Smith, 2000). Meanwhile the Evangelical movement in the US is dying.

About 75 percent of US churches are declining and only one percent growth results from conversion of the "unchurched" (Jim White, 2008; Johnson et al, 1993). In a survey of 200,000 churches in the US David T. Olson of *Ministry Today* notes that while the US population gained 52 million in 16 years, church membership in the US remains unchanged. One percent of churches disband annually, which amounts to a 3,750 mortality rate, similar to the human mortality rate (Olson, *Ministry Today*, 2010). What is the reason for this decline?

> "The least credible theory attributes their decline to the secularizing effects of industrialization, urbanization, and the spread of mass education. If secularization were the sole explanation, all but the most culturally insulated sectors of American religion would be losing members" (Johnson et al, 1993).

The counsel Ellen White gave regarding segregated worship during the time of heightened prejudice in America was similar to what Jesus offered to his disciples when he first sent them on their mission. The Twelve were told not to go to the Samaritans (Mt. 10:5), but later he sent the seventy two to go to the very people and places that he had earlier forbidden the twelve not to go (Lk. 10:1-11). His rationale for preventing the Twelve was that the Samaritan territory was not ready to listen to them when he sent out the Twelve because he had not yet prepared the way for them and their resistance would have discouraged the Twelve. By the time he sent out the seventy two, he had already gone through the territory (Jn. 4:4-26, 39-54) and prepared it to be receptive to their message (White, *DA*, 1898). The Samaritans were receptive to the seventy two disciples. Finally, Christ wants his remnant church to be united along racial and ethnic lines and in all other aspects. In unity there is strength. With strength, the three angels' messages may be proclaimed more forcefully. When God's people come together as one there is nothing he assigns us that we cannot accomplish. Those who belong to the remnant must see it as their Christian obligation to promote the common brotherhood/sisterhood of all humanity and oppose those who would seek to do otherwise. And this pertains also to segregated governance. Some argue that the Adventist Church in the US is not divided despite its obvious divisions along racial/ethnic lines. They point to the leadership of the General Conference, the North American Division, and a few other local conferences. Yet the divisions are obvious. You have only to visit our local churches and you readily observe that but for a few of our congregations (even those in large populations of Adventists), our congregations are more than eighty percent of one racial/ethnic group or other.

Latinos worship with Latinos, Blacks with Blacks, Whites with Whites, Asians with Asians and so on. In addition, our institutions (educational, health, others) are typically dominated by Whites, particularly in the higher paying positions and ethnic people are often covertly rejected (as "not a fit") when they seek employment at these predominantly White institutions. And when they are tokenized with employment, they often suffer unbearable discomfort resulting from the collegial and social isolation (from colleagues) they often endure. Many resign within a few years and move on to more welcoming environments. Further, we are largely segregated into local conferences that were racially designed, although in recent years some of them have experienced forced integration due to the in-migration of immigrant members.

4

Segregated Governance in the Remnant Church

Reconstruction and the Remnant Church- The period known as the Reconstruction in the US initially bore some marks of hope for minorities, but within a few years all hope soon fizzled out into thin air. Between the years 1815-1830 several theories of race circulated. They were not "scientific" as in later centuries, but came from uncensored and uninhibited discussions of ordinary people. The view advanced by Montesquieu in *De l'Esprit des lois* (Paris 1748) that the higher level of achievement among northerners can be accounted for in the temperate climate, was widely accepted. In the 1774 *History of Jamaica* by Edward Long, the author argued that Negroes came from a separate species and were halfway between humans and the higher apes. Charles White pointed out in another work in 1799 "that there was an ascending hierarchy of races" (Johnson, 1991) and that the least civilized Negroes were those with the most striking Negro character. He argued further that the Pepels, Nisagos, and Ibos, were the most savage and morally degraded of Natives. These he affirmed were the most likely to have deformed countenances, flat foreheads, and projecting jaws and other Negro peculiarities (Johnson, 1991).

The culture of the larger society tends to influence the religious culture of the churches in every society. In the modern era America was no different. The SDAC during this period bore a striking resemblance to the prevailing social intellectual climate. The Jim Crow laws which segregated Blacks and Whites in society were both unofficially (in the former) and officially (in the latter) applied to both the Adventist and the Evangelical movement. Consequently, Adventist congregants began to feel uncomfortable worshiping in mixed-race churches.

The ill effects of the segregation in society during the time of the Reconstruction were obvious. The Evangelical movement, including the SDAC, became victim to its dangers. Though it seemed un-Christian to segregate, many Adventists felt pressured to do so in order to avoid the ire of those outside of the Church. Meanwhile the Black Adventists wanted to prevent by legislation any further segregation within the ranks of the remnant. Writing about the resolution brought by the Blacks to the 1889 GC session, Ellen White offered the counsel:

> "At the General Conference of 1889, resolutions were presented in regard to the color line. Such action is not called for. Let not men take the place of God, but stand aside in awe, and let God work upon human hearts, both White and Black, in His own way. He will adjust all these perplexing questions. We need not prescribe a definite plan of working. Leave an opportunity for God to do something. We should be careful not to strengthen prejudices that ought to have died just as soon as Christ redeemed the soul from the bondage of sin" (White, *The Southern Work*, 1966).

Notwithstanding, Ellen White did not support segregation for reason of prejudice. During that time it was dangerous for Whites and Blacks to engage in mixed worship. Graybill maintains that Ellen White's statements regarding the separation of the races were made to avoid offending the prejudices of the Whites (Graybill, 1970). She exercised wisdom under the guidance of the Spirit of God and recommended--"Common association with the Blacks is not a wise course to pursue. To lodge with them in their homes may stir up feelings in the minds of the Whites which will imperil the lives of the workers" (White, *The Southern Work*, 1966).

Graybill has argued persuasively that Ellen White's first call for segregation came after White Adventists, working primarily with Blacks in Mississippi river towns, faced looting, shooting, and burning mobs of Whites. Ellen White "vigorously championed equality," Branson argues; she urged a moderate stance on race relations because of the social climate under Jim Crow laws. Her statements offered a concession to what she had hoped would be a temporary problem. She stated—"Let them understand that this plan is to be followed until the Lord shows us a better way" (Branson, 1970). At the appropriate time she counseled further—

> "You have no license from God to exclude the colored people from your places of worship…They should hold membership in the church with the White brethren. Every effort should be made to wipe out the terrible wrong which has been done them" (White, *The Southern Work*, 1966)…

While she discouraged mixed-race worship, she encouraged accepting Blacks into the fellowship of the Church even among the Whites. This problem of racial prejudice was not to result in keeping anyone out of God's kingdom. Her position was made out of "a desire "to maintain the work among Negroes" (Graybill, 1970). She realized that by going against the social "grain" could cause more harm than good in light of the ultimate goal of evangelizing Blacks. It is conclusive therefore, that Ellen White saw this as a temporary measure until the Lord would show us a better way (White, *9T*, 1948; Graybill, 1970).

Racial Dominance in Governance

The Adventist work in the US was started by people of primarily Anglo-Saxon descent. The majority of Americans in the early 1900s were of this racial background. The Millerite Movement was comprised primarily of the same race although as I showed earlier, there was much collaboration between the few Blacks and the Whites among the Millerites. Based on the historical literature available the racial divide of the believers did not become apparent until later, that is, decades after the SDAC was organized and into the early twentieth century.

Opposition to Shared Leadership- As the worked progressed, albeit under trying circumstances, thousands of Blacks accepted the Advent message and became a part of the SDAC. By the end of 1944 there were over 17,000 Blacks in the regional conferences alone (Baker, 1996). Prior to this time, however, Blacks were not given the opportunity to participate in the leadership of the local conferences. Blacks sought to integrate the Church but this was met with much White opposition. This is noted in the speech delivered to the GC session by Joseph T. Dodson, chair of the lay group that organized after Lucy Byard's death when she was refused treatment at the White Adventist hospital in Washington D. C. At the time Blacks wanted to be integrated into the whole and to be allowed to participate in the leadership of the Church at the local conference level. In apparent disappointment at their rejection Dodson remarked--"They gave us our conferences instead of integration. We didn't have a choice. In the end it was better to have segregation with power, than segregation without power" (Reynolds, 1984; Koranteng-Pipim, 2001).

An Embarrassing Development- Elder Charles M. Kinney was the first Black to be ordained as pastor in the SDA Church in the US. Kinney was born a slave in Richmond, Virginia, in 1878 and later moved west, where he accepted Christ through the preaching of J. N. Loughborough in Reno, Nevada. Showing much promise, Kinney was sent to Healdsburg College and after two years study there, was sent by the GC to work in Kansas among the Blacks there. It took nearly two decades of labor before Kinney was called to pastor the first Seventh-day Adventist Church that was organized among the Blacks. On the day of his ordination, Kinney and his wife were embarrassed by the racial prejudice that was shown against them. He vowed to address the problem (Reynolds, 1984; Baker, 1996).

Photo: C. M. Kinney (Adapted from History
of the South Central Conference)

Blacks Marginalized- For decades leading up to the 1920s the Church had been totally administered by White pastors and officials. During the 1920s Black leaders felt marginalized by their White brethren and requested involvement in the leadership of the Church. J. K. Humphrey and others led delegations to the Church's headquarters seeking redress on this issue but to no avail (Schwarz, 1979). Hospitals, educational institutions, and local conferences were supervised and staffed by Whites only. Capable, qualified Blacks were totally overlooked for leadership in the conferences to the point that it was socially suffocating for Blacks. Yet the message of the Church was so biblical and attractive that these committed saints dared not walk away from it. They were convinced that this was God's remnant church and remained committed members.

The leaders sought to preserve their leadership positions by various means ranging from the theological to the evangelistic and the social. To this day Whites continue to make the case against hiring Blacks for whatever the reason. A few decades ago, Roy E. Graham suggested that the demand of Blacks to make church appointments solely on the basis of a person's race "would be out of harmony with EGW's understandings" (Graham, 1985). Such suggestions should probably be construed in the light of his earlier statement that in every individual there exists "latent prejudice." If Graham were thinking fairly, why would he make such a conclusion without going on to point out that Blacks, who have been oppressed and marginalized, are due some restitution from society and even the SDA Church? When one considers the fact that for decades, Blacks and more recently, Latinos and Asians, have been making significant monetary contributions through local state conferences and union conferences of the church, which in turn supported our institutions, but they were refused admission to educational institutions and denied employment in the health and educational institutions because of their ethnicity. They were never receiving their fair share. Do the evils perpetrated by the racist society and racist actions of some church personnel not evoke the biblical principle of restitution, even in Christians (Lev. 6:2-5; Lk. 19:8, 9)?

In his unpublished work "Lights and Shades in the Black Belt," A. W. Spalding suggested that the work in the South would be hindered by trying to integrate the churches (Baker, 1996). Ellen White stated also that "Instead of wondering whether they are not fitted to labor for White people, let our colored brethren and sisters devote themselves to missionary work among the colored people" (White *9T*, 1948). This and other statements must be placed in the context of their socio-cultural milieu.

The Second Great Disappointment of the Remnant

Arguably the most unfortunate and disappointing thing that has happened in the Adventist Church since its 1844 first Great Disappointment in the US, is its decision in 1944 to divide into Black and White conferences (regional and state conferences). After Elder Kinney, the first Black ordained pastor in the US and his wife were treated discriminatingly by the Whites at his ordination in 1944, the Black members felt it was time to ask for the inclusion of Blacks in the leadership of the Church. That, coupled with the unfortunate death of a Black member of the church who, after falling ill and rushed to one of the White-run Adventist hospitals, was refused attention and abandoned in the corridor of the Washington Adventist Hospital, gave the move the appearance of urgency. Upon seeing the situation, relatives rushed her elsewhere in a frantic attempt to save her life. Recent research has uncovered credible information indicating that she actually died a few weeks (specifically, 38 days) after the incident as opposed to the widely believed account that she died before she could get to another facility across town. She was transferred to Freedman's Hospital, the current Howard University Hospital in Washington D.C. (Baker, Lucille Byard, 2020). This led to an increased push for inclusion of Blacks in leadership (Reynolds, 1984). The White members would have none of it. This being the case, Black Adventists felt forced to propose a resolution for separate conferences in order to adequately take care of their needs.

The following is the resolution passed at the General Conference session in 1944:

> **Whereas**, The present development of the work among the colored people in North America has resulted, under the signal blessing of God, in the establishment of some 233 churches with some 17,000 members; and

> **Whereas,** It appears that a different plan of organization for our colored membership would bring further great advance in soul-winning endeavors; therefore

> **We recommend**, That in unions where the colored constituency is considered by the union conference committee to be sufficiently large, and where the financial income and territory warrant, colored conferences be organized (Peters, 1944; Baker, 1996).

Regional Conferences Organized

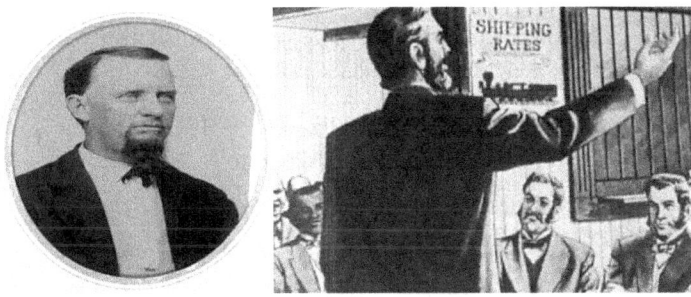

ELBert B. Lane preaches in Edgefield Junction. Adapted from History of the South Central Conference.

The first Black Adventist church was organized in Edgefield Junction, Tennessee after an appeal was made to the GC by R. K. Clune to send minister to evangelize the Blacks in the South. Elbert B. Lane was sent in response to the appeal and he was successful in baptizing several Blacks and arousing serious interest in several others. The account for the origin of the segregated governance structure by the General Conference is recorded in *Telling the Story…* by Delbert Baker (Peters, 1944; Baker, 1995). I refer to this as the Second Great Disappointment of the Remnant.

Members of the first Black congregation in Edgefield Junction, Tennessee (*Photo from the History of South Central Conference*).

The Vote to Divide- The Seventh-day Adventist Church in its spring Council meetings of 1944, voted to adopt the segregated governance structure. These meetings were convened "specifically to discuss the advisability of the organization of regional conferences" (Baker, 1996). The meetings were presided over by the president of the GC, Elder James L. McElhany. Although McElhany fell ill during the course of the meetings and remained sick in his hotel room, Elder George E. Peters, director of the Regional Office of the GC delayed the discussions until he had the opportunity to exit the meeting and dialog with Elder McElhany, in order to ascertain that the GC president had his input on this critical matter. Elder McElhany was persuaded by Peters to appear at the meeting; and he did. After several other influential members had spoken, the GC president clearly articulated his position at the meeting, indicating that he had a "deep interest" in the welfare of Blacks and fully supported the "wisdom of Black conferences" and he affirmed the capabilities of Black leadership (Baker, 1996). Thus the GC enabled the NAD in the formation of regional conferences.

The outcome of the premeetings resulted in union conferences being given the go-ahead by the GC, to form Black conferences within their territory. This came as a result of the refusal of Whites to allow Blacks even minimal participation in the leadership of the local conferences of the SDAC. Consequently, unions in the South, Northeast, and Midwest moved quickly to form regional conferences where Black churches were in sufficient numbers in their territories. While this was taking place in 39 of the 50 states in the US, all unions except the Pacific and Pacific Northwest Union Conferences organized regional conferences beginning in 1945 and the following years. The latter two unions set up Regional Affairs Offices instead (Baker, 1996; Land, 1998).

The first regional conferences that were formed in the years immediately following were: Lake Region was the first in 1945; Allegheny, 1945; Northeastern, 1945, South Atlantic, 1946, South Central 1946, Southwest Region, 1947; Central States, 1947 (Baker, 1996). The Allegheny Conference was divided and reorganized into

Allegheny East and Allegheny West in 1967. A decade and a half later the South Eastern Conference was organized in 1981 (Reynolds, 1984).

African American Initiatives- At the pre-meetings of the Spring Council of the GC in 1944, African American lay people drew up and submitted a list of grievances and recommendations to the GC (Baker, 1996). Among these were their dissatisfaction with the church's hiring practices, and recommendations for a nondiscriminatory admission to denominational educational and medical institutions and the establishment of Black conferences, staffed by Black officials (Land, 1998). Furthermore, between the years 1954 and 1966 under the leadership of Reuben R. Figuhr, African Americans succeeded in negotiating the appointment of a committee on race relations. These were passed at the General Conference autumn council of 1961 (Land, 1998).

The first African American SDA church was organized in Edgefield Junction, Tennessee, with a membership of ten and a first Sabbath offering of 24 cents. The work in the regional conferences has grown tremendously over the decades since. In 1933 over 10,000 African American members who gave $122,379.76 in tithe and $89, 181.70 in offerings ("SDA Race Relations," *Adventist Archives,* 1934). In 1944 the membership among the African Americans in Regional Conferences stood at 17,000 and 9% of the US; 220,000 and more than 25% in 1995 (Baker, 1996). In 2008 there were 232,456 (Adventist Archives, 2009); 2009 it was over 235,000. Yet this fact does not justify the segregation.

Dr. Barry Black's assertion nearly twenty years later in echoing the call for Black conferences to hire White pastors and for White conferences to hire more Black pastors, resonates with many Adventists today. Black posed the question in a *Review* article in 1992, "Could it be that, like Peter, God is blessing us in spite of ourselves" (Black, 1992)? But these are not to be placed according to race/ethnicity, but based on their spiritual /leadership gifts. By doing this a natural heterogeneity begins to occur. This is the "unity in diversity" which Ellen White envisaged in the SDAC (*9T*, 1948).

Ellen White's Views on Ethnic Conferences- Ellen White had this to say in reference to the letter of request she received concerning organizing German and Scandinavian conferences—

> Were those who seek to disintegrate the work of God, to carry out their purpose, some would magnify themselves to do a work that should not be done. Such an arrangement would greatly retard the cause of God. If we are to carry on the work most successfully, the talents to be found among the English and Americans should be united with the talents of those of every other nationality. And each nationality should labor earnestly for every nationality (White, *9T*, 1948).

This she asserts was given to her directly by the Lord several times. Since this was said of the German and Scandinavian conferences, would she not say the same about the White and Black conferences? Thus even with the growth that is quickly pointed out by some that defend the status quo, can we imagine how much more the remnant would have grown if we had not divided? Of over 307 million people in the US there are just over one million Adventists.

Black Union Proposal- In the decades following the divide, Blacks continued their efforts to seek further participation in the leadership of the church, which resulted in a recommendation by the North American Regional Department in 1969 to study the matter of Black unions. This proposal was rejected at the 1970 GC session on the basis that it could cause further separation of Black and White Adventists. The matter of Black unions came up again in 1978 and resulted in the creation of an office of Office of Ethnic Affairs to replace the former North America Office of Regional Affairs (*SDA Encyclopedia*, Vol. 11, 1976). This was later renamed the office of Human Relations, which remains presently. The move to elect more Blacks to leadership offices outside of regional conferences bore more fruit in the election of C. E. Bradford as vice-president of the NAD in 1979. The church also adapted a statement on Human and Race Relations to be included in the *Church Manual*. In this statement the church "pledged itself to promote workshops, literature, and textbooks on race relations…" as it sought to accommodate itself to pressures of social change (Land, 1998).

Failed Attempts by the SDAC- It is commendable that some attempts at reconciliation have been made in committee meetings and with written statements of the Church, yet these have been kept so quiet and pushed aside that even after decades, pastors and lay members do not seem to know about these developments. I had not known about them after nearly twenty years as an Adventist pastor, neither have I heard any reference to them in any meeting of the conferences, workshops, or seminars. Were these pledges put into effect? If so where? I still have not seen and cannot find, after diligent search, the literature that should be promoting anything on race relations, except for one book in a NAD series on race, sex, gender by Caleb Rosado in 1990. Besides, these statements in the *Church Manual* did nothing to address the "White flight" and "Black flight" issues.

"White flight" results from racial prejudice by Whites among other factors and "Black flight" results from Blacks feeling merely tolerated at traditionally White educational and health institutions of the denomination. What is being done to sensitize denominational workers to racial and ethnic peculiarities, to operate optimally in a diverse church environment? Have we been conducting diversity training at our institutions as the pledge above seems to recommend that we do? What is being done to teach or train members how to embrace diversity on the local church level?

In the 1970s attempts were made by the regional conferences to address the issue of racial reconciliation. In 1970 recommendations were sent to the GC by the regional conferences which recommended workshops to be held on race for ministers and workers across North America. This would include ministers sharing across racial lines as in an experimental living accommodations plan at Andrews University. It was also recommended that the churches in these conferences be asked to participate in "workshops exploring the terms and possibilities of exchange and fellowship at the grass roots" in 1971 (Reynolds, 1984). But we have not been hearing about these recommendations neither are we seeing anything being done. What is being done while the problems persist?

In the year 2000, the "regional conferences chose to create a Defined Benefits Retirement Plan rather change to the Defined Contributions Plan suggested by the NAD. This new Plan is being financed by all nine regional conferences without NAD and GC oversight. Nevertheless the "Regional Conferences contribute "more than $1 million per year towards the remaining benefits liabilities in the NAD" (Regional Conferences , 2020). After careful studying of the plan, at least one state conference found it to be a good plan and sought to participate in it. Pastors (including this author) and other conference employees of the Greater New York Conference voted to participate in this plan, after consulting with the Office of Regional Conferences.

This move, however, was discouraged by the leadership of the NAD, and the local conference leadership got cold feet and abandoned the pursuit. The then president of the NAD, told us at a meeting with local conference pastors that the plan was voted for the Blacks as a redress for the discrimination they suffered during the earlier years of the US and of the Adventist Church. He also argued that if other conferences should leave the GC's Defined Contribution Plan, it would collapse and leave the retired workers in a disadvantageous and desperate position. Thus, the latter would be unsustainable.

Several pastors (perhaps most employees of the Regional Conferences) have indicated to me that they do not want a change in the current governance structure that allows Regional Conferences to have their own retirement plan. Why? They admit that they do not want to lose their current retirement plan. Who would argue with their reasoning?

Clearly, the Regional Conferences' Defined Benefits Retirement Plan is a superior plan to the GC's Defined Benefits Plan. Many would question, however, whether that should be the reason to keep the church in segregated governance. And what about the matters of equity and inclusion? The ideal is for everyone to be treated equally in all sectors of the Adventist Church and create heterogenous local churches. Yet one must admit that only a change of hearts can make Whites and Blacks feel comfortable worshiping together regularly. The "White flight" phenomenon persists.

Blacks who support the maintenance of the status quo argue that it guarantees that they'll be included in church leadership all the while securing their retirement benefits. In their view, Whites remain as prejudiced as they have always been and things would return to where they were before, in which Blacks were ignored and marginalized. Why would we want that?

Segregation Results in Attrition

Early Adventists did not seem to make distinctions along the color line. This soon changed however, as White members in interracial congregations apparently began to fear for their safety and that of the entire denominational membership in the US (Branson, 1970). During a time of lynching and race riots, Whites left the First Church in Washington to organize other churches in the area. When word of this reached Ellen White, she accepted an invitation to speak at First Church. In letters written later, her reaction to this development was candid. She characterized it as prejudice against the Black minority and chastised the Whites for their cowardice. She wrote—"Let us as Christians… not be cowards in the face of the world… We should treat the colored man just as respectfully as we would treat the White man" (Reynolds, 1984)… A perceived attempt to make an all-Black church of an interracial group in 1903 evoked this response from Dr. Howard in a letter to A. G. Daniells of the GC:

'It is difficult to see why it is necessary to make a race line in the Adventist denomination in face of the fact that the truth involves a positive protest against any such thing in the church. It is even more difficult to see why there should ever have been a disposition… to experiment with this church in the interest of a policy of race distinction, or to deal with it in harmony with such a policy… We understand the awful meaning to us of the dealing of the General Conference…. It does seem… that there is a disposition among the General Conference Committee to make the Church colored' (Reynolds, 1984).

This unfortunate situation resulted in Elder Sheafe, who by then had been asked to pastor the People's Church in Washington, becoming disenchanted with the GC policy. He and the congregation later withdrew from the denomination (Reynolds, 1984).

At the turn of the century, as African Americans began planting churches in various states, the desire to be led by one of their own became strong. Lewis C. Sheafe was an outstanding preacher, who converted from the Baptist Church where he had been a minister. After being invited to hold meetings in Washington, he baptized numerous Negro members. With Negroes being the majority, he was asked to serve as their pastor (Reynolds, 1984).

Not surprisingly, throughout the history of the Adventist Church, many have left the denomination because of racial and ethnic tensions. The Church's racial policy toward Blacks between the 1920s and 1930s resulted in several Black leaders leaving its membership. J. K. Humphrey, a dynamic Jamaican pastor in Harlem, New York, left the denomination with his congregation of about six hundred members in 1929 (Reynolds, 1984).

In 1889 the first ordained SDA Black pastor, Elder C. M. Kinney, speaking on the concept of Regional Conferences, rightly affirmed that "...a separation of the colored people from the White people is a great sacrifice upon our part; we lose the blessing of learning the truth" (Schwarz, 1979)... For decades leading up to the 1920s the Church had been totally administered by White pastors and officials. During the 1920s Black leaders felt marginalized by their White brethren and requested involvement in the leadership of the Church. All the local and union conferences, educational and medical institutions in the US were homogeneous. Several Black ministers made repeated appearances before the White leaders to include some Blacks in the leadership, but to no avail. Among these was J. K. Humphrey, a charismatic and influential leader originally from the island of Jamaica, who had a church of 600 members in Harlem, New York. Humphrey eventually got discouraged, took his congregation, and left the organized work. He remained outside the ranks of the Church until his death in 1952 (Schwarz, 1979; Baker, 1996). How unfortunate that this unresolved racial issue should lead to such great attrition from the Lord's church.

Photo: J. K. Humphrey (from History of South Central Conference).

Just prior to the Spring meetings in 1944, a female mulatto member from Brooklyn, New York fell ill while visiting relatives in Washington D. C. and was rushed to our denomination's Washington Adventist Hospital, a segregated facility then. She was admitted at first until it was observed on her paperwork that she was Black at which time treatment was abandoned while contact was made to Freedmen hospital a considerable distance away. Her conditioned worsened while she awaited treatment and she died. This incident was very painful to Black members and minister alike, who used it to make another push for integration of all institutions. The GC committee which studied the proposal rejected it as being unfeasible.

Yet as some declared during the pre-meetings to the GC session, their insistence was for an "organization (structure) that will give us a future" (Reynolds, 1984; Baker, 1996). During these meeting Elder G. E. Peters insisted that the sitting GC president and facilitator of the discussions, Elder James L. McElhany, be a part of the deliberations, but he lay sick in his hotel room. After requesting for a delay of the discussions, Elder Peters also asked leave of the meeting to visit with Elder McElhany in his room.

During his visit he impressed upon the president the need for his personal input on the discussions, as the perception was that the issue would not be settled until he voiced his positions on it. Elder McElhany appeared and addressed the meeting in which he spoke in favor of organizing conferences for the Blacks. On the second day McElhany supported his position by suggesting that he supported organizing conferences for the Blacks so that they could take leadership and in order to preserve unity. Two prominent White delegates, William A. Spicer and Jay J. Nethery spoke in favor of this move along with a prominent Black pastor, F. L. Peterson. Twenty two persons spoke on the issue; seventeen spoke in favor of it, three against and two asked for clarifications. The move was overwhelmingly supported (Baker, 1996).

Throughout the history of the co-existence of Whites and Blacks in the US, the Black-White relation has been atrocious at worse and tolerable at best. The SDA Church has arguably been very similar. From the earliest years since its formation out of a splinter group of the Millerite Movement, the Church has had serious challenges embracing diversity. Whites out rightly refused the request to share the leadership with Blacks in the local state conferences. This resulted in Blacks calling for the formation of regional conferences.

Whites flee to join or form new congregations whenever the number of Blacks gets to a certain percentage ("tipping point"), usually thirty percent (Rock, 2006). Over the years many Blacks who visited White congregations have been informed without request where they may find Black houses of worship. Some Whites still do **not** want to have Blacks in their local churches; without a doubt it also goes vice versa. Hence the attrition of many Adventists may be accounted for in racial discrimination.

Much has been said about the timely, vigorous discussions and eloquent speeches by church officials that preceded the vote to divide. Baker, Knight, and others provide ample evidence of this (Baker, 1996; Knight, 1993, 1994, 2005), but none has any record of time being taken to earnestly seek the Lord's counsel in the matter after the emotional debate and before the vote was taken. The result, therefore, is not surprising, giving the omission of divine guidance. This serves as a frightening reminder of what Ellen White counseled in *Testimonies for the Church Vol. 9,*

> Because the president of a conference suggested certain plans, it has sometimes been considered unnecessary to consult the Lord about them. Thus propositions have been accepted that were not for the spiritual benefit of the believers and that involved far more than was apparent at the first casual consideration. Such movements are not in the order of God. Many, many matters have been taken up and carried by vote, that have involved far more than was anticipated and far more than those who voted would have been willing to assent to had they taken time to consider the question from all sides (1948).

Summary- The institution of slavery was no longer present at the time when the Adventist Church voted its segregated governance structure, but America was still reeling under the debilitating throes of Jim Crow laws. Everything was segregated. Yet this was no excuse for God's people to go the way of the other Evangelical Christian churches of the day. This was not God's ideal for his church. He wants no "wall of partition" to divide us, but rather for us to come together as one and unite our efforts in laboring for him.

The period of Reconstruction was probably the most difficult time for Blacks in America. They knew they were free, but enjoyed little freedom. The tyranny of discrimination and oppression served to make their lives miserable. They felt almost as if they were better off in slavery. The Evangelical movement did not make it any better for them, neither did the SDAC. The segregation in society was unbearable in the spirit, but the segregation in the Church was a torture of the soul.

Black Adventists in the SDAC were very involved in evangelism and general church life. They now wanted to participate in the leadership of the Church, but the Whites were totally opposed to it, except in leadership of their own race. Educational and health institutions were dominated by Whites while Blacks were being rejected from employment. Several attempts were made by Black leaders to resolve this but to no avail. It all came to a breaking point when a Black sister was denied treatment at a Church-owned health institution and died while being rushed to another that would admit her across town. This together with the poor and embarrassing treatment shown at the ordination of the first Black Pastor in the following year caused Blacks to ask the Church for their own conferences. The action to form regional conferences was voted in 1944 and has remained in place since. Much growth has taken place in these conferences and, but the Church remains divided. Each race is becoming more entrenched and can hardly be found worshiping in the same congregation. As the years roll on there is no end to this segregation in sight. Ought this to continue in the Church of God?

The second Great Disappointment resulted from the reluctance of Whites to unite with Blacks along racial lines and share the leadership of the Church with qualified Blacks leaders. That resulted in much attrition then and continues to do so now. "White flight" is still prevalent and occurs whenever the ethnic membership of a White congregation gets to about thirty five percent. This problem remains and continues to hurt the Church in its missional appeal. Meanwile, many believers are asking: "Why can't we all just get along?"

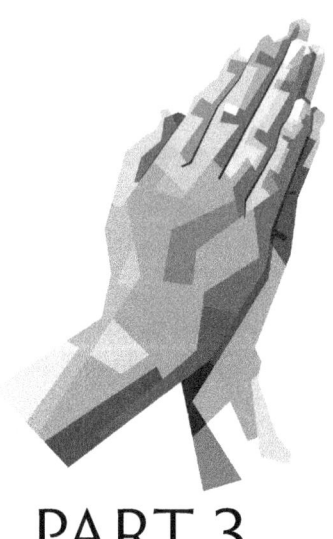

PART 3

Why Can't We All Just Get Along?

The reconciled

"And God raised us up with Christ and seated us with him in the heavenly realms in Christ Jesus… But now in Christ Jesus you who once were far away have been brought near through the blood of Christ" (Eph. 2:6, 13, NIV).

"There is neither Jew nor Greek, slave nor free, male nor female, for you are all one in Christ Jesus (Gal. 3:28, NIV).

5

"Why Can't We All Just Get Along?"

"There is neither Jew nor Greek, slave nor free, male nor female, for you are all one in Christ Jesus" (Gal. 3:28).

Historical Challenges to the Unity of the Remnant

It has been over one hundred and sixty years since the first Great Disappointment. As I write, numerous voices are crying "genocide" because of the mass displacement and current death toll of over 23,000 people killed in "indiscriminate bombings" by the Israeli Defense Force in Gaza. The United Nations (UN) has called the Israeli confinement of Gazans in the Gaza strip apartheid and the collective view of member states of the UN (prior to October 7, 2023) has been that the Israelis have made Gaza "the biggest open-air prison in the world." On July 11, 2023, a Reuters report stated—"A United Nations expert on Tuesday said Israel had transformed the occupied Palestinian territories into an 'open-air prison' through widespread detentions of Palestinians, an assertion swiftly dismissed by Israel" (Reuters, 2023). Meanwhile in the US, ethnic citizens (particularly Blacks, also Jews and Asians) are of the opinion that racism has significantly increased. Racially motivated attacks specifically on the latter two ethnicities are widespread, having increased exponentially.

In the ecclesiastical arena, presently racial and ethnic forces dispersed throughout their respective ethnic camps are plotting for the next local conference triennial session, union and division sessions, as well as the next GC session, in hopes of electing members from their racial or ethnic groups this time. Like all politicians do, they rationalize that if they do not do this they will be left without proper representation at the various levels.

Meanwhile the years roll on and younger members are being drafted into their respective ethnic ranks to be acculturated, brainwashed, and trained for conflict with the rest of the church that does not look or speak like them. The vicious cycle continues from session to session, while on the off times we halfheartedly preach—"Jesus is coming again; prepare to meet him." And distasteful, ungodly, and eternally fatal as this friendly fire is, no end seems to be in sight. Like the African American man, Rodney King, during the 1992 Los Angeles uprising that resulted from his arrest and brutal beating by several White police officers, I pose the question—"Why can't we all just get along?"

What W. E. B. Du Bois said of the US in the twentieth century is true of it also in the twenty-first century. In *The Souls of* Black *Folk*, Du Bois postulated that "the problem of the Twentieth Century is the problem of color line" (1969). As indicated earlier, Billy Graham expressed a somewhat similar viewpoint when he remarked years ago that America's greatest problem is the problem of race (Emerson and Smith, 2000). The culture of the Adventist Church has traditionally mirrored that of the mass culture in America in the social aspect. Hence the racial and ethnic problem of the US holds true for the Adventist Church. And regrettably, the Adventist Church does not typically engage the culture, certainly not in the matter of racial and ethnic issues. It does not perceive its saltiness as being inclusive of agitating against systemic injustices. That may be due partly to the fact that the Adventist Church is Evangelical in essence and currently about fifty percent White. The Evangelical movement, being the dominant protestant (one-third of population) religious persuasion in the US, sets the tone for the religious culture in America (Kyle, 2006). And the adherents to evangelicalism and their forbears are largely the benefactors and current perpetrators of the racial oppression of the past and systemic injustices of the present.

I refer to such injustices as those which they sought to justify theologically by maintaining and perpetuating the oppressive system of slavery with clear consciences and to the demise of a people (s). Current research points to the fact that the White Evangelicals are identical in their approach to race as the rest of White America in the larger society (Emerson and Smith, 2000). It is no different in the Adventist Church whose members generally share the same geographic and social characteristics as other typical White Evangelicals. Could this account for the dearth of literature on racial reconciliation in the Evangelical Church in general and the Adventist Church in particular?

Ethnic Challenges Ahead for the Remnant- The African American community is plagued with numerous social problems in the larger society. The Adventist Church generally does not appear to be appealing to this community. Those within its membership often feel tolerated and marginalized, particularly when they are in predominantly White churches and White educational and health institutions. Cornel West pursues this philosophical position on the state of Black America—

> "The accumulated effect of the Black wounds and scars suffered in a White-dominated society is a deep-seated anger, a boiling sense of rage, and a passionate pessimism regarding America's will to justice. Under conditions of slavery and Jim Crow segregation, this anger, rage, and pessimism remained relatively muted because of a well-justified fear of brutal White retaliation. The major breakthroughs of the sixties—more physically than politically—swept this fear away. Sadly, the combination of the market way of life, poverty-ridden conditions, Black existential *angst*, and the lessening of fear of White authorities has directed most of the anger, rage, and despair toward fellow Black citizens " (1993)…

Black-on-Black violence- The incidence of Black-on-Black crime is alarming. West's argument is persuasive as he attributes the sad state of Black Americans partially to the ignominious history of domination by Whites in their country of birth. Coupled with the psychological defects that they have, with terrible schools and undesirable home conditions, they are placed into the marketplace to compete with privileged Whites. They cannot. The frustration that results is unfortunate, however, as they take this frustration out on each other, often their women (West, 1993) but clearly on the streets in violence against other Blacks.

"Previous studies have shown that the Black population does indeed experience higher rates of violent crime due to segregation as well as other social disadvantages"(Mecom, 2002). The Black on Black Crime Coalition released statistics indicating that in 2007, with African Americans being 13.5% of the population, they were victims of 43% of the murders committed. 24.3% of African Americans were victimized in violent crimes such as rape/sexual assaults, robbery, aggravated and simple assaults in 2007. The percentage (38%) was highest among those ages 15-24 (Raynor, 2008). Homicide was the leading cause of death among African Americans males, ages 15-24 years nationally in 2008. It was the second leading cause of death among Black women.

These statistics serve to accentuate the need for intervention, even reparations to mitigate the effects of centuries of oppression throughout which the neglect of an entire race in the US was perpetrated. Reparations can be used to provide better education, training, housing, health, business investments. "Reparations can trigger a new set of countervailing processes to effectively negate the forces that maintain racial inequality" (Williams and Collins, 2004). The same is not true of other minorities, which have not been as traumatized by the systemic deficiencies, but who came to the US with a determination to improve their lives. Dialog among church members can bring about an understanding of the effects of oppression and convey a sense of neighborliness that will cause Whites to come alongside Blacks and other minorities in effectuating these changes that could improve their situation in life.

Tension Between African Americans and Immigrant Blacks- An unfortunate challenge we face is that Blacks in the Adventist church in the US have never been totally integrated among themselves. They may worship together, play together, pray together, but each group has its own sense of national identity. African Americans generally do not consider Caribbean Americans and immigrant Africans as a part of their ethnic group and vice versa.

An interesting challenge is posed by the fact that immigrant Blacks were generally evangelized to worship like the White missionaries who proselytized and initiated them in their respective islands, countries, and so on, but could not teach them how to develop their own liturgy. African Americans, on the contrary, due to their prolonged enslavement and ongoing oppression by Whites, developed their own liturgy, which is markedly different from the Whites' and that of the immigrant Blacks. This results in much tension whenever they integrate. Consequently, many, particularly the uppity immigrant Blacks, flock to White churches in the suburbs where they often live and find similar worship patterns to their homeland churches', or start their own ethnic churches. In the last two decades, however, the immigrants have learned to appreciate the African American worship and preaching styles and have even begun to comfortably identify with them.

Another critical factor that is noteworthy is that it appears that African Americans generally view these immigrant groups as a threat to their advancement and control of the leadership of the Black sector of the Adventist church in the US. Thus their failure to hire these immigrant pastors in the regional conferences even to pastor totally Caribbean or African congregations is not surprising, but unfortunate. The hiring of immigrant Blacks in regional conferences is more common nowadays as the hands of African Americans are forced by the number of immigrants in the regional conferences, as well as by the growth in the relationship between the two groups.

The "White Flight" Phenomenon- After years of dealing with this unfortunate situation of apparent irreconcilable differences with African Americans, these immigrant peoples have more recently taken their membership and tithe to the predominantly White churches in the White conferences. Very often they move to congregations in the suburbs where they are then met with "White flight" when the number of them increases to a certain percentage. The "White flight" on the religious front mirrors the "White flight' in the larger society, which, for decades saw Whites moving out of neighborhoods when a Black family moved into a house in their suburban neighborhood (Rothstein, 2017, p. 56, 123-124). Yet these resilient people groups, along with the Hispanics, who engage in aggressive evangelism, are rapidly becoming the majority of the Adventist church membership in North America.

It has become the new joke of these immigrant communities now that they need not build or buy churches; rather, all they need to do is simply move into an existing White church and within a few years or less they will have the church for themselves because all the White members will be gone elsewhere after the percentage of non-Whites gets to about thirty five percent of the congregation. This "White flight" phenomenon impacted an entire conference: the Greater New York Conference. The once totally White Greater New York conference now does not have one US born "White church" (not because they have integrated) and has only a handful of White members (usually immigrant Whites— Italians, Romanians, Russians, Ukrainians) scattered here and there throughout predominantly Black congregations.

When Caribbean Blacks, Africans, and Hispanics began to move into the conference, the White members moved further north to upstate New York, and became members of the New York Conference and South to Georgia-Cumberland and Florida Conferences. The Northeastern Conference (Lawson, 2018) had a predominantly immigrant ethnic membership of 25,000 between the years 1990 and 2005. Today they comprise over ninety percent of the conference membership (Lawson, 1998). In his latest (2018) study of the membership composition of these conferences,

Lawson's research findings indicate that Whites comprise only 2.7% of the membership of metropolitan New York with African Americans at 8%. The bulk of the membership is the "new immigrants" (Lawson, 2018).

Immigrant In-fighting- Among the Caribbean people groups, Jamaicans, Trinidadians, Bajans, and other islanders, typically identify themselves with their respective country. The bond among the peoples of the Caribbean appeared to be tenuous in years gone by and nationalism had been known to split churches down the middle along national lines. The bond appears to be getting stronger over more recent years. Also, Latinos from the various countries in the Americas have been jostling among themselves for prominence in their communities over the years, but have generally given the appearance of a closely-bonded group.

Immigrant Asians have their own tensions, even rifts among the various nationalities (North versus South Koreans, Chinese versus Vietnamese, and so on). Immigrant Africans are often seen as one people by those outside of them, but among themselves, they are Ghanaians, Kenyans, Nigerians, and so on. More recently they have begun founding country-specific African churches. The very first Ghanaian church in the *US* was spawned by the Grand Concourse Church in the Bronx, New York, in 1992, while I was an assistant pastor there. It had huge support from the local conference leadership and apparently the General Conference, one of whose officers visited and addressed them on several occasions in their infancy. These ethnic congregations (Ghanaian, Spanish, Korean, Romanian, and so on) are now the new fad among Adventist immigrant, but are not known to thrive necessarily because of their mono-ethnicity.

Evangelism by Race/Ethnicity- Evidently, it appears that the Adventist Church has inadvertently adapted the "homophily principle"—the strategy of planting churches that are homogeneous, a strategy which has been developed and used for years by the Southern Baptist Convention (SBC). About ten years ago the NAD sponsored an evangelistic team which was sent to Westchester County New York to plant a "White church" using that principle. White evangelists came and met with the White pastors and members in the conference but did not even inform the entire conference that they were launching a crusade. Blacks comprise more than ninety five percent of the Adventist Church in New York. After the first week, however, they realized that their audience was predominantly Black. Interestingly, they ran out of money and had to ask for help in housing it at a nearby Black church (First White Plains SDA Church) for the final two weeks. Blacks were upset with this conduct by church officials not realizing that they were apparently following the HUP model.

African American Blacks are equally as likely as Whites to choose an Adventist church that is at least 80 % Black (Anderson, 2004). Whites flee to join or form new congregations when the non-White population gets to about 35% and Whites do not usually choose to join an ethnic church. Although current research has shown that Asians and Hispanics assimilate more easily into heterogeneous congregations (Emerson and Smith, 2000), yet they still choose to form their ethnic churches when they become of adequate numbers to do so at any location. Is this how the remnant church ought to be? Indeed there is a better way for the remnant people of God if we will heed the counsel of the apostle Paul in Galatians 3:28—"There is neither Jew nor Greek, male or female, bond or free; for we are all one in Christ Jesus." We need to see ourselves as One New Humanity in Christ and live as such.

The Greatest Challenges- The greatest challenges that the remnant face with respect to racial/ethnic reconciliation, as we prepare for the return of Christ are the challenges to love and forgive. This was apparently what G. Ralph Thompson had in mind when he affirmed years ago-- "Beyond all these issues, the greatest challenge we face is spiritual. Only the Holy Spirit can bring unity in diversity" (1994). It was hatred that led to the annihilation of Native Indians, enslavement and other forms of oppression of Blacks. White Adventists need to corporately and in some cases, individually, confess their sins to and show love for Blacks and other minorities in the SDAC. This will ultimately result in the cessation of "white flight" and "black flight" in our churches and the Adventist health and educational institutions. In addition, Blacks need to forgive Whites if even Whites do not seek their forgiveness corporately or individually, if Whites would seek their forgiveness for the bygone oppression in society and the SDAC. The ability to forgive comes from Christ. And Christ extends the invitation to all Christians to "learn of me" (Mt. 7:30). As he hung on the cross and contemplated the heinous acts of his crucifiers, he declared "Father, forgive them for they know not what they do" (Lk. 23:34, KJV) Forgiveness was also an admirable trait of the Indian sage, Mahatma Ghandi. He avers, "The weak can never forgive. Forgiveness is the attribute of the strong" (Berger, 2010).

After Nelson Mandela was elected president of South Africa, he did something remarkable. Besides appearing onstage with his predecessor, F. W. DeClerk, in 1995 Mandela invited all the widows of the former presidents of the country along with the widows of leaders of the Black liberation movement to lunch. Betsie Verwoerd, who was ninety-four years old at the time, opted out but mentioned in passing that Mandela could stop by for tea on another occasion. Within two weeks Mandela and his entourage of over two hundred arrived in the white supremacist *volkstaat* (homeland), Orania, South Africa, for tea with Mrs. Verwoerd. After spending forty five minutes with her, Mandela emerged with her to address the media and press. As she struggled to read, Mandela assisted her in reading the statement which asked for Mandela's compassion (DeYoung, 1997). History confirms that he granted her request. But someone, in this case, the victim, had to take the first step. What grace; what forgiveness.

Reasons Cited for the Racial/Ethnic Divide

The divide in the SDAC is not singular; it is multiple. With the widespread immigration of various nationalities to the US (especially since the 1970s) in an attempt to classify everyone, the social scientists have applied social designations to several ethnic groupings in the larger society. Upon becoming members of the SDAC in the US, immigrants encountered two distinct, entrenched groups of saints forming the existing Black/White divide. In an attempt to survive, the immigrants have taken cover in their social groupings.

The current divisions into Asians, Hispanics, Franco-Haitian, Blacks, and Whites in many local conferences are the result. Hence we now have several racial/ethnic divides in the NAD. The "White flight" and "Black standoff" that currently exists in the SDAC is regrettable and this is multiplied with the emergence of numerous other groups. Yet the major problems are being caused by the existing divided governance structure, which fosters division, hence the absence of integration in the local churches. In an attempt to justify the divide, the foremost rivals (Whites/Blacks) posit numerous reasons, which I examine in the segments below.

Theology- Centuries of differing history in the US have resulted in Blacks and Whites having different theological focuses. White Evangelical theology tends to focus more on living the "clean hands and pure hearts" lifestyle with little reference to and apparent hope for the return of Jesus, perhaps due to their privileged status and wealth in this society. Blacks, on the contrary, focus their theology on the pain they suffer here and a longing for the day when it will end. Michael G. Cartwright takes the leads in our pursuit here with the question: "Can Euro-American Christians & African American Christians learn to read Scripture together" (Okholm, 1997)? African American professor, James H. Cone, insists that if Christ is to have any meaning to the Blacks in the US, "he must leave the security of the suburbs by joining Black people in their condition" (Cone, 1970). He argues further that "if Christ is White and not Black, he is an oppressor, and we must kill him," so that he does not get in the way of "our revolution" (Cone, 1970).

Much of Black liberation theology has crept into the remnant. One needs only visit a local African American SDA church in any city a few times and this becomes obvious. This kind of Black theology may appear to have a harsh, even offensive tone to White Adventists and other evangelicals. Whites typically find this theology offensive and challenging to their status, theology, and comfort in a worship setting. Yet the legitimate cries from this theological perspective must not go unanswered. The prophets (Isaiah, Jeremiah) of the Old Testament and the New Testament prophets and apostles (John, Jesus, James) were just as fierce and forthright (even offensive) in their rhetoric against systemic evils (Isa. 1: 15-17; 10:1-4; Jer. 2:19; 5:28-31; 7:5-7, 16; Mk. 6:17-29; Mt. 23; Jam. 5:1-6). The pain of Blacks, and more recently, Hispanics and Asians in the US is real and is not self-inflicted, neither is it divine punishment for the sins of their ancestors. It originated from avarice, developed into hatred and has been inflicted with malice by Whites, while White evangelicals stuck their proverbial heads in the sand and because this theology forces them to see the evil of which they are benefactors, Cartwright avers that they seek to evade it (Okholm, 1997).

In the article "Blacks and Religion in the United States," Werner Hass asks—

> What is different about Black theology? It is "'due exclusively to the failure of White religionists to relate the gospel of Jesus to the pain of being Black in a White racist society'" (Haas, 2006; see also Cone, 1970).

While this difference is generally true among Blacks in the US, it is observable in the SDAC in the US also. After over three hundred years of enslavement and severe oppression during Reconstruction and under Jim Crow laws, while being forced to listen to their masters' music, prayers, and so on, Blacks, who were worshiping mainly among Whites in their masters' churches, felt a need to separate from them and sing their own songs, pray their own prayers, and fellowship in their own styles. Haas maintains that the exodus of Blacks is due to the failure of Whites to make the gospel real to the Black community (2006). His conclusion echoes with precision the argument of Vincent Bacote in the preceding decade that "This [Black] theology emerged because of racism and the failure of classical or White theology to address issues at the core of African American existence" Okholm, 1997). The theology even in the SDAC, like all evangelical denominations, is essentially classical theology, which upholds the status quo on matters of race, justice, and freedom with little or no challenge to them. Such theology bears neither relevance nor appeal to the Black community.

I concur with Haas after being a part of a White congregation for the last five years. Frankly, based on conversations with other Blacks of all regional descent (African Americans, Afro-Caribbeans, Africans immigrants, Black Latinos) over the years, it is obvious that Blacks do not believe that Whites understand their pain an d understand that the system that they created for us is tilted in their favor as shown by sociologists (Emerson and Smith, 2000). It appears to stem from the pain it causes most White Americans to think of the heinous past. Michael G. Cartwright maintains that this pain makes them want to do almost anything to avoid confronting it (Okholm, 1997). Also, some Whites are aware, but seem either fearful of change or are content to be benefactors of a lopsided system without any concern for their fellow human being.

In the wider evangelical movement, this is because of the "social vision" of dispensational premillennialists who wrestled with God in the nineteenth century in a desperate attempt to control history, much like the prophet Habakkuk did. In their erroneous approach to Scripture, some evangelicals diminish the reading of the Psalms to the church and thereby psychologically exempt themselves from the eschatological judgment in order to situate themselves as controllers of history. In doing so they content themselves that Christians will not have to suffer. Cartwright alludes to this as a cultural fantasy on the part of Euro-American Christians (Okholm, 1997). But they are wrong! It is true that Adventists are neither dispensationalists nor premillennialists and therefore do not subscribe to an exemption of Christians from the final judgment. On the other hand, however, Adventists teach the participation of the saints (saved Christians) in judgment after the millennium. But that fact elicits the question: With what judgment will we judge if we ignore the pain of fellow saints while traveling together on this pilgrimage? Or, will we be among the judges?

This leads to the most important conclusion on classical or White theology. The White evangelical approach to social issues is the self-designated "engaged orthodoxy" but one, I submit, in the context of a theology that is disengaged "from the history of earthly struggle in the church and in the world" (Okholm, 1997). Is this true of White Adventist theology?

Leadership- The same problem that led to the divided governance structure still haunts us. Among the most frequently cited reasons that African Americans present for favoring the status quo is the fear that everything will revert to what it was like before 1944. Blacks generally do not believe that their White counterparts in the SDAC and in ministry in particular, see them as competent. Of course, this harks back to the legacy of slavery during which Blacks were taught by their White superiors that they were "no good" and were forced to do only the menial tasks. In addition, in more recent years it has been the trend that when any organization of the Church is forced to integrated, it is the perception of Blacks that their White colleagues believe that a White person must be in charge of the treasury, since Blacks do not know how to manage funds or are dishonest and cannot be trusted with the funds. They point to instances in various aspects of the Adventist Church organization as cases in point.

While this is difficult to solve, it ultimately has to do with seeking the Lord's guidance in these matters. When we trust God and approach him for guidance in making decisions such as these, he offers assistance. Unless we are truly converted so that we have a faith relationship with God and trust ourselves, it will be impossible to trust others. When we do, there is no anxiety. The author of the Proverbs says it succinctly--"Trust in the LORD with all your heart and lean not on your own understanding; in all your ways submit to him, and he will make your paths straight" (Proverbs 3:5-6, NIV).

Communication- It is challenging to communicate effectively. The inability of members of different races/ethnicities to communicate well with those who are not of their race/ethnic group has the potential to cause serious racial/ethnic misunderstandings. Communication takes places through various channels, which could have barriers such as mental images, verbal symbols, unclear objectives, irrelevant presentations (Skinner, 1971; Du Preez, 2000). Gottfried Oosterwal propounds that communication is the sharing of messages. In the sharing of messages there are distortions. Distortions occur even when communicating within one's culture. Only about 45-60 percent of all communication is effective within one's culture; in cross-cultural communication the percentage falls to 20-25 (Pollard, 2000). That being said, it becomes critical for members of different races/ethnicities to be sensitized to racially divisive communication, which could add to the distortions that are inherently present in cross-cultural communication.

Oosterwal recommends some principles of cross-cultural communication for leaders of multicultural organizations that I suggest would be helpful to everyone in a multicultural setting. These are:

- While words do have meaning of themselves, they are subject to people's values, perceptions, and other underlying cultural assumptions from which they derive their meaning.
- In addition to content, the context of one's message should be carefully considered.

- There are culturally-specific modes of communicating in every culture.
- One should be fully aware of the true purpose of communication.
- Every communication has identification; none is without (Pollard, 2000).

By adhering to these and other pointers, members of the remnant may assist in healing and in bridging the divide between the races/ethnicities. Notwithstanding it must be realized that even with the best communication among us, if some other crucial elements are absent it will be of no avail. Be mindful though that we can beat the odds with the help of God.

Status- Emerson and Smith have shown that the same factors militating against reconciliation in the larger society are having the same effect on the church (2000). Two hundred years of slavery and subsequent decades of marginalization during Reconstruction and beyond have resulted in generations of Blacks being far less educated than Whites. The high school drop-out rate is much higher in the Black community. The number of college graduates among Black is considerably lower than in the White community. The rate of incarceration among Blacks surpasses by far that in the White sector of society. How can Blacks compete? How can they be expected to climb the social ladder and raise themselves out of poverty? Their inability to do so have made them less desirable company for their more educated, affluent, and upwardly mobile White counterparts. Despite these handicaps, however, ought this to be the reality in the remnant?

The epistle of James speaks to how statuses should be viewed and dealt with in God's church. In James 2:1-11 the apostle denounces the preferential treatment of the more privileged class in the society during the period of the first century church and exhorts the saints to practice equal respect and treatment of all members of the household of faith. That none ought to consider himself/herself higher or better than the other is well established in Scripture—"For by the grace given me I say to every one of you: Do not think of yourself more highly than you ought, but rather think of yourself with sober judgment" (Rom. 12:3, *NIV*). It is also noteworthy to reference Jesus' statement in Mt. 23:11—"The greatest among you will be your servant." No status is of any significance in the church of God: "There is neither Jew nor Greek, slave nor free, male nor female, for you are all one in Christ Jesus (Gal. 3:28, *NIV*).

Trust- Given the history between the races/ethnic groups, it has been extremely difficult for African Americans, in particular, to trust Whites. This is true in the larger society and even in the remnant church. In theory it is the Christian thing to do, they admit; in spite of this they are reluctant to risk losing what they have gained "through many danger toils, and snares." They fear that if they let their guards down it could revert to its former state when Whites led in everything and Blacks and everyone else simply followed. Yet our ultimate trust should be in God. This is God's Church. When we trust him with his work; he will do what is best for it.

Much can be done to build trust, however. Trust is something that is earned; it is not automatic even among Christians. In a recent survey that was reported in an article in the Archives of Internal Medicine entitled "Distrust, Race, and Research" the authors found that Blacks were significantly more distrusting of medical research than Whites. The objectives of the research were—"To examine possible differences in distrust by race and to determine to what extent other sociodemographic factors explain any racial differences in distrust." The researchers examined 527 Blacks and 382 Whites in a national telephone survey on participation in clinical research. The research data showed the following results—

> African American respondents were more likely than White respondents not to trust that their physicians would fully explain research participation (41.7% vs. 23.4%, *P*<.01) and to state that they believed their physicians exposed them to unnecessary risks (45.5%

vs. 34.8%, *P*<.01). African American respondents had a significantly higher mean distrust index score than White respondents (3.1 vs. 1.8, *P*<.01). After controlling for other sociodemographic variables in a logistic regression model, race remained strongly associated with a higher distrust score (prevalence odds ratio, 4.7; 95% confidence interval, 2.9-7.7); (Smith et al, 2002).

Based on the research, this was true even after controlling for social class markers (Smith et al, 2002).

In another survey conducted by Katrina Armstrong et al, pertaining to the distrust of physicians among racial/ethnic and geographic variation in the US, the researchers found that Blacks and Hispanics reported higher levels of distrust than did Whites (Armstrong et al, 2007). Similar evidence of a higher level of distrust among Blacks and Hispanics can be found in the areas of politics (Michelson, 2001), religion, finance, business.

Several factors influence if and how much people trust each other. Alberto F. Alesina and Eliana La Ferrara observed that in US localities, the strongest factors associated with low trust on an individual level were:

> i) a recent history of traumatic experiences; ii) belonging to a group that historically felt discriminated against, such as minorities (Blacks in particular) and, to a lesser extent, women; iii) being economically unsuccessful in terms of income and education; iv) living in a racially mixed community and/or in one with a high degree of income disparity. Religious beliefs and ethnic origins do not significantly affect trust. The role of racial cleavages leading to low trust is confirmed when we explicitly account for individual preferences on inter-racial relationships: within the same community, individuals who express stronger feelings against racial integration

trust relatively less the more racially heterogeneous the community is (2000).

Lack of trust is a huge factor among African Americans. Distrust can cause one to ruin opportunities that one would otherwise have taken advantage of to one's benefit. It destroys relationships. It has an adverse psychological affect. Meanwhile, on the contrary it may cause one to exercise necessary caution. Lack of trust for middle class Blacks is evident among the African American youth.

Dale P. Andrews maintains that this lack of trust is their reason for the disparagement of Black churches by the Black youth (2002). Despite these realities the SDAC would do well taking note of these trends and attempt to develop a strategy to counteract them. It appears that trust must be engendered in order to attain the optimal performance. While in society it may be incumbent on those who seek to be trusted to first earn trust, in the household of faith, based on the *philos* (brotherly love), which should come naturally between believers, it is reasonable to expect that one would be trusted without having to earn it. We all need to allow our trust in God to assist us in our ability to trust others among God's remnant. In the end God will distribute adequately to every ethnic sector all that it needs.

Geographic Factors- Racialization in the US has resulted in Whites and Blacks being geographically removed from each other in most states. After the end of the Jim Crow laws, Whites fled urban areas and relocated in the suburbs, as a part of the deliberate strategy to counter industrialization and urbanization (Williams and Collins, 2004), thus leaving behind the Blacks and other ethnic groups who need to stay close to places of employment, cheaper housing, and so on. This was the second wave of segregation in the US. Not only has this hypersegregation resulted in poorer housing accommodations for minorities, but also horrible road conditions. Williams and Collins further argue that it results in inadequate health facilities and poorer health for them (2004). Church goers tend to choose places of worship close to their home. This racial isolation usually makes it an easy choice for Blacks to worship where they live and for Whites to do the same. Hence Whites worship in the suburbs, where only few middle class Blacks can afford to live and Blacks worship in the cities, where they work and can find adequate and affordable housing.

With the embourgeoisement of many minorities, more recently many suburban churches are being flocked by them. As an example, almost all the Adventist churches in the New York suburbs of Lower Westchester County and Nassau County, Long Island are made up of predominantly minority members from the Caribbean and Africa. The Metropolitan Atlanta area is also similar; Miami, LA, and many other large US cities. It has become more difficult for Whites who chose to remain Adventist in these large metro areas to avoid worshiping with minorities. "White flight" is now more than an escape to the suburbs. It means going deep into the countryside or relocating to another more rural state with little employment opportunities. Interestingly, with the population of the US becoming majority non-White, what will the prejudiced White Adventists do when they are surrounded in every suburb by minorities?

Wealth- The disparity in wealth between Whites and Blacks in the U. S. has been alarming. In more recent years there has been an accelerating wealth gap. Somehow this factor seems to adversely affect the integration of the Adventist Church. A survey conducted by the University of Wisconsin shows that Whites ages 61-70 with a college education or higher were worth over $450,000.00, while Blacks and Hispanics with similar qualifications were worth just over $200,000.00 in 1998. John Karl Sholz and Kara Levine discovered further that in 1998 one percent of American families owned 34 percent of the country's wealth (2003). In 2007 the median wealth of Whites was $100,000 and that of Blacks was under $10,000.00. Based on a study by the Brandeis University, between 1984 and 2007, the median wealth gap between White families and Black families widened from $20,000.00 to $95,000.00, with

Blacks being at the lower end of the wealth gap and Whites at the top (Shapiro et al, 2010; Cottrell, 2010).

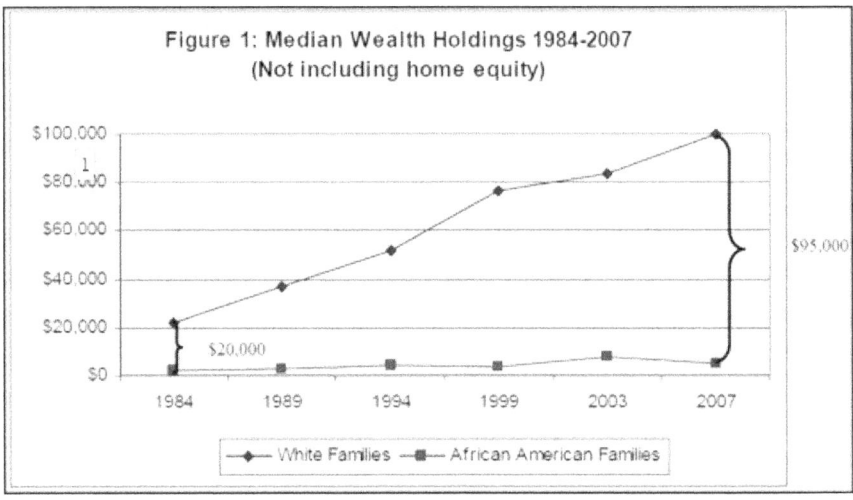

Figure 1 Adapted from the Institute on Assets and
Social Policy web site (Shapiro et al, 2010).

A recent CNN Black in America segment revealed that in 2010 the gap is $28,000.00 for Blacks and $140,000 for Whites. In an opinion by Dr. Boyce Watkins, this college professor averred—"The dominant reason for the Black/White wealth gap is simple: For 400 years, America built itself into a multi-trillion dollar empire on the backs of Black people without paying them hardly a penny for their labor" (2010). Presently, few Blacks are recipients of inherited wealth, while Whites inherit significant wealth from their ancestors. Most ancestral Blacks did not have wealth to pass on to their descendants, while Whites did because of their privileged position over the centuries. Yet while it is a disconcerting disparity, wealth should not be a hindrance to integration unless we are storing up treasures on earth instead of heaven (Mt. 6:19, 20). All of scripture point us to a stewardship which encourages God's servants to use their wealth for the advancement of God's kingdom (1 Jn. 3:17).

Consequently, an ever-widening gap is obvious. African Americans have been becoming increasingly poorer over the last 23 years (Shapiro,

Meschede and Sullivan, 2010). This wealth gap impacts where people worship. The wealthy live and worship in the suburbs, while the poor live and worship in the cities. The poorer sector of the population in the US is comprised of predominantly Blacks and Hispanics. Faith does not seem to be the primary deciding factor of where Adventists worship, but wealth plays a major role in that decision.

More and more members seem to be more comfortable worshiping with those of comparable worth. Ronald Sider suggests--"Christians certainly ought to live in the suburbs as well as in the inner city" (1997). How did Evangelical Christians contribute to this disparity and ever-widening gap between the wealth of the people groups? Can the Evangelical movement assist in reversing this trend? The issue of racial economics is at the heart of our social dilemma and probably unlike the larger US society, it warrants definite spiritual solutions for Adventists. It elicits the question, therefore, are reparations in order for the US and the Evangelical denominations including Adventists? The issue of reparations by denominations further study.

A few decades ago, the term *lifeboat ethics* was popularized by the distinguished University of California biologist, Garrett Hardin. His ideology suggested that the poor should be allowed to starve instead of helping them with food or aid. By helping them, he argued, we will all starve together, but if they were allowed to starve they would check their "irresponsible" reproduction.

While it is true that the Bible suggests penalties for the indolent (2 Thess. 3:10), this approach is wrong. Christians must have a sense of responsibility to their distance and immediate neighbors. "If anyone has material possessions and sees his brother in need but has no pity on him, how can the love of God be in him?" (1 Jn. 3:17, NIV). Besides, in most cases the rich only became so wealthy because the nation's wealth has been unfairly distributed, either by the laws of an oppressive system or by exploitation. Ronald Sider provides a detailed rebuttal of the *lifeboat ethics* theory (Sider, 1997).

Fear- Whites fear Black rage and retribution. Some Whites who were around in the 1960s and during the Rodney King L.A. uprising, are familiar with Black rage and fear encountering it personally. Famed African American thinker, Cornel West legitimizes this rage and sanctions it in some forms of its expression (1993). While retribution is unnecessary and would be inconsequential, the thought of it is a source of great fear for many White Adventists. The fear of retribution in turn retards integration. They fear that if Blacks should be given a level playing field and should one day become too prosperous, they would return the favor of the heinous, debilitating, and inhumane treatment that was meted out to them (DeYoung, 1997). Yet the Bible informs us that "perfect loves casts out fear." When we learn to love, love looks beyond fears and sees friendship of family. That is what we now are in Christ. We are family; we ought not to live in fear of each other.

W. E. B. DuBois observed this fear among Whites and asks rhetorically-–"Is this the life you grudge us, O knightly America…? Are you so afraid lest peering from this high Pisgah, between Philistine and Amalekite, we sight the Promised Land" (1969)? Calvin Rock alludes to this fear also and identifies several aspects of it: fear of loss of wealth, of status, fear of loss of job (1970). More recently, other social scientists and reconcilers observed the fear factor among Whites (Emerson and Smith, 2000; Yancey, 2001).

Culture -Essentially, culture is "who we are and how we do what we do." The church has a religious culture. Religion is an integral part of culture. There are cultural norms and mores for people of differing classes in society. The Christian may choose to identify with or practice them or he/she may refrain. Our culture inevitably and seriously impacts our worship style and involvement in church activities. There is an obvious distinction in the worship preferences of Blacks and Whites and all ethnic groups in the Adventist Church. The way we sing, instruments we use, style of our music, the length of service, style of preaching, and so on; differ greatly among most racial/ethnic groups in the SDAC. Some argue that this is the reason for the segregation. Yet I have observed huge variations between worship and preaching styles within a single ethnic group. This suggests that while the general ethnic group differences play a role, it is still individual preferences that result in the segregation we now experience. Each person chooses to accept one or the other. In other words, many Whites like "high church" worship, others prefer the contemporary vineyard liturgy, others, cowboy worship; likewise Blacks, Asians, Latinos differ just as widely. Yet as a mission-focused remnant our focus ought not to be so much on what we like but on what advances the cause of God. Black is right, "The time has come to break the shackles of custom. Remembering Peter's dream will help us do it" (Black, 1992).

Culture: Dress, Jewelry, Recreation- This was one of the challenges to unity in the South Africa Union Conference. Members of the Black and colored sectors offered some resistance based on culture. They were afraid that the Whites' liberal style of wearing slacks to church, wearing jewelry, and visiting theatres would be a bad influence upon their members, particularly the jewelry. It poses a serious challenge here in the US also.

Frankly, this is a challenging issue. The SDAC continues to officially prohibit the wearing of jewelry among its membership, except for wedding bands in the US. This is enforced at our educational institutions from elementary to tertiary as one of the distinctive marks of the church. Generally, our educational and health institutions and denominational agencies prohibit students and employees from wearing other than the accepted jewelry to class or work. Yet for the most part, White members do not appear to take adhere to this practice outside of those settings. Many younger Blacks, particularly those who worship in predominantly White congregations, or who were educated at the predominantly White Adventist institutions, do not see it as a doctrinal issue either and have chosen to wear earrings, and so on.

Blacks, Hispanics, and Asians, seem to advocate generally strict observance of the Sabbath, while Whites, on the other hand generally do not seem to. As an instance, Whites seem generally comfortable making regular, planned visits to the restaurant on the Sabbath; they plan hikes, play ball games, and engage in other recreational activities on the Sabbath, but not so for the other groups. Practices of this nature are subject to official reprimand in some ethnic churches and possibly church discipline in the case of prohibited jewelry. These, therefore, would need much discussion and will pose serious challenges to the reconciliation and ultimate unity.

Assimilation- While there are a few examples of this throughout the US, very rarely does a White Adventist choose to become a member of a predominantly African American Church. Typically, the few Whites that are a part of predominantly Black congregations are the vestige of the "White flight," which occurred earlier. While many suburban Whites welcome Blacks and other ethnicities into a predominantly White church or institution and conference, they seem to expect them to simply assimilate. The observation of these other groups is that there is no attempt to integrate the cultures by trying to understand and accommodate them. Rather, the expectation is that they would assimilate, which is essentially to "become like the rest of us," by acting White, listening to Anglo music, always enjoying an Anglo worship style, without any thought of diversifying the liturgical menu. This is not the preferred way to promote diversity and reconciliation.

There needs to be serious efforts on the part of all parties involved in these situations, to learn from each other and conduct the business of the church, institution, or conference in a manner that validates other cultures and people groups by participating in activities that are from other than one's culture and even partake of foods that are from the other cultures. By following this approach, acceptance and not tolerance (a negative energy) is promoted. When acceptance is realized, participation is encouraged, spiritual gifts may be utilized optimally, and the cause of God greatly advanced.

Absence of Dialog- As sinful humans living, working or worshiping together in the same space (denomination), we inevitably do each other wrong. The way to resolve those wrongs is not to avoid dealing with them, but to dialog about them. This dialog has been nonexistent in the SDAC and has been for some time. The GC made some attempts to create meaningful dialog in the 1970s and the NAD called a summit in 1999, but since that we have been silent. The dearth of literature in our publications speaks to this absence of dialog. How can we reasonably expect to solve this problem without dialog? God counsels us to engage each other in dialog.

The Bible recommends dialog as a viable approach to resolving issues among us. Jesus recommended this is Mt. 18 for when we sin against each other. The ultimate goal and outcome of such dialog should be forgiveness and reconciliation. In the epistle to the Galatians, the apostle Paul makes specific reference to dialoging with those who have done wrong (Gal. 6:1-6). Some of the benefits of dialog are 1) it creates the opportunity to share ourselves, our ideas as gifts to each other; 2) it assists us in discovering offensive words, judgment, and conduct and helps in eliminating these in our interactions with each other; 3) identify faults in the relationship and address them; 4) It could help us in realizing the brotherhood of all humanity (Butler, 2010).

Since the appalling public execution of George Floyd (the Black man that was killed on May 25, 2020, with a knee to his neck by a White Minnesota police officer), the people of America were summoned to a racial reckoning. For the first time in recent years, the callous, cold-blooded execution was caught on cameras and shown to the world. The incident forced the conversation on race relations in the US. Every television network as well as internet discussion was on the topic of race for the next several months. Protests erupted, not just in the US, but worldwide, as Whites, Blacks, Asians, Latinos, and all other people groups in one voice, called for an end to racism and its attendant social ills. And for the first time, Adventist leaders from the grassroots to the GC engaged each other in substantive dialog on the issue, some resolving to be vigilant and attentive to the reality of the existence of systemic ethnocentrism and racism and implement measures to mitigate and eradicate it.

Such dialog was long overdue and heartening. Yet it ought not end there. The harder tasks follow—continuing the dialog, building relationships, being sensitive to the inadvertent marginalization of others, being deliberate about including other ethnic groups, seeking equality in allocation of the church's resources, intentionally seeking qualified candidates of other ethnicities for vacant positions at our institutions and so on. These, among other measures, intentionally implemented, will ultimately help to bridge the divides. In fact, they will foster integration and organically facilitate dialog as people of all ethnicities interact daily.

The epistle of James admonishes us to be "quick to listen, slow to speak" (1:19). There is no peace in the Middle East between the Israelis and Palestinians, but the good thing is that when they engage in dialog, they keep progressing toward reconciliation.

Black and White Sexuality In a June 26, 2009 study of Black and White college students conducted by David Knox and Marty E. Zusman entitled "Sexuality in Black and White: Data from 783 Undergraduates," the authors discovered some significant findings in

1. Blacks and Whites had very similar sexuality. Ninety percent of both groups had marriage as a goal.
2. Blacks are significantly more conservative in their sexuality than Whites.

In the US, Blacks are usually stereotyped as "slutty, orgiastic, and hedonistic with out-of-control libidos" (Knox and Zusman, 2009), as portrayed in the US press and media. Research shows that Blacks have more children outside of marriage, have a higher rate of divorce, and more single-parent households than other ethnic groups. In 2008, the percentages of children in single family homes by race in the US were as follows:

Non-Hispanic White 23%; Black or African American 65%; American Indian 50%; Asian and Pacific Islander 16%; Hispanic or Latino 38%.

The total number of single-parent homes in the US was 32 percent (The Annie E. Casey Foundation, 2009). Yet Whites are more likely to have sex on their first date and are more prone to hedonism (Knox and Zusman, 2009). Furthermore, during slavery, it was White slave masters who indulged themselves sexually with Black women, after they had whipped their husbands out of their huts to go and work on the plantation and sometime while they were fast asleep after being overworked on the plantation. After slavery, Whites disparaged Black sexuality in an attempt to further denigrate them (West, 2001).

In the Adventist Church, as in much of society, both groups generally discourage intermarriage because of the history between the races. It appears that Whites (men in particular) now fear retribution. The sexuality of both Whites and Blacks with their attendant stereotypes and fears, serve as major deterrents to integration in the Church.

Recently, when I suggested to a White acquaintance at my church that some of us were interested in starting an intentionally diverse congregation, his first response was--"Does that mean that I have to divorce my wife and marry a Black woman?" Of course, he followed by stating that he was just kidding. And he was. Yet, that that was his first thought suggests to me that this is one of the greater fears of Whites, as they contemplate racial integration. The issue of interracial marriage is one that is largely between individuals, even though there are social issues that impact these unions. This is to be determined by those who are so inclined. While aspects of interracial marriage could be perceived to be negative, yet if God is leading two heterosexual

Adventist individuals of different races/ethnic groups to marry, who has the right to say no because of race?

Ethnocentrism- The White racism of the pre-Civil Rights Movement era has more recently morphed into an insidious ethnocentrism in the US as well as the Adventist Church in the US. No longer can the overt racism of the bygone era be practiced with impunity. For this reason, many in our ranks have resorted to subtleties created in the image of racism, but manifesting as domiciliary isolation and cultural insensitivity. Whites and Blacks have harbored racial prejudices, which are displayed in their race-centeredness. Some Whites conduct themselves with an air of Eurocentric superiority and Blacks seem to find refuge from societal denigration in Afro-centrism.

Ethnocentrism (Euro-centrism) on the part of Whites, results in their reluctance to develop close affiliations with Blacks, Hispanics, and Asians frequently, except in the case of a few wealthy, powerful or well-educated ethnic people. Meanwhile, Blacks emphasize their need to promote the interests of Blacks in a racist society. West identifies this as a recent approach to expressing Black rage (2001). In addition, we have Latinism, Asianism, and so on. These "isms" may be collectively construed as Satanism They are essentially self-centered, ethnic-centered, and diabolic, all the while purporting to be focused on bringing about a better good for "my people". Additionally, the "isms" further divide the remnant. Ought we not on the contrary to be focused on reconciling the remnant? I submit that we must all work to discontinue the "isms" and instead seek and promote the oneness of us all.

The Corinthian schism referenced in the New Testament was an unfortunate development in the church of Corinth (1 Cor. 1:10-17). When Paul recognized it and visited there, he called it what it was and totally denounced it, even though some of the believers claimed allegiance to him for evangelizing them. Paul would have none of it because he had not evangelized them for his glory, but God's. If only our church officials today would allow the Lord to imbue them with the

Pauline boldness, what a difference we may realize in the racial/ethnic dilemma of the SDAC!

The above challenges are numerous and varied. Many of them are also internal challenges to the various ethnic groups, but they still manage to get along in the same conferences and often in the same congregations. On the larger scale, they may not appear to be as manageable, but why can we not approach them and see what the Lord can do? Despite their daunting nature, let us remember that the SDAC is the remnant church and God stands ready to assist us all. But he unleashes his power to assist only when we fully surrender and come to him in humility. Shall we?

A Call for Racial and Ethnic Reconciliation

There is a dearth of literature calling for racial/ethnic reconciliation in the remnant. Ninety percent of Evangelical Americans are members of congregations that are eighty or more percent homogeneous (Marti, 2005). More recent experimentation with intentionally forming diverse congregations has been hugely successful. Examples of these are Mosaic in Los Angeles (SBC), Ambassador Bible Church, Vienna, Virginia (non-denominational), Antioch Bible Church, Seattle (non-denominational), Bridgeway Community Church, Columbia, Maryland, New Providence Community Church, Nassau, Bahamas, Redeemer Presbyterian Church, New York, Willow Creek Community Church, Chicago (Marti, 2005; Anderson, 2004); I would also add All Nations S.D.A. Churches, in Berrien Springs, Michigan, McAllen, Texas, Chicago, IL, and numerous other denominational and non-denominational congregations elsewhere. Many well-meaning converted saints of various denominations are engaging the racialized culture of this society and the status quo of their denominations and are planting heterogeneous congregations in both urban and suburban America. The planters of these congregations reject the HUD and under the aegis of the Spirit of God, are stepping out in faith to develop a new paradigm for church planting.

Of interest is a recent article in *Christianity Today* by David Swanson. In it he affirms,

> Again, we need new churches of all different types. Thanks be to God that whatever the shortcomings of our strategies, it is his church and mission. Even so, we must continue to choose church-planting models whose very essence displays, as Paul puts it, 'the mystery of Christ' (Swanson, 2009)

The desire for reconciliation is not peculiar to the sphere of Adventist Christians. Numerous peoples, factions, tribes, ethnicities all over the globe engage daily in its pursuit. That is because it does something good to the individual soul and for the collective interest when it is achieved. The resultant peace that accompanies reconciliation is covetable.

Some church planters still support the HUP. A recent article in *Christianity Today* magazine suggests

> I believe our approach to ministry has to be in and through a given culture. If the Good News takes root properly, it can flow naturally to family and friends within that culture. If it doesn't flow naturally through the culture, the Good News suddenly becomes the Bad News. It doesn't go beyond one person.

> Of course, there is an inherent danger with a mono-cultural approach: ethnocentrism. I know from my 30 years of experience how mono-cultural ministries can easily violate kingdom principles like justice, humility, and unity. Followers of Christ could wrongly apply mono-cultural thinking to condone new types of apartheid. Yet Jesus modeled for us a culturally-focused ministry that never showed bias or favoritism, culturally, socially, or economically. He was both culturally

bounded and sensitive, yet he always operated in a 'kingdom-culture-mode.' This must be our approach, if we are sent as he was (Swanson, 2010).

Much attention should be given to DeYmaz's disagreement with Steer in suggesting that the latter's findings are neither theologically nor scientifically persuasive. Besides, they are confined to a small portion of the population of the US. His assertion that the unbiased oneness that Jesus prayed for in John 17:20-21 is potentially modeled in mono-cultural congregations is at best faulty as it decontextualizes the prayer of our Lord (Steer, 2010). Evidently, Steer also overlooks the socio-demographic milieu of the churches that Paul planted. Paul was evangelizing at times in regions that had peoples of the specific cultures only. When they did, he planted churches among those who came to Christ as a result of his ministry. Paul's interest was in planting churches and he did so among the people in each specific geographic region. He was never intentional about planting mono-cultural congregations and he never asked them to segregate. In reality, he did the opposite (Eph. 2).

Benazir Bhutto coveted reconciliation for her beloved Pakistanis and Pakistan from whom and which she was exiled for eight years, but to which she returned in 2007 knowing that her life was in great jeopardy. In *Reconciliation: Islam, Democracy, and the West,* Bhutto addresses the need for Muslims to "rediscover the values of tolerance and justice that lie at the heart of her religion." In her quest for reconciliation she was assassinated in a motorcade on the streets of Rawalpindi two months after her return to Pakistan. She contends,

> There is much that Muslims can do to reconcile the internal contradictions that badly divide their communities in the twenty-first century...The Islamic states, in my view, can both accommodate and reconcile with one another and with the West. It is an ambitious undertaking, but it can be done (Bhutto, 2008).

What the Muslims of the East desire is what the Christians of the West need: reconciliation. It has been oft-repeated that the Evangelical movement in the US is the most segregated place on a Sunday morning. The same may be correctly said of the SDAC on a Saturday morning also. I showed in chapter four that the Evangelical and SDAC *Apartheid* generally existed way before South Africa's and persists in evangelicalism after its abolition in South Africa. Members are still occasionally being pointed to churches of their ethnicity in the SDAC. Note—"…the Seventh-day Adventist Church in South Africa appears to have practiced racial discrimination to a greater extent and for longer, than the church in other parts of Africa" (Crocombe, 2006). Further, Du Preez and Du Pre maintain,

> The Adventist church was always far ahead of the government of the day in applying racial segregation in the church, and far behind when it comes to scrapping racially discriminatory measures. By the time *Apartheid* was introduced in law after 1948, Adventists had been practicing it for twenty or more years (1994).

Gerald Du Preez avers that rather than suggesting that the Church in Southern Africa was ahead of the state in applying *Apartheid*, it is more accurate to say that the church "uncritically imbibed and adopted the policies of the government of the day," while admitting however, that there were some instances of this egregious error by the Church (Du Preez, 2010). This call for reconciliation in the remnant is not the first. After the April 12, 1954 meeting in which the "Current Issue" committee of the NAD was considering the question of whether to allow colored people into Columbia Union College. W. H. Branson sent a letter to the NAD Union and local conference presidents and managers of institutions on April 13, 1954 stated—

> The Christian churches of North America are altogether outstripping us in the matter of racial segregation. Many of them are moving forward toward the goal of total integration of all races into Christian fellowship on the

basis that 'All ye are brethren.'... He continued, "'Shall
we wait until our hands are forced on this matter, or
shall we move forward carefully but surely as men who
believe that 'All ye are brethren'" (Haloviak, 1999)?

Summary- The problem of the racial/ethnic divide in the Adventist
Church is a part of the bigger problem in the Evangelical movement and
the American society. The church has allowed itself to be molded into
conformity with the culture of the larger society. Adventists do well to
contextualize this social if spiritual blight but not condone it as status
quo. We are to rise to the challenge it poses to the church and access
the divine assistance that is available to help us.

While there are numerous countervailing reasons for prolonging
the status quo because of the peculiar enculturation and socialization of
each race/ethnicity, none of them is beyond our ability to appropriately
address and resolve our differences amicably. Whether it is theology,
trust, fear, geographic factors, wealth, status, culture, or any other,
if we would undertake the painstaking process of working toward a
resolution; with divine assistance it would be attainable. We can do
all things through Christ; things which strengthen us (1 Cor. 4:13).
Meanwhile, Adventists have been far too silent on the issue at hand.
We need to arouse ourselves and take action to reconcile God's people.

The practice of apartheid in the Adventist Church in South Africa
was similar to what was previously and to a lesser degree being currently
practiced in the NAD (although much has changed) as I will show at
this juncture. Could this evil practice have been exported to the South
Africa Union Conference of the SDAC by Adventists? This is an area
for further historical research. Excursus I peeks into the subject just
enough to pique the curiosity of the inquisitive mind.

6

The Third Great Disappointment of the Remnant

Admittedly, the title of this section does sound like a misnomer. For how can the Seventh-day Adventists be the remnant and yet become the disappointed? Nevertheless Adventists must understand that although we have the right doctrines, and many may practice the right lifestyle, our refusal to reconcile could lead to many among us being bitterly disappointment when Jesus returns. I will show in the paragraphs below that the third great disappointment of the remnant is still future and will be at the second coming of Christ.

As the remnant prepare for Christ's return, we must deal with this issue and wrestle with this reality as suggested by Rosado:

> "The major problem confronting the last-day church, which is also threatening the validity of the gospel, is a resurgence of the old problem, but in a new garb and on a global scale—the conflict between Whites and non-Whites" (Rosado, 1990).

This has existed in the US for centuries and plagues God's remnant Church today. We have not learned how to get along and totally unite our efforts optimally in doing the work of God.

In her account of the North-South war in the US, Ellen White wrote, "God is punishing this nation for the high crime of slavery. He has the destiny of the nation in His hands. He will punish the South for the sin of slavery, and the North for so long suffering its overarching and overbearing influence" (White *Vol. 1*, 1948). Was Ellen White referring to the North and South of her day (Civil War era) or was she referring to the final days before Jesus returns to earth for His own? I submit that the South of her day was in question, but the answer is really immaterial. The point of her warning is that racial/ethnic discrimination and segregation are sinful. This is affirmed more explicitly in another statement--"God is punishing the North..." for allowing the sin of slavery to exist. And further, "God is not with the South, and he will punish them dreadfully in the end" (White, *Vol. 1*, 1948). The North did not join the war in sympathy to the slaves, but joined the war only because it wanted to preserve the Union. Consequently, it was as guilty as the South for perpetuating slavery because it did not do all it could to prevent slavery from continuing so long (White, *Vol. 1*, 1948). Is Ellen White suggesting that God's punishment in the end will be the Third Great Disappointment that was prophesied by Christ in this parable of the ten virgins?

To all who profess Christ, Jesus' parable of the ten virgins in Matthew 25:1-12 is instructive. The virgins were all waiting for the Bridegroom with their lamps trimmed and burning, but only some of them had adequate oil and enough extra oil. Jesus teaches here that many will be awaiting his return, but not all will be ready. They were all initially in the house to which the Bridegroom came, but because some had run out of oil, they had gone out to purchase more when he came. Not all were inside when they should have been and when they knocked, he replied, "I do not know you." They were sorely disappointed. The fact is, not all Israel is Israel. Despite the fact that the remnant Church remains imperfect and incalcitrant, the Lord continues to use her. Why else did Ellen White make the following statements in 1898--"The Church is in the Laodicean state. The presence of God is not in her midst" (Olson, 1986; White, MS 156, 1898). In 1903 she stated elsewhere—

"The Lord will always have a chosen people to serve Him. When the Jewish people rejected Christ, the Prince of life, He took from them the kingdom of God and gave it unto the Gentiles…But, if these in turn do not purify their lives from every wrong action, it they do not establish pure and holy principles in all their borders, then the Lord will grievously afflict and humble them and, unless they repent, will remove them from their place and make them a reproach" (Olson, 1986).

Note again her counsel in 1904:

> In the balances of the sanctuary the Seventh-day Adventist Church is to be weighed. She will be judged by the privileges and advantages that she has had. If her spiritual experience does not correspond to the advantages that Christ, at infinite cost, has bestowed on her, if blessings conferred have not qualified her to do the work entrusted to her, on her will be pronounced the sentence: 'Found Wanting.' By the light bestowed, the opportunities given, will she be judged (White, *8T*, 1948).

As we prepare for the return of our Lord, Jesus Christ and contemplate the path ahead of us, we must seek daily to do the works of him who has sent us. Jesus has sent us on a mission to call others to be reconciled to God. Yet when we bring them into the Church they come only to see the remnant church segregated: local conferences segregated by race and local churches segregated by ethnicity. For this reason some have returned to their former ways. Like Ghandhi, they admire Christ, they are intrigued by Christianity, but they are turned off by the lifestyle of Christians. On the basis of our doctrines we boast that we are the remnant. **And we are**. But when those outside of our denomination look at our lifestyle, who do we appear to be? As Adventists the affirmation below may be said of us—

> "There is an arrogance to which we are all liable. It is the arrogance of thinking that only we have the truth. God's truth may well be greater than all of our 'truths. Until we

come into that larger truth, we must be true to the truth we have embraced'" (Pierce and Groothuis, 2005)...

The Need for Unity- Unity is critical to the mission of the Church. Koranteng-Pipim avers, "Christ's chief concern in His last prayer was for unity" (Koranteng-Pipim, 2001). Unless those to whom we are witnessing can sense unity among us, they will be turned off. History is replete with examples of such. They see us as hypocrites because we profess love and unity, but we merely feign its practice. Calls for unity are proliferated throughout Scripture and the writings of Ellen White (Jn. 17:20-21; Eph. 4:1-16; 1 Cor. 1:10). Five times Jesus prayed for this among His disciples (Jn. 17: 11, 21a, 21b, 22, 23), yet it remains sadly lacking among his remnant today. But unity comes at a cost.

Unity existing among the followers of Christ is an evidence that the Father has sent His Son to save sinners. It is a witness to His power; for nothing short of the miraculous power of God can bring human beings with their different temperaments together in harmonious action... It should be understood that perfect unity among the laborers is necessary to the successful accomplishment of the work of God (White, *9T*, 1948).

This unity is not simply doctrinal unity, as difficult as that is to achieve, but spiritual unity, which comes only by the presence of the Holy Spirit in our hearts (Koranteng-Pipim, 2001). We often attain it only at the expense of pride. It requires a measure of humility. Above all it costs us love. We must show genuine love in order to be genuinely united.

Ellen White suggests,

> "But never, never forget that you are either servants of Jesus Christ, working strenuously for that unity of believers which Christ prayed might exist, or you are working against this unity and against Christ" (White, *5T* 478.3).

The apostle Paul reminds us in the epistle to the Ephesians that we are all a part of one body. Each part of the body is important in its proper function and has a significant role to play in accomplishing its ultimate goal, which is building up the body of Christ. No part can say to the other "I do not need you," for each has its unique role to play (Eph. 4:1-16). Neither can all work as if alone, for we are a part of the body; a team. Collaboration and unity are critical. The time is short and we cannot afford to duplicate the roles. The greater the unity we enjoy, the greater our chances of minimizing any duplication. And all of this is done with and out of love. Unity is usually achieved in conjunction with love.

Anger and Hatred- The issue of rage is a major one in this dilemma. Many Adventist believers are still angry with one or another race. Some Blacks are still very angry about what the Whites did to their forebears and about their (Whites') current privileged positions in society and the SDAC, due to economic inequities, political clout, structural imbalances in society, and unfair advantages and racial discrimination in the SDAC. A few Whites may be angry because of isolated incidents of racial discrimination or violence against them, Affirmative Action, or about incidents in which their relative (s) were hurt by Blacks, Hispanics, or Asians. And all these may be justifiable anger, since anger is a legitimate emotion in instances when one was wronged. Yet what is the mature Christians attitude toward anger?

Not many years ago, a retired African American Adventist pastor, whom I knew from the Northeast relocated to the South to enjoy his retirement years, after the passing of his wife. His adolescent son relocated with him also. But after about a year, I saw him again and he informed me that he had moved back to the North. "Why would you?" I enquired. He went on to inform me that his son became so angry every time he saw White people and so many of them were living in his subdivision, he felt that he was going to attack one of them. He relocated in order to avoid that situation. Cornell West addresses this "Black rage" issue in *Race Matters*, as one which has a legitimate place, given the oppression meted out to Blacks in the US over the past centuries (2003). Nevertheless as Christians we ought to channel our anger in the appropriate direction and not let it adversely impact our missional obligations.

There is real anger among Adventists, particularly Black Adventists. And God allows us to get angry in cases of injustice, abuse, exploitation, and other sins. God also gets angry (Ps. 7:11); Jesus got angry (Jn. 2:13-18); the apostles experienced anger (Gal. 2:11-14). Despite that, we are discouraged from harboring hatred. Besides the fact that anger and hatred (grudge) could cause us to hurt others, they definitely hurt us. They prevent us from "engineering a real solution to the problem." Behavioral Therapist, Barry Lubetkin, affirms that "anger—induced by your grudge—can cause tremendous psychological stress" (Lubetkin, 1996). That is the reason the apostle Paul admonishes us--"In your anger, do not sin; do not let the sun go down while you are still angry" (Eph. 4:26, NIV). Whenever we become so consumed by anger as in the example above, we are in danger of sinning. Let us pray for the power of forgiveness, so that we can let go and move on.

Lack of Love- What is it that keeps us apart? I submit that it is lack of love for one another. Jesus illustrated this in the parable of the Good Samaritan. When the young man asked, "And who is my neighbor?" Jesus replied, "He who fell among thieves?" The lack of love for each other is the reason we have been unable to unite. Ellen White identifies the lack of love as the root of the remnant's problem. She writes--

> "Men may have both hereditary and cultivated prejudices, but when the love of Jesus fills the heart, and they become one with Christ, they will have the same spirit that He had... If Jesus is abiding in our hearts we cannot despise the colored man who has the same Savior abiding in his heart" (White, 1948)...

Christ requires all of us to be neighborly. "Every man is potentially every man's neighbor. Neighborliness is non-spatial; it is qualitative. A man must love his neighbor directly, clearly, permitting no barriers between" (West, 2003). One who fell among thieves in the parable may be likened to Blacks and Indians and more recently Hispanics and Asians to a lesser degree, in America. These ethnic groups have been robbed, exploited, extorted, and simply wronged, yea, oppressed for centuries by White America with no reparations: they fell among thieves. The society and the Christian church in America, including the SDAC ought to offer reparations to the oppressed Blacks (Williams and Collins, 2004).

The church must be the voice of the oppressed; it needs to speak for them. But even such atrocities must not cause the oppressed to hate the oppressors or the descendants of their oppressors. Instead, love must prevail in their relationship. Howard Thurman posits, "the religion of Jesus makes the love-ethic central'" (West, 2003). Love was what drew us to Christ and love is the only thing that can bind us together as a remnant people. But it appears love is sadly lacking among us. This is not an indictment of one race, but of all of us.

Ellen White appeals to the saints in Healburg—

"Do not forget that the most dangerous snares which Satan has prepared for the church will come through its own members who do not love God supremely or their neighbor as themselves. Satan is continually striving to wedge himself in between brethren. He seeks to gain control of those who claim to believe the truth, but who are **unconverted** (emphasis mine); and when he can influence these, through their own carnal nature, to unite with him in trying to thwart the purposes of God, then he is exultant" (White, *5T*, 477.1).

If we truly loved each other, we would hear thousands, perhaps millions more Adventists calling for reconciliation in the remnant. But no, those who do are often scoffed at and called names. We are often told--"You do not understand the history of the Adventist Church in America…" as if to say that the sordid history justifies hatred and segregation. Ellen White counsels, "Unless we daily cultivate the precious plant of love, we are in danger of becoming narrow, unsympathetic, bigoted, and critical, esteeming ourselves righteous when we are far from being approved of God" (White, *5T*, 1948). "As a people we are sadly destitute of faith and love" (White, *5T*, 1948)… The genocide in Rwanda is a sad testament to our destitution as former GC president, Jan Paulson, notes—

> And it is with sadness that the Seventh-day Adventist Church must also acknowledge that in the midst of this tragedy, many church members -- people who should have known better -- failed to display basic love and care for their brothers and sisters" (*Adventist News Network*, May 11, 2005).

We become brothers and sisters at baptism regardless of the color of our skin, our gender, or our status. And we are one. Adventist Christians would do well heeding the word of Bonhoeffer—

> And if we grant the baptized brother the right to the gifts of salvation, but refuse him the gifts necessary to earthly life or knowingly leave him in material need and distress, we are holding up the gifts of salvation to ridicule and behaving as liars. If the Holy Ghost has spoken and we listen instead to the call of blood and nature, or to our personal sympathies or antipathies, we are profaning the sacrament (Bonhoeffer, 1995).

In *The Southern Work*, Ellen White States, "I want you to think of this and of the burden that rests upon the White people to help the colored people" (Baker, 1996; White, *The Southern Work*, 1966)… She further counsels,

> "I call upon every church in our land to look well to your own souls. 'Examine yourselves, whether ye be in the faith; prove your own selves. Know ye not your own selves, how that Jesus Christ is in you, except ye be reprobates?' God makes no distinction between the North and the South. Whatever may be your prejudices, your wonderful prudence, do not lose sight of this fact, that unless you put on Christ, and His Spirit dwells in you, you are slaves of sin and of Satan. Many who claim to be children of God are children of the wicked one, and have all his passions, his prejudices, his evil spirit, his unlovely traits of character" (Ellen White, 19…)

In his message to the 2009 Fall Counsel, Elder Jan Paulson, then president of the GC, noted four core elements to the gospel through the message of reconciliation 1) there is only one way; 2) death to death; 3) a reconciling ministry; 4) the certainty of his return. Based on the entirety of the epistle to the Hebrews, Paulson understands Jesus to be involved in an ongoing ministry of reconciliation in heaven now. Paulson posited, "Without this ministry, we cannot effectively be set free from our past or present failures, or from the impending destruction of the future. It is the ministry of reconciliation which Christ is engaged in today that gives us access to the "'power of His resurrection'" (Annual Counsel of the GC committee, 2009).

Philip Yancey suggests four steps that Whites and Blacks must take in order to reconcile. First, they need to develop primary relationships among individuals of the different races; 2) White must recognize the existence of social structural inequalities and the need for all Christians to resist them; 3) White must view themselves as benefactors of a racialized society and "must repent of their personal, historical, and social sins;" 4) when Whites ask, Blacks must be willing to forgive them individually and corporately (Yancey, 2010). But only the love of God in their hearts can lead individuals of the different races to takes these steps. These are hard sayings. Yet they are not too hard for those who have been call to sacrifice (Romans 12:1). And unless we do, we will individually suffer the Third Great Disappointment!

A Final Segregation- Dietrich Bonhoeffer's makes a compelling argument--"the Church is marked off from the world not by a special privilege, but by the gracious election and calling of God" (1995). Yet when God calls, not all who answer saying, "Lord, Lord...are his but those only, who "do his will" (Mt. 7:21). Currently there is a great divide in the remnant and this will become more evident in the last days. The line of demarcation is fuzzy now; it is not for anyone to judge who is in and who is out. Instead we must do the works of righteousness and be prepared. Those who "confess his name" will then be segregated from those who "do his will" (vs. 22). Bonhoeffer goes on,

> The word of the last judgment is foreshadowed in the call to discipleship. But from beginning to end it is always *his* word and *his* call, *his* alone. If we follow Christ, cling to his word, and let everything else go, it will see us through the Day of Judgment. His word is grace (1998).

Bonhoeffer's understanding of these texts is correct. His assessment is scripturally supported and is corroborated by the leading Adventist theologians of all era, as well as Ellen White (LaRondelle, 1983; Rodriquez, 2009).

In answering the apostle Peter's rhetorical question in 2 Pet. 3:11, 12, Elder Ted Wilson affirmed in the September 23, 2010 issue of *Adventist Review* that "You ought to live holy and godly lives—revived lives, reformed lives, lives filled with the power of the Holy Spirit" (Wilson, 2010). And what impact will such lives have? Wilson maintains that consequently "...individuals everywhere will be attracted to his remnant church as they see the fruit of the Spirit in the lives of those who are waiting for His soon appearing" (Wilson, *Adventist Review,* 2010).

The apostle Paul offers the counsel in Rom. 15:1-2—"We who are strong ought to bear with the failings of the weak and not to please ourselves. Each of us should please his neighbor for his good, to build him up'" (NIV). That unity and love are requisite for membership in the body of Christ is evident in Scripture. Paul affirms this in Col. 3:14--"And over all these virtues put on love, which binds them all together in perfect unity" (NIV).

More counsel comes from the pen of inspiration:

> What shall I say to arouse the remnant people of God? I was shown that dreadful scenes are before us; Satan and his angels are bringing all their powers to bear upon God's people. He knows that if they sleep a little longer, he is sure of them, for their destruction is certain (Goldstein, 1994; White, *Christian Service,* 1947).

Dybdahl again notes that Western Christians, in particular, want to hear about love, but cringe at the mention of judgment. Those disappointed in the final day will be weeping and wailing and gnashing their teeth (Revelation). I conclude this exposition with an admonition for reconciliation in the remnant, uttered by the apostle, Paul in Rom. 15:5-6--"May the God who gives endurance and encouragement give you a spirit of unity among yourselves as you follow Christ Jesus, so that with one heart and mouth you may glorify the God and Father of our Lord Jesus Christ" (NIV).

Summary- The final great disappointment is alluded to in Scripture. Jesus spent much time assuring his disciples that there will be a final judgment at the end of time. In that judgment, not all who expect to be saved will be saved; it will be a time of great disappointment for many, including members of the remnant church. None of us can judge who will be among the disappointment, but we know for sure that without love for our fellow humans, it is impossible to be among the saved. Rather than trying to determine who will be disappointed and who will be saved, the question we should ponder is--"Am I showing the genuine love of God to my fellow human beings inside and outside of the church in thoughts, words, and actions?

7

Reconciliation: A Christian Moral Imperative

What is Reconciliation?

J. J. Blanco in his Ph.D. dissertation, "A Critical Analysis and Comparison of the Doctrine of Reconciliation...," examines the varying definitions of reconciliation. Blanco notes that reconciliation "originates from the social-societal sphere (cf. 1 Cor. 7:11) and speaks in general of the restoration of the right relationship between two parties" (Blanco, 1970; De Witt, 1975). The William Webster's Dictionary defines "reconciliation" as "the action of reconciling: the state of being reconciled" (Mirriam-Webster, 2010).

A Theology of Reconciliation

Definition: The English noun "reconciliation" is used to translate the Greek words, *katallasso, katallage, apokatallasso. Katallasso* and its derivatives occur only six times in the New Testament; *katallage,* four times, and *apokatallasso,* three times (Eph. 2:16; Col. 1:20, 21). The Greek verb *katallasso* means "to reconcile," and denotes "bringing together" or "making peace" between two hostile or estranged parties (Moo, 1996; Geisler, 2004). It also carries the meaning "to change," "exchange," and in the passive voice—"to be reconciled." Meanwhile the noun *katallage* means "an exchange," "reconciliation," "restoration to favor" (Moulton, 1990). The Greek verb *apokatallasso* is a compound word from both the particle *apo* and the verb, *katallasso. Apo* means "from," "off," "away from"; *katallaso,* "to reconcile". The translations "to reconcile completely," "to reconcile back again," "bring back a former state of harmony" are preferred. In Col. 1:20, 21 it is a cumulative aorist and denotes an action which ended at a certain point in the rendition (Thayer, 1996). Thus "reconciliation" connotes a finished action.

Its New Testament Usage- By its use of the word "reconciliation" the New Testament introduces a concept to the group of words that was foreign to Greeks. In Greek society subjects did not reconcile with their gods. It was customary to use the words in the context of human to human relationships. They are used in Mt. 5:24; Acts 7: 26; Rom. 5:10, 11; 11:15; 1 Cor. 7:11; 2 Cor. 5:18, 19, 20; Eph. 2:16; Col. 1:20, 22. With the exception of Mt. 5:24, the words "reconcile" and "reconciliation" do not appear in the New Testament outside of the Pauline epistles. In every instance except 1 Cor. 7:11 (reconciliation between husband and wife), reconciliation is an action of God (Gallagher, 1988).

In the writings of Paul, reconciliation is not a mere act but an activity. Thus the "ministry of reconciliation" is an activity of Christian servitude. The Greek noun *diakonos*, "ministry," is employed in 2 Cor. 5:18 instead of *leitourgia*, which is used elsewhere in the New Testament and is translated "ministry". The words are not used interchangeably in the Greek because *leitourgia* denotes a "ministry at one's own expense," (as in the case of Christ's sacrifice or a priest fulfilling the sacrificial cultus) while *diakonia* refers to a ministry carried out at the command of someone else. Thus "the waiter at a meal" (Jn. 2:5, 9), "the servant of a master" (Mt. 22:13), is a *diakonos*; they both perform their duties as the discharge of their obligations to those whom they were called to serve (that is, God and fellow human) out of love. Likewise, "the servant of a spiritual power," whether good or evil (2 Cor. 11:4f; Kittel, 1993) is a *diakonos*. The *leitourgia* fulfills his/her sacrificial duties to God, while the *diakonos* fulfills them to both God and human.

The "ministry of reconciliation" (*diakonian tes katallages*, 2 Cor. 5:18) is not listed among the *charismata* in 1 Cor. 12:28; it is not a spiritual gift, such as those divided among the saints—prophecy, service, tongues, and so on. Neither is one elected to it or selected for it. Rather, it is a ministry that is enjoined on all the saints by God. Taken from the sphere of the common meal, it makes every saint "a servant at the table" to each other, without regard to race, ethnicity, gender, status, age, color, nationality caste, or any other distinction.

Reconciliation has close association to the following concepts: peace with God" – (Rom. 5:1; Col. 1:20); access to God" - Eph. 2:18; 3:12; Col. 1:22); fellowship with God" - I Jn. 1:3); justification" - Rom. 5:19; II Cor. 5:19,21); adoption" - Rom. 8:15; 9:4; Gal. 4:5; Eph. 1:5); restoration" - Acts 3:21); spiritual exchange - Acts 26:18); spiritual union - I Cor. 6:17); indwelling of Holy Spirit - Rom. 5:5); identity as "new creature" - II Cor. 5:17); saving life of Christ - Rom. 5:10); joy - Rom. 5:11); times of refreshing - Acts 3:19); love - Rom. 5:5; II Cor. 5:14 (Fowler, 2004).

The New Testament presents Christ as the fulfillment of the Old Testament type. The history of ancient Israel is a type of Christ's mission. The name "Israel has been symbolic of reconciliation with God since its origin: Jacob's name was changed to Israel after he wrestled with and began clinging to God's messenger (White, *Patriarchs and Prophets*, 1958). His clinging to God and declaring—"I will not let you go until you bless me" is indicative of the development of a reconciling relationship. At times we may wrestle with each other over various issues in the church, but while wrestling has its place, it must end when the love of God constrains us to reconcile.

Among all the New Testament writers, reconciliation as an emerging theological construct is most evident in the writings of Paul. The apostle Paul is very forthright on the subject of our oneness as members of the body of Christ; oneness which becomes possible only through reconciliation, since we were formerly two estranged parties. Christ created "One New Humanity" by his sacrifice on the cross. The oneness is of such that it removes the need for one member to litigate against another of the household of faith. Any conflict which arises is settled within the jurisprudence of the commonwealth of faith (1 Cor. 6; Gordon, 2008). Why? In the civil courts, the judges are unjust, but in the commonwealth of faith, they are presumed just. Hence the no-brainer, why would a Christian want to go before one of the unjust judges when he has the just ones among us? "What the church binds on earth is bound in heaven (Mt. 16:19) because the Holy Spirit guides the church. The church judges righteously.

Paul likens reconciliation to justification. In Rom. 5:9, 10 he employs a parallelism in affirming that we are "justified by His (Christ's) blood" and reconciled by His death. In 2 Cor. 3:9 and 5:18 he alternates the "ministry of righteousness" with the "ministry of reconciliation." Reconciliation is foundational to and the sum total of the Christian life (De Witt, 1975).

George Yancey propounds in the Journal of Christian Ethics that Jesus went seeking to reach Samaritans for his kingdom (Jn. 4:1-26) even though they were generally despised by members of his ethnic group. He was a Jew. The Jews despised the Samaritans because they were of a mixed race (2 Kgs. 17:24-41). Jesus was not prejudiced and would have none of it.

Jesus' sacrifice removed the barrier between us as individuals and collectively as races/ethnic groups. Galatians 3:28 pinpoints the common ancestry of all who accept Christ without respect to race, gender, or social status. Ephesians informs us that in Christ we are "One New Humanity" (Eph. 2:5-8). All over the New Testament the followers of Christ are represented as a unit: the kingdom of God (the Gospels), the body of Christ (1 Corinthians), and the bride of Christ (Revelation 22). The notion of separateness is foreign to New Testament Christology and theology. Christ provides the connectivity among all races and ethnicities. His Spirit lives in us all. Hence as Christ's, it is not "us" and "them," but "us" alone: family; the family of God. The church should "function as the locus of (and pattern for!) the reconciled world" (Col. 1:18; Dunn, 1998).

The doctrine of reconciliation is central to Pauline theology. Paul sees reconciliation as the overarching goal of redemption. It is the "fundamental motif of Paul's preaching" (De Witt, 1975). The reconciliation motif is at the core of the epistle of Romans (Jews reconciled to Gentile; both reconciled to Christ). In the Corinthian epistles (1 Cor. 1) he contends that no schism ought to exist between saints (fellow Christians). Each saint is to be reconciled to the other (brother to brother, man to wife) no matter what their differences may be (1 Cor. 1:10-17). The epistles to the Ephesians (2:16ff) and Colossians (1:20, 21) highlight the reconciling sacrifice of Christ, which makes possible and warrants the reconciliation of Jews and Gentiles and by which God reconciles all things to himself. In Philemon, slave is reconciled to master and vice versa (vss. 15-17). Essentially, through reconciliation God removes the enmity (between fellow humans, between human and God) and restores peace (between fellow humans, between humans and God).

The apostle Paul suggests that the "word of reconciliation" is the gospel (2 Cor. 5:19, NIV). It is good news to those who are at enmity. Those who are at enmity are hurting; hurting because of the lost friendship and fellowship with their estranged other. James A. Fowler identifies the "ministry of reconciliation" (2 Cor. 5:18, NIV) as evangelism (1999). Paul announces God's invitation to reconcile with him (2 Cor. 5:20).

Although reconciliation is preceded by justification, it is a personal concept, not a forensic one, as in the former. Thus no legal requirement is entailed. There is, however, a meeting of the minds that is often symbolized by a handshake, embrace, or other physical contact. It is an agreement reached between people to overlook differences, hurt, or disagreements, that may have resulted in estrangement.

> Reconciliation also has an eschatological nuance. The essence of reconciliation is justification; the work of reconciliation is sanctification; the result of reconciliation is necessary for translation and the ultimate goal of reconciliation is glorification. Neither are the results of

reconciliation limited to humans, but they impinge on the restoration of the world. Reconciliation precedes and is requisite to the new creation: the passing away of the old and the advent of the new (2 Cor. 5:17, 18).

The world as a cosmic material entity is under the dominion of Satan and cannot be reconciled to God without the sacrifice of Christ. But let us not lose sight of the fact that Christ created us before he re-created ("redeemed") us. We were in a reconciled state at creation because there was no estrangement between righteous humans and their righteous God. We were in a reconciled relationship before we needed redemption (Blanco, 1970). Now that we are justified by Christ it becomes even more encouraging to us that we are reconciled (Boers, 1994).

In Pauline theology there is one ministry that is enjoined on all the saints, that is, the ministry of reconciliation (2 Cor. 5:18-21). Every believer is gifted to be reconciling ministers. In light of this ministry assignment Paul counsels that we should owe nothing else to anyone but love (Rom. 13:8-12); we make peace with one another (Rom. 14:19-21); we share with one another (Gal. 6:2); we speak kindly of and to one another (1 Thess. 5:15; Jam. 3:1-12); we bear each other's burden (Gal. 6:2); we serve one another (Gal. 5:13; 1 Cor. 12:25). All these requisite acts of the Christian, serve to show that the Christian life is all about reconciliation. After we have been reconciled, we engage in reconciling others: to God and to each other; that is ministry.

Reconciliation

Figure 2 The process of reconciliaition

Figure 2 above suggests that reconciliation, individual and corporate, is a process. It is always necessitated in this life because of our sin nature. We constantly do wrong against each other and always need to make amends.

In summation, it is noteworthy that reconciliation among humans is multivalent. On the one hand it is a finished action, but on the other it is a dynamic process (DeYoung, 1997). It is linear (continuous) even while it is punctiliar (at a point). It is a goal, yet it is a journey. It is an act and an activity. Reconciliation is an ongoing ministry in which believers are to be engaged daily (2 Cor. 5:18). We have victories each step of the way as we engage regularly in personal reconciliation and ultimately corporate reconciliation.

The nuance of unity is present in the noun reconciliation. To be reconciled is to be restored to oneness. This oneness suggests unity--atonement. It is something that God does with us. Thus God restores us to himself or to each other. Jesus' sacrifice is the reconciling factor and his love constrains us to reconcile. Only he really can reconcile us.

God as Reconciler

In the epistle to the Romans, Paul establishes the sinfulness of all humans. Firstly, "there is none righteous, not even one" (Rom. 3:10, NIV). Then later on in that chapter he says it explicitly--"all have sinned…" (Rom. 3:23, *NIV*). The presence of sin in any humans results in their separation from God and ultimately in the death of the sinner (Rom. 5:12). Thus the need for reconciliation as the means of escape from an ultimate eternal death is amplified.

Reconciliation with God has been initiated by God. Decades ago, the Jamaican-American preacher and reconciler, Samuel Hines, argued that reconciliation is God's one item agenda (Emerson and Smith, 2000). God, therefore, having made the provision for this possibility before the founding of the world, sends Jesus (Jn. 3:16) to be the Reconciler *par excellence* (Rom. 5:8-10). Jesus did this while we were "dead in our trespasses and sins" (Rom. 5:8). Jesus reached out to humans while we were still enemies of God (Rom. 5:10). Consequently, we may rejoice in God through Jesus Christ "whom we have now received reconciliation" (Rom. 5:11).

Not only are we able to rejoice now, we may also be at peace, because Jesus is our peace (Eph. 2:16). This peace is both vertical and horizontal. His sacrifice gives us peace with God and with our fellow humans. In the light of vertical peace, Jesus becomes our "peace offering" to God by which we are "saved from God's wrath" (Rom. 5:9). With respect to the horizontal peace: he removes the dividing wall of hostility and becomes the peace bridge between fellow humans (Eph. 2:14). Being at peace allows us to fellowship freely since we can now trust each other.

If you should drive from Jerusalem to Cairo via the Suez; in order to get to downtown Cairo, you would have to go across a bridge, which takes you over the river Nile. This bridge was built after the 1967 war between Israel and the Arab nations. Egypt signed a peace accord with Israel and this bridge was built as the memorial of their peace accord. Christ is that peace bridge between us and God and between us as humans. Any hostility between us is removable by Christ!

This refers to either real or contrived hostility. The hostility is sin: sin which no human can expiate, but which Christ's blood eradicates. The idea of a change in attitude or relationship is embedded in the word reconciliation as rendered in the Greek. *Katallage* and its Greek cohorts imply that something or someone was either separated, broken, fragmented, or alienated and needs to be brought back into a wholesome relationship. Thus Christ brings "all things in heaven and on earth together under one head, even Christ" (Eph. 1:10, *NIV*). Christ is the reconciling agent. He initiates reconciliation and guarantees it. When we approach the Father through him, our reception is guaranteed. As a result we may now approach the throne of grace with confidence (Heb. 4:16).

The concept of reconciliation is a New Testament one. The concept does not have an Old Testament parallel. The Bible uses reconciliation only in the context of God doing something for or with us. Jesus makes reconciliation possible (Rom. 5: 15-21). He is the reconciler *par excellence* (DeYoung, 1997). He orchestrated reconciliation on the cross and demonstrated it in his ministry. He mingled with sinners, publicans, Samaritans, poor, rich, males, females, old, young, everyone, without regard as to ethnicity, age, gender, education, wealth, class, caste, or status. Then he sent his disciples out to do the same (Lk. 10).

Why Should We Reconcile?

A Biblical Mandate Reconciliation is a biblical mandate for Christians. Both Jesus and Paul are very clear on that fact. Jesus' prayer in Jn. 17:20-21 is to be understood to be a prayer for reconciliation among His disciples. Paul builds a lengthy argument for reconciliation among Christians in the epistle to the Ephesians. Ephesians 2 affirms that Jews and Gentiles who were previously apart from each other have been brought nearby. Christ's sacrificial act on the cross, removed the wall of partition, thus reconciling them. And he now becomes their peace (vs. 8). This fact applies not just to the Jews and Gentiles, who were Paul's contemporaries, but also to every disciple of Christ today.

When members of all ethnicities become a part of the body of Christ, we are reconciled to both Christ and to their fellow human. We are all reconciled to Christ by His death (2 Cor. 5:19), which also has the power to reconcile us to each other. Though we may be from warring factions, upon being reconciled, we are instantly at peace, we lay down our arms, and we begin to pursue individual reconciliation. Further, we join together as siblings and engage in the ministry of corporate reconciliation. This entails saying to our fellow Christians, "We are friends now," even though we look different and talk differently, "Let us lay our arms down." Thus, we are no more "us" and "them," but simply "us." We become "One New Humanity," the new creation of Christ (Eph. 2:15-16; 2 Cor. 5:17 NKJV).

Jesus also gives us the "ministry of reconciliation" (2 Cor. 5:18, NIV) because he wants us to enjoy the beauty of leading others, our enemies, to him, so that they may enjoy sweet fellowship with him and with us. We each ought to be engaged daily in this ministry, appealing to our fellow humans on Christ's behalf--"Be reconciled to God" (2

Cor. 5:20b). It should occur to us that it is Christ's desire to make this appeal through us to each other. As we learn to labor together for the salvation of each other here, we will eagerly anticipate eternity together in the same heaven.

The all-encompassing nature of reconciliation is intimated in 2 Cor. 5:18-19, in that no where else in Scripture are believers explicitly counseled to engage in any other ministry for Christ. Reconciliation is the sum total of what Christ calls us to in him. It is the sole reason for which Christ died on the cross for us. Everything that Christ calls us to engage in is a part of the ministry of reconciliation. God is first engaged in this ministry (reconciliation). It is both subjective and objective. God is the one whose righteous indignation must be appeased and Christ is the only one who can at once appease God and expiate humans. Then having demonstrated it by giving all he had to save us he now calls us to engage with him in the ministry to save others!

A Testament to our Humanness- Besides being biblical, the call to reconcile is humane. The South African Anglican Bishop, Desmond Tutu, took the position that the struggle against apartheid served as a barometer of one's humanness. He further affirmed that "'our humanness is measured by the extent to which we are moved by the suffering of other people'" (Ateek, 2008).

Robert Banks makes a persuasive point in his examination of the writings of the apostle Paul on this subject. In *Paul's Idea of Community...*, Banks propounds that the Christian faith joins all Christians into a community of believers who are interdependent (Banks, 1980). Just as we all share in the sacrifice of Christ through fellowship (*koinonia*) with Him, Christ wants us to share in struggles, pain, challenges of others as we fellowship with them (Gal. 6:2). *The Theological Dictionary of the New Testament* suggests that "fellowship with Christ leads to fellowship with Christians" (Kittel, 1965). This fellowship is mutual among members of the community.

Reconciliation is Costly

Our reconciliation cost God "his only begotten Son" (Jn. 3:16). It will come only at a cost to each of us (DeYoung, 1997). It comes at the ultimate spiritual cost to both Black and White Adventists, as well as to all ethnic groups in the SDAC. Potter rightly posits that it requires death (Okholm, 1997), spiritual death. A death which results in all of our being "living sacrifices" (Rom. 12:1, 2). The SDAC will not realize unity without sacrifices.

It is not the nature of humans to work together in a unified manner. This is exacerbated by the history of oppression of one race by the other in the US. Issues of trust, of culture, and inferior/superior attitudes combined with societal pressures are mitigating factors against reconciliation. Slavery and Jim Crowism did not simply disappear in America because the White ruling class felt that they were terribly wrong in perpetrating oppressive serfdom and segregation against Blacks, Indians, and Jews and then pitied the disadvantaged minority peoples. The abolition of slavery and the outlawing of the Jim Crow laws came at huge costs. Some 620,000 soldiers lost their lives during the Civil War (Davis, 2004).

The Antislavery Society and Abolitionist Movement of the nineteenth century and the Civil Rights Movement of the 1960s which championed the cause of the oppressed, cost many all that they had. There was much bloodshed and thousands of lives were lost as hundreds of thousands marched, litigated, and fought for equal rights and justice. These were not just Blacks, Jews, and Indians, but Whites and Hispanics; thousands through whom the blood of Christ flows. Black Adventists were a part of the Civil Rights Movement (London, 2009). Many Adventist and other Christian Whites were also involved apparently to a lesser degree (Branson, 1970; Haloviak, 1999). And God was on the side of the oppressed. That is what made it a "war of liberation" (White, *Vol. 1*, 1948; Reynolds, 1984). Abraham Lincoln's Gettysburg Address spoke to the sacrifices of all of these.

Moss Ntlha, head of the Evangelical Alliance of South Africa asserts that "Reconciliation is not cheap grace, but is attended by a willingness to suffer in solidarity with victims" (Okite, 2010). Yancey's observation is correct—

> "There are also minority-group members who fear that their racial cultural distinctiveness will be lost if Whites are allowed to intrude upon their lives. Historically, oppressive racial relationships can lead to paternalism in contemporary minority relationships. Interpersonal racial relationships can no longer be hierarchical, with Whites controlling the lion's share of power. We must seek new egalitarian racial relationships" (George Yancey, 2001).

Similarly, it has been observed that a fear exists among Whites. Emerson and Smith observed a fear of losing status and wealth (Emerson and Smith, 2000). DeYoung posits that Whites have a fear of retribution (DeYoung, 1997). Yancey hints at this fear factor among Evangelicals also (Yancey, 2001).

The time has come once more for all racial and ethnic groups in the remnant church to rise up and be united. We need to raise every believer's awareness of the need for racial and ethnic reconciliation in the remnant church. This unity will come only at a cost to the adherents of truth and seekers of righteousness. But did Jesus not say we "must leave father, mother, sister, wife to follow him" (Lk. 14:26)? The discipleship of Christ is costly. Christians must sacrifice if they would even approximate the lifestyle requirements of their faith. In an article about the political expediency characterizing the SDAC leadership, a recently retired vice-president of the GC noted in 1970--

> Many White leaders do have an understanding and conviction but they refuse to act because they fear loss of prestige, loss of finance, loss of status, and even loss of

job. This results in an unfortunate vacuum of leadership which leaves White lay members lock in their deep, dark prejudices (Rock, 1970).

In the *Cost of Discipleship*, Dietrich Bonhoeffer argues--"In such times as these, Jesus requires his disciples to distinguish between appearance and reality, between themselves and pseudo-Christians" (Bonhoeffer, 1995). Christ challenges Christians to a closer fellowship with God and to be more loyal disciples.

Of much import is the sacrifice that God made to achieve this. The sacrifices we are being called on to make will not be easy. David Swanson, an Evangelical pastor of a church-plant on Chicago's South Side understands this well. Swanson writes,

> "There are good reasons to be hesitant about cross-cultural church planting. As a White man pastoring a multi-ethnic church in a historically African-American neighborhood, I've become exceedingly aware of the perils. Anxieties about patriarchy, inexperience with racism, and ignorance about other cultures and histories are realities I must deal with directly and repeatedly. Additionally, most of us are keenly aware of how difficult it is to bridge racial and class divisions. The amount of humility and patience needed to do so can seem super-human and—to be frank—not worth the effort. In fact, if not for the nature of the Gospel itself, the pitfalls of non-homogeneous ministry are enough to dissuade even the most cross-culturally adept church planter" (Swanson, 2010).

The estrangement between humankind and God resulted from humankind's dethronement of his Creator from the Lordship of his life. We rebelled against God; we rejected him. Thus God becomes the injured party of this estrangement. Yet God did not merely send Jesus to do the work of reconciliation, but though being the injured party, "God was in Christ reconciling the world unto himself" (Rom. 5:19). The point here is critical: Blacks have been dehumanized, debilitated, and discriminated against by Whites for centuries, but no amount of abuse justifies a permanent standoff between God's people. Indeed we may get angry, but even in anger we should not allow our anger to rise to the level of sin (Eph. 4:26). The fact is, Jesus is our peace (Eph. 2:14) and we are his new creation (2 Cor. 5:17, 18).

In Christ's relationship with us, he (the injured party) actively seeks us out in order to reconcile with us. His reconciling love constrains the abused to not look upon the abuser with contempt; rather it moves the abused to release the abuser from his guilt. We all need each other. Martin Luther King, Jr's statement was correct—"The Negro needs the White man to free him from his fears. The White man needs the Negro to free him from his guilt." Scripture counsels oppressed Blacks not to hold the transgression of Whites against them.

The urgent need to reconcile with God coupled with the need for reconciliation among humans, make reconciliation central to the Christian faith. All of Scripture is highlighting the sinfulness of humans and the provision that God has made to rid them of it. Hence the first dimension of reconciliation is vertical. Our sinfulness has estranged us from God and necessitates a blood sacrifice (Jesus Christ) to remove the penalty of God's wrath from us. That having been done, we are then invited to fellowship with God again. That is reconciliation. The second dimension of reconciliation is horizontal. In this, our sinfulness has resulted in enmity between us as humans. That was not God's original intent. By Jesus' death on the cross, he created the possibility for us all to be re-created in him, be reconciled to each other, and thus become the One New Humanity (Eph. 2:14-16) he desires. A third dimension of the reconciliation process is that he wants to reconcile the rest of creation to himself (2 Cor. 5:19). The reconciliation with and of his creation is the ultimate goal of all that God has been doing throughout salvation history.

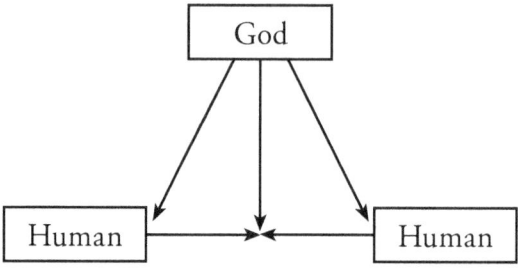

Figure 3 Reconciliation

In figure 3 I illustrate the vertical and horizontal reconciliation in which Adventist Christians must engage. The figure shows that while we were still unrighteous sinners, at the cross God reached down to reconcile with humans. As a result of God's reconciling act, we are moved to reconcile and fellowship with each other. Upon reconciling, we then collaborate in the ministry of reconciliation for others.

It requires the willing participation of the parties at enmity to achieve reconciliation. Sin estranged humans from God; we needed to reconcile but he had to initiate it by reaching down to us. Humans (Whites/Blacks) are estranged from each other and both need to reach across to each other in order to reconcile. 1 Jn. 1:3 suggests this triangular fellowship, but it can only be effectuated by reconciliation. As they both become reconciled to God in Christ, his Spirit prompts them to reconcile with each other.

In dealing with the present divide in the Adventist Church it is instructive to note that "this reconciling work is what it means to be the church—a community that would break through all cultural and racial barriers" (Church, 2008). The cross being the central message of the remnant, has also served as the symbol of reconciliation in the writings of Paul; for whether Jew or Gentile, no more are we twain, but one in Christ Jesus.

Curtis DeYoung suggests that in order to achieve this, Christians must become reconcilers. In order to become agents of reconciliation, we must be "visionary activists, serious empathics, courageous prophets, patient mediators, and compassionate advocates" (DeYoung, 1997). To this list I would add loving, self-sacrificing neighbors. All this seems impossible unless Christians resolve to love one another. No meaningful or genuine reconciliation is possible without genuine love for one's neighbor. On the surface it could look like reconciliation has occurred and sound like it, but it will not be experienced in the daily lifestyle of those involved without love.

In his statement on the reconciliation process in the aftermath of apartheid South Africa, Ntlha avers further, "Politics has a tendency of emptying the term *reconciliation* of its rich spiritual significance, which would include confession, repentance, restitution, and reparation" (Akite, 2010). This is true of the church also. Yet the Bible is very clear on the fact that reparations are in order after wrongs have been committed (Lk. 19:1-10).

Is Reconciliation Possible?

When ask recently by *Christianity Today* if Evangelicals are doing a good job at racial integration, some experts in the area offered the following responses:

> "Evangelicals over the past couple of decades have been the most purposeful when it comes to racial integration. We see this from the 1990s with the racial reconciliation movement, and after that you began to hear a lot about wanting to move toward racial integration in religious organizations. There's a movement out there. Evangelical churches are hearing about it, and some are committing to it" (Edwards, 2010).

> "If you look at straight numbers, Evangelicals and all churches are not doing well. On the other hand, when you see that evangelicals emphasize that one's religious

identity should be more important than anything else, they have a very interesting capacity for creating a new identity that rallies people of different races and ethnicities. Individuals are willing to accentuate religious identities over ethnic identities within some local churches" (Marti, 2010).

"We have the best potential, in that Christians have the capacity to think transcendentally, beyond ourselves. That should lead us to an understanding of how cross-cultural multiethnic relationships can work. We have theological language that should move us in that direction. We have in recent history done a relatively poor job of integration, so in that sense we're starting behind compared to the rest of society. But ... the Church is becoming more diverse at a faster rate than American society" (Rah, 2010).

Assuming that conversion has already taken place, reconciliation can only become possible when two things happen: the first is the responsibility of White Adventists; the second, the responsibility of Black Adventists. In sum, both parties must "die." Potter correctly affirms that the near genocide of Native Americans and the centuries of oppression of Blacks constitute America's "'original sin'". Until White Evangelical (Adventists) admit this truth, understand its moral gravity, genuinely repent of this past and seriously work toward the "new birth of freedom" that Abraham Lincoln envisaged reconciliation is impossible. On the other hand, when White Adventists confess and repent of this past, the responsible Christian response of Black Evangelicals (Adventists) is forgiveness (Okholm, 1997).

In a recent conversation with the Office of Human Relations at the NAD earlier this spring, the hope of reconciliation was expressed by personnel with whom I spoke. This hope was based on the effectiveness of prayers, however, not on any other substantive efforts being undertaken by anyone or any entity in the SDAC. In that conversation, it was also brought to my attention that while Elder Alfred McClure presided over the NAD, he apologized to the African Americans for the unfair treatment that was meted out to them by the church in the US. In that conversation no document was cited where record of this occurrence could be found. In my research, I discovered no such apology or any corresponding response from African Americans. Assuming that our NAD beloved late president had made an apology, would it not have been great to see this disseminated throughout the Church so that all could have been informed of it? And while that was being disseminated, would it not have been wise to capitalize on the opportunity to promote similar exchanges of apology and forgiveness among local churches as an appeal for reconciliation was highlighted? Despite this, is reconciliation still possible? Yes!

Gary W. Deddo insists—

> Resisting reconciliation is not just a violation of an abstract commandment; it is resistance to the essence of who we are and who God is. Resistance can only mean the rejection of the grace of God. and it constitutes a threat not just to the relationships among the races but also to our being and becoming. It is a rejection of God's essential purposes. Those unreconciled cannot enter the kingdom of God (Okholm, 1997)

Old and New Testament Racial/Ethnic Struggles

The Old Testament does not directly address the issue of racial discrimination. The apostle Paul focuses much of his epistle to the Ephesians on the ethnic tension between Jews and Gentiles of his day.

Moses' Siblings

Miriam and Aaron had a problem with the ethnicity of Moses' wife (Num. 12:1). Moses' wife, Zipporah, was an Ethiopian woman. Miriam and Aaron complained to him about her and Miriam became leprous as a result (Num. 12:10). The argument has been made that Miriam and Aaron complained about her because of her racial/ethnic background. That their racial prejudice caused God to afflict Miriam and not Aaron with leprosy seems doubtful. Why would God show partiality? It has also been suggested that the issue was one of pride. But that response still raises the question, if that was the case, why was Miriam alone inflicted with leprosy?

The passage does not make any references to the color of Miriam's skin, except after she was made leprous, although it mentions her nationality (Ethiopian). Moses and his siblings were Hebrews. Thus Moses and his Israelite siblings had different nationalities/ethnicities/races. What motivated Miriam and Aaron to make this statement? It appears that Miriam was the instigator and main perpetrator of this grievous act; for that reason God targeted her in order to make his point.

Ruth, the Moabitess- The story of Ruth is one that portrays racial/ethnic unity (Ruth 1, 2). Naomi was an Israelite and Ruth was a Moabitess. Naomi and her husband Elimelech were living across the river in Moab. The peoples of these nations worshiped different gods. But upon the death of Naomi's husband and eventually her sons, who were married to Ruth and Orpah, she decided to return to Israel, her homeland. Ruth refused to return to her people because she had been convicted by the true God. She asked to migrate to Israel with Naomi because she wanted to be with those who served the God whom she now worshiped. Naomi granted her request, she went to live with her, and ultimately married Elimelech's relative in Israel. Though she was a foreigner (Gentile, Ruth 2:11), it did not seem to matter to either Naomi or Boaz. What mattered was that she had begun serving their God, Yahweh.

This story suggests racial reconciliation occurred. It portrays a sense of oneness among those who are of the household of faith regardless of race, ethnicity, or nationality.

Samaritans- During the time of Jesus' ministry and throughout much of the New Testament writings, there was an overtone of segregation. The Jews did not get along with the Gentiles. The Gentiles were primarily Samaritans as seen in the Gospels. For this reason Jesus does not send his twelve disciples to evangelize them (Mt. 10:1, 5-8) until he had prepared the way, but later on he sends the seventy two because the Gentiles would be more receptive then. Essentially, Jesus is using a strategy to prevent a total rejection of the gospel message and the discouragement of the disciples. No prejudiced segregation is being promoted; rather reconciliation is being sought as they were sent to every town of the Gentiles.

Jesus takes the gospel personally to the Gentiles in Jn. 4. Although he was a Jew, he entered a Samaritan town when they were still segregated from the Jews. His intent was to interact with the Samaritans and share with them that the Messiah had come and reconcile them to God and each other. He succeeded by using an outcast woman; she told others, they believed and the kingdom was opened to the lowly Samaritans as equals with the Jews.

Throughout Scripture, God seeks to reconcile race, ethnic groups, and genders even after the worst sin had separated them. His intent is to bring everyone together in him, especially those who are of the household of faith. Is the remnant divided in Black, White, yellow, and brown? Ellen White suggests, "We are to demonstrate to the world that men of every nationality are one in Christ Jesus. Then let us remove every barrier and come into unity in the service of the Master" (White *9T*, 1948).

"...That They All May Be One"

> [20]My prayer is not for them alone. I pray also for those who will believe in me through their message, [21]that all of them may be one, Father, just as you are in me and I am in you. May they also be in us so that the world

may believe that you have sent me. [22]I have given them the glory that you gave me, that they may be one as we are one (Jn. 17:20-22, NIV).

Evidently, as Jesus said His final prayer for his disciples, he had a burden for them to be reconciled to each other. He had heard their squabbles as they jostled each other for power, popularity, and prominence in His kingdom. In response He had cautioned them that the greatest among them "shall be your servant" (Mt. 23:11, KJV). As he gets ready to depart from them, He still senses this great need; they need reconciliation. Thus His prayer—"That they may all be one..." (Jn. 17:20-21, NASB).

Unity is not simply for unity's sake. The ultimate goal of this unity which Christ seeks for His followers is salvific. It impacts our salvation and that of others. When we unite we assist in taking care of each other's needs, spiritual or other. When we unite we enjoy a peace which is beyond our understanding. When we unite we can witness more effectively (Williams, 2009). Unity is a witness in itself. They (proselytes) will know we are Christians by our unity.

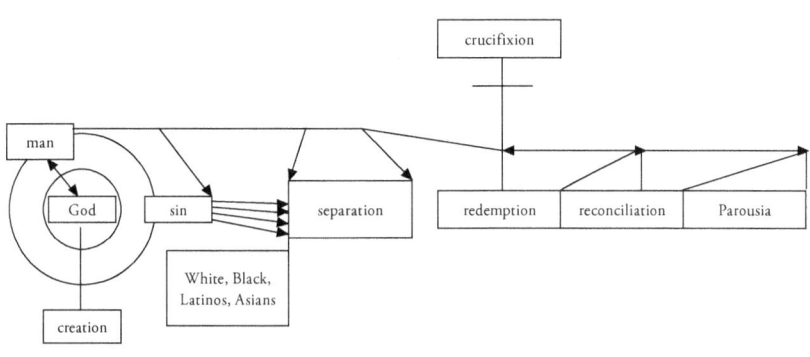

Figure 4

Figure 4 suggests that at creation, God and humans were fully reconciled. The incidence of sin resulted not only in the separation of man from God, but also the separation (estrangement) of man and fellow man (White Black, Latino, Asian). At the cross, Jesus offered himself as the sacrifice for the penalty of sin and invited humans to reconcile with God.

Upon accepting this invitation to reconcile with God, humans (without regard to race, ethnicity, culture, gender, age, creed, caste, or class) are equipped and empowered (by God) to reconcile with each other and engage in the ministry of reconciliation. The ministry of reconciliation is a process which continues until Jesus returns. It is a ministry in which all Adventist Christians ought to be involved (2 Cor. 5:18).

A Proposed Resolution for Reconciliation

WHEREAS the Lord Jesus Christ prayed in His final prayer on Earth in John 17:20-22 for all His people to be one, regardless of race, tribe, gender, caste, ethnicity, status, as He, the Holy Spirit, and the Father are One

WHEREAS we are a body of biblical Christian believers from every race, caste, gender, ethnicity, tribe, color, status, baptized into God's remnant Church and are commanded to love, confess, repent, forgive, reconcile, and unite as one

WHEREAS throughout the history of the Seventh-day Adventist Church, we have struggled with fully accepting and integrating all races, tribes, genders, castes, ethnicities, statuses

WHEREAS the sanction, practice, and perpetuation of racial, ethnic, or other forms of discrimination are unchristian and undermine our mission as a Church, we humbly urge the following of the leadership of the SDA Church at all levels:

- A corporate admission and apology for the wrongs committed against minority groups within our church

- A concerted effort to abandon all prejudicial practices throughout our institutions, conferences, and our organization by embracing diversity and inclusiveness

- That we implement changes in our church structure at all levels that create a climate of openness and acceptance of all believers in the faith to participate in the governance and execution of its mission, regardless of race, ethnicity, culture, gender, tribe, caste, and status.

- That we intentionally create opportunities and implement initiatives that foster lasting, genuine unity within our church by intentionally reaching across racial, cultural, ethnic, and economic lines

- That all racial and ethnic groups collaborate individually, locally, and corporately in worship, fellowship, and in evangelizing the world in preparation for the coming of our Lord, Jesus Christ.

May the God of love, peace, and unity instruct us in our efforts to become a more loving and unified body of believers, who through His strength, and by the power of His love, will more effectively accomplish His mission in these last days (Birch, et al, 2010).

Jesus and Paul on the Racial/Ethnic Divide in the Christian Church

Jesus- Neither Jesus nor Paul had any place in their theology for the preeminence/subservience or superiority/inferiority of members of Christ's Church. Jesus' death on the cross eradicated those distinctions; it was the seminal act of reconciliation. Without this sacrifice, we could not be reconciled to God; we would not have the desire to and neither could we reconcile with each other. It is because of his desire to realize his ultimate goal of reconciling the crowning products of his creation to Father that he calls all to come to him and find rest (Mt. 11:28-30). This rest suggests peace; peace with God and each other; rest from our cares about the penalties, power, and ultimately, the presence of sin. It is the ultimate rest that humans need.

In Mt. 5, Jesus counsels his disciples regarding how to handle their disagreements. They should not hold grudge after wrong has been done, but should reconcile. In vss. 22-24 he says, "But I say unto you, that whosoever is angry with his brother without a cause shall be in danger of the judgment: and whosoever shall say to his brother, Raca, shall be in danger of the council: but whosoever shall say, Thou fool, shall be in danger of hell fire." Essentially this is about reconciliation. In Mt. 18 Jesus enlarges on this concept as he instructs his disciples that when one member sins against the other it is the responsibility of the offended to seek reconciliation. If after speaking one on one no agreement is reached, take another member with you; if the member still does not listen then you have the right to "treat him as you would a pagan or tax collector" (NIV). Yet it must be kept in mind that he must still love the pagan and tax collector as a neighbor and always relate to him as such. Finally, this passage recommends that the final step should be to disfellowship the offender from the church. Disfellowship then qualifies him/her as one to be pursued for readmission to the fellowship of the body. We are never justified to live in estrangement or malice.

Paul In Eph. 2:1-17 Paul goes straight to the heart of the Jewish/Gentile racial tension. The Jews were the circumcised and the Gentiles, the uncircumcised. The Jews felt themselves to be superior to the Gentiles because of their election by God. But Paul denounced the heresy, even while identifying himself as a Jew (Acts 23:6). On one occasion he confronted Peter publicly for showing prejudice against the Gentiles during a visit from other Jews from Jerusalem (Gal. 2:11-14). Peter had refused to eat with the Gentiles during the visit because they were uncircumcised; a cultural bias. But he used to eat with them when the men from Jerusalem were not there. At the time of the occurrence, Jesus had already died and offered himself as the ultimate sacrifice for our sins. Hence circumcision was obsolete (Gal. 5). It was not to be enjoined on the Gentiles. In fact, Jews are released from their obligation to practice circumcision now that Jesus has come as the fulfillment of the types, of which it was a part.

In the epistle to the Romans Paul totally rejects the notion that there is any difference between Gentiles and Jews in the Christian church, thus the kingdom of God. In Rom. 3:1 the apostle asks rhetorically—"Then what advantage has the Jew? Or what is the value of circumcision" (RSV)? Further along he asks pointedly—"Are we Jews any better off." He answers himself—"No, not at all; for I have already charged that all men, both Jews and Greeks, are under the power of sin" (Vs. 9, *RSV*)… Paul would have none of the discrimination or segregation of his fellow Jewish Christians. Both Jesus and Paul are very clear on the fact that racial/ethnic segregation, discrimination, and prejudice are unacceptable because they are unchristian.

Paul appropriately moved to reconcile his fledgling slave believer, Onesimus, who had run away from his master (Philem. 8-21). He called for corporate reconciliation in the church of Corinth (1 Cor. 1:10-17). Paul reconciled with John Mark after his quarrel with Barnabas (Acts 15:37 cf. Col. 4:10; Philem. 24).

Jesus Desires Racial/Ethnic Recon@ciliation among His Followers

The essence of Jesus' prayer in Jn. 17 is reconciliation. The gospel of Jesus Christ is a gospel of reconciliation (Okholm, 1997). To genuinely be one suggests forgetting differences, hurts, pain; putting aside prejudices and accentuating the sameness that makes us more alike. On the surface this would appear easy for the people of God, considering that we all have the Spirit of God assisting us. But no; it is not. The "old" person of sin (Rom. 7) is still with us and like a condemned prisoner tied to a decomposing corpse (Bruce, 1963), we wrestle to extricate ourselves from our sinful tendencies, but it just appears that we can't. Yet if in our desperation, we would cry out for help like the apostle, we would find that not only is there "no condemnation for those who are in Christ Jesus" (Rom. 8:1) Indeed we would find rescue from our prejudices!

Jesus helps in the process of reconciliation. He does not call us to a ministry (2 Cor. 5:18) for which He does not equip us and for which He does not provide assistance. He sends His Spirit to succor us in our weakness (Jn. 14-16). His Spirit comes to strengthen us, guide us, and keep us from falling--even into our old habits of ethnic discrimination, segregation, demonizing, and lack of forgiveness.

Reconciliation does not require the nullification of race, ethnicity, status, and wealth, but it does require shifting the focus from our dissimilarities to our commonalities; from what we possess to what we ought to give. It makes race of mere relative significance with a focus on the inclusiveness of all humans in Christ. It suggests constantly and proactively exploring ways to enhance the relationship that exists between two former foes (Whites/Blacks) and current strangers. Perhaps a semblance of Benazir Bhutto's recommendation for reconciliation between the West and the Muslim world may be adapted to the Adventist Church.

Bhutto recommends the creation of a Reconciliation Corps modeled on the United Nations Peace Corp. The young members of this Corp could be appropriately trained for various technical tasks and posted in Muslim-majority countries to demonstrate that Muslims, Jews, Christians, and Hindus can live together peacefully (Bhutto, 2008). If this model for reconciliation were adopted by Adventists in the US, we could train and empower the youth and young adults in the task of breaking down longstanding racial/ethnic barriers and in building new bridges that transcend color or ethnicity. As an example, we could train and mentor the younger generation of Whites, Blacks, Hispanics, and Asians and expose them to the technical operation of the Church under the supervision of the experienced adults. We could also empower them to execute the changes necessary to bring about the reconciliation. This would make it easier to reconcile.

A critical characteristic which the youth possess that is requisite for reconciliation is a change-friendly attitude. Adults are chronically change-averse. Hence the structural inertia that currently persists. With well-trained, spirit-led young adults, the fear factor is minimized, the energy level is high, and the desire to achieve reconciliation is greater because these (Black and White young adults, Asians, Hispanics, and all) have not experienced the unbalanced relationship between their respective forbears that has resulted in the segregated structure that we now have. They are more trusting of each other and they more easily look beyond skin color to the individual's heart.

> Ellen White offers further counsel on the subject. She wrote—

> I warn you, brethren, and sisters not to build up a wall of partition between different nationalities. On the contrary, seek to break it down whenever it exists … We are to demonstrate to the world that men of every nationality are one in Christ Jesus. Then let us remove every barrier and come into unity in the service of the Master (White, *9T*, 1948).

> Do we expect to meet our brethren in heaven? If we can live with them here in peace and harmony we could live with them there. But how could we live with them in heaven if we cannot live with them here without continued contention and strife (White, *9T*, 1948)?

Summary- The concept of reconciliation is a New Testament one. It was introduced to the primitive Christians as something that God does. God initiates reconciliation with us because of our estrangement through the first Adam. Through the second Adam, Jesus, he has earned the right to reconcile with us (Rom. 5). Now that we have been reconciled to God, he enjoins on us reconciliation with our fellow humans, a very costly undertaking. Yet it is necessary and possible. It was practiced throughout the Old Testament without the designation and in the New Testament we are call to the "ministry of reconciliation." Reconciliation, not redemption is the overarching theme of the entire Bible. Jesus demonstrated it (Jn. 4), Paul illustrated it (Eph. 2), now the Spirit of God empowers us to coordinate it (2 Cor. 5:18). It is not an act but an activity; one in which Adventist Christians ought to be daily engaged.

Jesus' prayer was sincere. He observed the problems that resulted from disunity among his disciples. He badly wanted to see a change for the better among his followers and that was the reason for his prayer. Ellen White's counsel corroborates the prayer of Christ: "That they all may be one." In our church today, the problem of the divide is not to be blamed on just one race, but on all involved. We must work together to eradicate it.

While Whites need to be humble and see themselves as who they really are before Christ, that is, mere sinners saved by grace; Blacks need also to be humble and cultivate the spirit of forgiveness, all the while realizing also that they are sinners, who need God's forgiveness. This goes for all ethnic groups in the Adventist Church as well. Pride on every side is hurting us individually and corporately. As Adventist Christians we are all too ethnocentric. Only by losing our pride and assuming the humility of servants can we realize this oneness which Christ craves for his church. Unity is evasive; reconciliation is costly; but these are not optional for the remnant people of God.

After the resolve to reconcile, comes the praxis of reconciliation. Admittedly, this is not nearly as easy as it appears on paper. Yet there are helpful biblical guidelines for this. We do not need to search long and hard to find them either; they are found in some of the most well-known passages of Scripture. Recommendations for bridging the racial/ethnic divide are in order at this juncture.

8

Bridging the Racial/Ethnic Divide

The story of two farming brothers at loggerheads goes like this: These two men, John and Tom would quarrel so often that John decided that he did not want to see his brother, Tom again. Tom dug a creek between their farms and one day John saw it. He immediately thought that his brother did this just to get him angry, so he decided that he would build a fence to block any view of Tom's property. John hired a carpenter to build the fence. While John was off going about other business, instead of building a fence, the carpenter built a bridge over the creek which Tom had dug. When Tom saw this he was so delighted that John had built the bridge. He began walking across the bridge. Just then John returned and saw that the carpenter had not built a fence but a bridge instead. Nevertheless he decided to walk across the bridge. As John walked across he met Tom in the middle of the bridge. They both embraced. Meanwhile the carpenter was packing his tools. They attempted to engage him in a conversation, but he quickly packed up and hurried off saying, "I'm on my way to build more bridges."

In the move to bring reconciliation, it is critical for both parties to be confident that the other is sincere (Anderson, 2004). If this sincerity exists and is not clearly articulated and adequately communicated, lack of trust could develop and mar the process.

Approaches to Racism- Yancey contends that there are two approaches to racism that are typically used by non-Christians. The first is the "color-blind" model. In this model it is assumed that everyone can be treated as if he does not have a skin color and none should be given economic or social advantage over the other because of skin color. The approach is usually used by Whites who would prefer to ignore the history of racism and its deleterious effects upon minorities. They mean well, but are naïve to the fact that ignoring the problem does not make it go away (Yancey, 2001). The second approach is called the "politically-correct" model. Unlike the previous model it does not ignore the problem of racism but seeks to reverse its effects by deliberately institutionalizing them. In so doing they provide more employment and economic opportunities for minorities. It seeks to overturn the effects of centuries of racial oppression by empowering minorities. Those who advocate it would typically call for affirmative action.

Neither model is without its shortcomings. Both ignore the nature of sin, Yancey rightly affirms. The first "places too much confidence on the willingness of White Americans to seek justice in a meaningful way" and overlooks the advantages that they have gained from their oppressive institutions. The second downplays sinful occurrences among minorities and tends to shift the blame to the majority (2001). Thus it is overly optimistic of humanity and their inability to compensate for the powerful effects of sin.

Theological Solutions

A theology of racial reconciliation that acknowledges the past sins is more likely to succeed in achieving the goal of reconciliation; and rightly so. For if one refuses to acknowledge he is wrong, he is prone to keep repeating it without any sense of transgression. Meanwhile the injured party is being perpetually hurt. In light of this Yancey suggests that in order to achieve reconciliation Blacks and Whites should 1) make attempts to positively interact with members of the other race/ethnic group; 2) that regardless of race or political persuasion, Christians should oppose social structures that create or perpetuate inequality among races/ethnicities; 3) that Whites, as the benefactors of historical and structural oppression of others, should corporately admit it, repent of it, and make amends (Neh. 1:6-7; Dan. 9:5-6); Williams and Collins concur with Yancey on this point (2006); 4) racial minorities must have an attitude of forgiveness to Whites (Mt. 6:14-15).

R. R. Wright, Jr., editor of the *Christian Recorder* (1909-36), branded as an apostate from the slave religion, issued a call for a new kind of Negro in the early twentieth century. In 1915 Wright's editorial took a turn to militancy. He called for a kind of Negro that would fight for the right. Right must precede peace, he insisted. He advocated that Jesus came with a spiritual sword to combat evil. He further argued that "'A man who shuns a fight with evil, with a lawbreaker, or a robber, or a corruptionist, is not a peaceful Christian but a sinful coward'" (West and Claude, Jr., 2003). But Wright's theology of militancy is not entirely biblical. While his argument that Jesus came with a "spiritual sword" holds true, it must be noted that Jesus did not wage a war to achieve what was right. He did not physically hurt anyone. He fought against many "right" things (Sabbath laws, hypocrisy, segregation of Jews and Gentiles, and so on) in Jewish laws, in order to attain righteousness. Righteousness was his goal. That "right" must precede peace in Wright's theology does not follow in Jesus'. For Christians, "Jesus is our peace" (Eph. 2:14). He gives us peace amid our persecution and hardship. Hence we may put down our swords against each other and be at peace, even when it is right to fight back based on our culture.

In *Multicultural Ministry*, David A. Anderson uses the dance analogy to suggest ways that reconciliation may be achieved. He sees the racist and the reconciler on either ends of the racial reconciliation continuum. Anderson parallels this with the continuum of faith (babe, child, teen, adult, to a reconciler) in which the racist moves along the continuum from an agnostic, to a cynic, to a seeker, and finally to a converted soul (2004). The logic and progression are clear though I would rather place an emphasis on Jesus sacrifice on the cross and his reconciling work in us. The following trajectory illustrates my point:

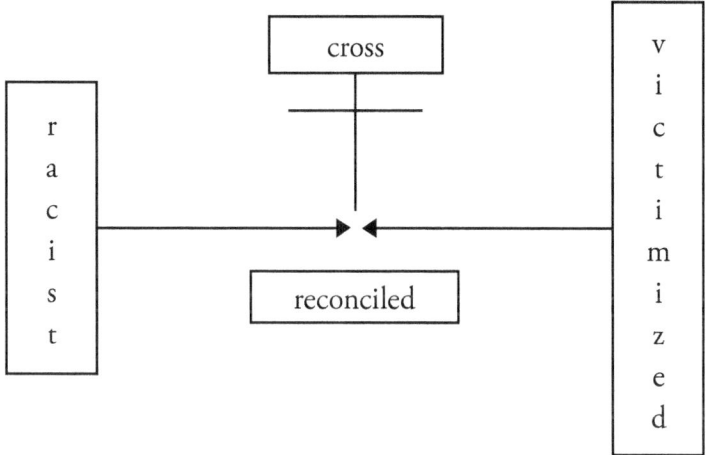

Figure 5 Racial Reconciliation Trajectory

In figure 5 Jesus becomes the central person in the process of reconciliation—the Reconciler *par excellence*. Having offered himself as a sacrifice for us, Jesus is now engaged in the work of reconciling humans to the Father and to each other (Heb. 8:1ff). The cross represents the connectivity which Jesus becomes between the racist and the victimized other. The two were initially at enmity with each other, because of wrongs committed, but Jesus, by the power of his sacrifice on the cross, draws them to each other and connects (reconcile) them as one in himself. In this, Jesus brakes down the barrier (s) between the racist and the victimized and replaces it/them with a bridge. Thus is created the One New Humanity that Paul alludes to elsewhere (Eph. 2:11-18). And there is no reason to boast, except in the cross of Christ, by which we all should crucify self and all the earthly reasons for boasting and pride (Gal. 6:14). Jesus is the bridge personified between estranged humans.

IDENTITY

The unbeliever: is earthly (3:5, NIV) Choice of clothing--	The believer: died to Christ (3:3, NIV) Choice of clothing--
• Sexual immorality • Impurity • Lust • Evil desire • Greed	• Compassion • Kindness • Humility • Meekness • Patience • Forgiveness • Love • Peace • Thankfulness
Exhibits: Anger, wrath, malice, slander, verbal abuse, lying	**Exhibits:** wise teaching, thanksgiving, submissiveness, spiritual songs

Figure 6 A Diagram on Colossians 3:1-17. Partially adapted from *Multicultural Ministry* (Anderson, 2004).

When we are "in Christ," as figure 6 shows, he clothes us with different garments than we choose wear when we are "of the world." As others look on us, they see our clothes. The clothing of the believer is the virtues he displays, while the unbeliever is clothed in all manner of vices. Our identity in Christ, that is, our faith identity, transcends all other identities that we may have. It is like clothes. Unlike the worldly people, who worship other gods, we accept Christ's clothing and others can see the difference in the garment.

The identity of the unbeliever is fornicator, sexually impure person, lustful person, one who desires evil, and greedy. Conversely the identity of the believer is that of a compassionate, kind, humble, meek, and patient one. He practices forgiveness, shows love, is peaceful, and thankful. Whether she/he is Black or White (Greek or Jew) it does not matter; they are known by the virtues they clothe themselves in. Above all else, that is what others see.

When the believer opens his mouth regarding another race or ethnic person, there flows from his lips: wise teaching, thanksgiving, submissive speech, and sweet spiritual songs (3:15-17). The unbeliever, on the other hand, spews out anger, wrath, malice, slander, and verbal abuse regarding those of other races/ethnicities. When Adventists begin to wear the clothes of reconciliation, others will recognize it in mixed congregations and total integration in our institutions. What a difference one's identity in Christ makes!

It is Good Christian Practice to take the First Step

Blacks in the Adventist Church ought not to wait until the Whites change their ways before loving and forgiving them and choosing to reconcile with them. Nowhere in Scripture are Christians expected to do this. The converted must take the first step and keep stepping toward reconciling with the other party. Many Blacks still as, however, why must we always be taking the first step when we are the victims? The facts suggest that it is true that Blacks have been initiating reconciliation among the Evangelicals and in the SDAC (Galbraith, 2006; Baker, 1996). As an encouragement, the apostle reminds us, "While we were still sinners, Christ died for us" (Rom. 5:6-8, NKJV). Paul admonishes further, "Brothers, if a person is caught doing something wrong, those of you who are spiritual should restore that person gently. Watch out for yourself so that you are not tempted as well" (Gal. 6:1). Meanwhile, White Adventists must understand that they are the benefactors of the oppression of Blacks and others and ought to have a sense of Christian obligation to take the first step. Other reconcilers affirm this position (DeYoung, 1997).

Freelance writer Debra Akins, writing for the *Kyria.com* website suggests we seek to cross the racial/ethnic divide by:

1) Thinking beyond our comfort zone. This may mean physically moving into an area that you otherwise would not have, but you do so in order to be among those who are different than you are. 2) Being intentional. By participating in ministry activities with other races/ethnic groups and making the effort and taking the time to get to know them, we can build bridges. 3) Signing up for the long haul. This requires a long time commitment to the goals of racial reconciliation (Akins, *HomeLife,* 2005).

Principles for Corporate Reconciliation

Note the eight principles recommended by Promise Keeper for corporate racial reconciliation:

Principle One: The Call (Key Word: Mandatory) II Corinthians 5:17-21. We are called to be involved in the ministry of reconciliation, but some have a special call to minister in diverse situations.

Principle Two: Commitment to Relationships (Key Words: Conflict Resolution) Ruth 1:16, 17. Reconciliation is built upon the foundation of committed relationships.

Principle Three: Intentionality (Key Word: Perseverance) Ephesians 2:14, 15. Intentionality is the purposeful, positive and planned activity that facilitates reconciliation.

Principle Four: Sincerity (Key Words: Trust and Transparency) John 15:15. Sincerity is the willingness to be vulnerable, including self-disclosure of feelings, attitudes, difference and perceptions, with the goal of resolution and building trust.

Principle Five: Sensitivity (Key Words: Knowledge and Understanding) Ephesians 4:15, 16. Sensitivity is the intentional acquisition of knowledge in order to relate empathetically to any diverse situation, person, place or organization.

Principle Six: Sacrifice (Key Word: Cost) Philippians 2:3, 4. Sacrifice is the willingness to relinquish an established status or position in order to facilitate diverse relationships.

Principle Seven: Empowerment (Key Words: Repentance and Forgiveness) II Corinthians 8:9. Empowerment is the use of repentance and forgiveness to create complete freedom in diverse relationships.

Principle Eight: Interdependence (Key Word: Equality) II Corinthians 8:12-14. Interdependence recognizes differences but realizes that each offers something that the other needs, resulting in equality in that relationship (2008). As we practice these principles we will find greater collaboration occurring and significant enhancement of the mission of the Church.

One's desire to reconcile does not necessarily coincide with a desire on the part of the other person to do the same. Even when both parties are interested in reconciling, there still are factors that could potentially hinder or slow the process. Nevertheless it is worth the effort and is required of all Christians. Ellen White counsels the remnant,

"The God of the White man is the God of the Black man. The Black man's name is written in the book of life beside the White man's. All are one in Christ. Birth, station, nationality, or color cannot elevate or degrade men. The character makes the man" (White, *The Southern Work*, 1966).

We are neighbors of each other. After we have attempted to do all of the above, unless we decide to love, it will all be in vain: we will not achieve reconciliation. It is, therefore, incumbent on all members of the remnant to love and because we love, we all should desire reconciliation among us.

Love

In order to reconcile as Christians of all races/ethnicities we must decide to love one another regardless of racial/ethnic backgrounds. To love is not optional for Christians. "Whoever does not love does not know God, because God is love" (1 Jn. 4:8, *NIV*). Christ enjoins this on every Christian by giving the directive to "love your neighbor as yourself" (Jn. 13:34-35) He identifies one's neighbor as every person, especially those whom one has the opportunity to interact with. The apostle Paul underscores *love* as the only character trait that really matters in the end (1 Cor. 13).

Love will elicit a willingness to admit past and present wrongs. Undeniably Whites have perpetrated much wrongdoing against Blacks and other minorities in the Adventist Church and vice versa to a far lesser degree. If this were openly confessed and repented of by the current generations of Whites, it could potentially begin the process of healing the relationship between the two races. Meanwhile, the wronged (Blacks, Indians) should acknowledge being wronged, but express a willingness to forgive and move on. The evil perpetrated against Blacks and Native Indians in society range from physical and sexual abuse to economic and social oppression, among other atrocities. These ought to be admitted and confessed. Most Whites may be quick to argue that individually they did no wrong and even dismiss the historical oppression and structural inequities as nonexistent. But the facts are well established that Whites are the benefactors of such systemic wrongs even in the twenty-first century (Yancey, 2001; Horsman, 1967; Emerson and Smith, 2000; Bennett, 1987).

Love constrains Adventist Christian Whites to admit these failures of the system and corporately repent of them. The objective of such repentance is to build trust among Blacks. Without trust Blacks will never freely associate with Whites or vice versa. And all must decide to love each other.

> E. E. Cleveland says it succinctly— "Christianity requires that a bond of unselfish love unites believers all over the earth, and under the sanction of this requirement no man can think ill of his neighbor or wish his neighbor ill, nor does differing culture or skin pigmentation constitute sufficient grounds for coldness and apathy" (Cleveland, 1969).

While I was a student at the Andrews Theological Seminary, in a conversation with a friend, we touched on the subject of love. It was very enlightening to me when she declared that she could "choose" to love whomever she wished. It just knocked me over the head. I had never heard it said or ever thought of it that way before. But I pondered it long and hard and came to the conclusion that it is true. As I look at marriage relationships that fall apart, I realize that this happens because two people decided not to keep loving and forgiving each other anymore. And when another couple decides to stay together, it is not because none ever wronged the other, but it is because they have decided to keep on loving and are not holding each other's wrongdoing against them.

Forgive In the model prayer that Jesus gave to his disciples he instructs us to ask for forgiveness as "we have forgiven" our debtors (Mt. 6:12). He informs us further that unless we do this our heavenly father will not forgive us of our sin (Mt. 6:15). And we all have sinned (Rom. 3:23). Forgiveness is therapeutic. Blacks and other minorities will find healing in their souls as they decide to forgive Whites for their atrocities and forgive each other. A few Whites may have experienced discrimination from Blacks and other minorities too and would need to forgive them.

This must be one of the most difficult things that God has enjoined on Christians. And I know this firsthand. It is not easy to forgive especially when you feel like you have been terribly wronged and the other person is neither willing to admit it nor repent of it. Yet Christians must forgive.

Make Peace- Peace comes only from God. Although much talk of peace can be heard throughout the electronic and print media, no genuine, lasting peace is attainable without God. God is the author and sustainer of peace. In fact, Jesus is our peace (Eph. 2:14). Paul highlighted this fact to the Jews and Gentiles of his day, who were as racialized as we are in the US today. Even the synagogues were segregated in first century Christianity. A physical wall divided between the seating and worship areas of the races (Eph. 2; Rosado, 1990). Paul denounced this practice, informed them that there is no need for animosity between them, and invited them to enjoy the universal peace in the borderless commonwealth of the new humanity that Jesus created by His death on the cross (Eph. 14-16). We must resolve to be at peace with each other.

Whites, Blacks, and all ethnic factions in the US need to declare that the war is over. We need to have a meeting of the minds and resolve to tear down our twenty-first century walls that divide us. These are walls of hostility that cause reproach upon the cause of God and could potentially lead to the eternal demise of many Adventists.

Have you ever observed two children at play? One takes a toy that the other wanted to use. The one who lost it gets upset and begins to frown. The one who has it does not want to have an unpleasant play time because of one toy, so she asks what is wrong and as soon as she realizes, she decides to let her friend have the toy back. Immediately there is peace and they run along and keep on playing as if nothing happened. It is not as easy as this in adult racial reconciliation, yet it serves to remind us of the importance to admit wrongdoing and make amends.

Interact- You could hardly get to know others unless you interact regularly with them. Emerson and Smith's survey of Americans indicates that the racialization of our society poses some challenges to interaction (Emerson and Smith, 2000). Yet interaction is necessary in order to understand each other. This could often prove difficult for both Blacks and Whites and every ethnic group at first but it can be gradually achieved. Cleveland suggests starting with a "smile and a cheery good morning the next time you meet someone who is not of your racial background" (Cleveland, 1969). And unless we understand each other, we can never be sure of the things that matter to, hurt, or offend each other. Neither can we learn to appreciate each other unless we understand each other's personality, culture, challenges, and so on. For this reason, instead of deliberately avoiding other persons of another race/ethnic group, we should seek them out (Cleveland, 1969). The process of racial reconciliation necessitates interaction among the races and ethnic groups in the Adventist Church. By constant interaction we get to understand, know, and appreciate with each other.

Fellowship- *Koinonia* is the Greek noun that is translated "fellowship" in English. The Christian is called to fellowship with God and with fellow believers (1 Jn. 1:7, 8). You cannot build community without fellowship. This fellowship is what Paul refers to by his use of the Greek *koinonia*. In addition to being a social and spiritual fellowship, it should also be understood to be an economic *koinoinia (1 Cor. 19)*. Just as all Christians shared in the imputed righteousness of Christ freely, wrought by his self-sacrificing love, so ought we also to share our means freely with others regardless of race or ethnicity (1 Cor. 10:17); or, maybe, because of race/ethnicity. It suggests taking time to visit with each other on the phone, at each other's home; playing together, sharing a meal occasionally, and taking time to hear each other's concerns, frustrations, victories, and so on. The primitive Christian community knew what this meant as may be observed in their generosity: "The disciples, each according to his ability, decided to provide help for the brothers living in Judea" (Acts 11:29). Instead of segregating and withholding, the wealthy fellowshipped and shared (Acts 2: 44-47). Robert Banks affirms this in his examination of the *koinoinia* of the primitive Christian church (1980).

Appreciate- When you are appreciated by someone, you usually know it and it usually brings out the best in you. Someone who appreciates you, compliments you, looks for the positive things you do and commends you on them warms your soul and lifts your spirits. Appreciation has the ability to sometimes overlook the unpleasant, or that of informing you of those unpleasant mannerisms in an inoffensive if cordial way. Appreciation is not to be confused with toleration, which gives the impression--"I do not really want you here, but I cannot do anything to get you out of here, so I'll put up with you." Appreciation seeks you out and makes much of your presence.

Pray- The need for constant praying cannot be overestimated. This kind of praying is to be personal. We often want to pray for the other person whom we perceive to be prejudiced, but we must pray that we ourselves will have the right attitude. We must pray for a heart to love everyone regardless of race, color, status, tribe, caste, gender, and other potentially divisive peculiarities. I have found that when I pray for something or someone who has done me wrong, it helps me. Prayer has the ability to assist us through our challenges. Perhaps while enduring a challenge God will change us during the process, as we open ourselves up to him in prayer. And he certainly can move on the hearts of those for whom we pray. I like the counsel of this preacher--"On our knees day by day we must pray that God will give us a wholesome, healthy, loving attitude for that day toward all men" (Cleveland, 1969).

Is racial/ethnic reconciliation in the SDAC possible? The opinions vary. Yet reconciliation is a biblical mandate; it is the fundamental reason that Christ died on the cross for us. Christ has now enjoined on his followers (the remnant) the ministry of reconciliation. Despite this fact, no substantive official effort is being made to promote or facilitate reconciliation, even with the formation of an Office of Human

Relations at the NAD. I submit that we carefully consider the approach suggested in our next section.

Several attempts have been made by individual members of the Adventist clergy and lay people. The president (Pastor Fredrick A. Russell) of the Allegheny West Conference of SDAs started a petition for reconciliation on the internet, which attracted numerous signatures. Just prior to the 59th quinquennial session of the GC in Atlanta, Georgia, in 2010, I, in concert with a so-called committee on diversity in Collegedale, Tennessee, initiated an internet-based petition drive to call for a resolution on racial/ethnic resolution at the GC session. It received 200 signatures from numerous countries and states within a few months. Some of the signatories were pastors, professors at Adventist universities, among other church employees and a majority of regular lay members. Many expressed that they viewed the present governance structure and the segregated worship setting as racist. The committee has increased in size and diversity and we continue to meet presently. I am including below some of the comments that were posted on the internet petition site with minor editing (spelling, punctuation).

Comments from Petition for Racial/Ethnic Reconciliation in the SDA Church

Petition Comments:

200 10:22, Aug 08, Samuel Guto, Kenya

"Racial and ethnic differences anywhere but particularly within the church are unnecessary evils"

195 19:47, Jul 14, Renee Hernandez, CO

I believe we are endowed with the ministry of reconciliation and meant to have unity. We are to love one another & display God's love before the world.

191 16:44, Jul 11, JoAnne Houston, PA

We, as Seventh-day Adventists, must break down these racial boundaries which have long plagued the Christian community: SDA included. How can we 'love our neighbor' as Jesus taught when there is so much hatred and contempt within the walls of some of our churches? When I became an Adventist, I was privileged to worship in a church which was multicultural and extremely loving. I was not yet aware of the existence of an undercurrent of racism until our church school board hired a prejudiced teacher for our new and growing diverse elementary school. This teacher treated the non-White students with ridicule and subjected them to mental, emotional and physical abuse. This unacceptable behavior from the teacher was immediately brought to the attention of the school board and the church. The Caucasian teacher was supported. The abused children begged to be removed from the school which was promptly agreed upon by their parents. We lost one-half of the school children that day. I tell you this story to reiterate the need to remove the enemy's tool of racism from our churches. We must pray for the outpouring of the Holy Spirit to bring revival to the remnant church. Praise God from Whom all blessings flow! Hallelujah!!!

183 08:45, Jun 28, Jose Reid, MD
The true church of God will not practice the principles of discrimination and racism. You shall know them by their fruit.

179 21:51, Jun 24, Cheryl George, TN
Racism and discrimination have NO place in God's church. I recently moved to a new city and visited a church there. I was told by the White pastor that there was a Black church in town I might want to visit. That was so disappointing to me. I was not raised Adventist but Catholic and I'm relatively new to this faith but I must say I'm ASTOUNDED at the blatant racism in the Adventist faith. :(

173 11:29, Jun 23, Cypriana Smith, GA
Many of the people of color are complacent with the way things are, and will not take a stand on this issue. Our leaders, they know better, they need to do better.

167 01:58, Jun 22, Michael Campbell, IL

The Adventist church structure, its policies and its constitution and certainly its practices, should reflect the spirit of unity, and capitalize on the synergy of talent regardless of race or origin to accelerate its mission -- just because we wish to demonstrate a genuine love for God which is reflected in our love for each other. Prejudice is a naturally sinful human phenomenon and it requires letting go of self to overcome. With the almost exclusive claim that we place on God's power, this should be much easier for us than for the government and certainly other denominations... .and if this is the case, Satan will be working much harder against us because when we do it, it will be because of a genuine love, much different from others who have a show of desegregation, make a political policy statement and still connive differently with practices that really are not just or fair or loving. Unfortunately, it is primarily with policy that we can begin to heal and make structural changes as we meet those who have already begun genuinely loving their brother and sister regardless of background and promote/encourage/support them for higher levels of authority and encouraging loving, open acceptance of all peoples. So, let's get started this year (2010) at the GC session. Let's get this on the agenda and make a change for the God we say we love so dearly - no matter what the fallout, anger, loss of power, embarrassment, uncertainty of the end product and relational dynamics. What if Jesus had politicized His work? Note that He did exactly the opposite. Let's be like Him. Let's move forward this year to step out of the way and allow many to see Christ's power at work to prayerfully eliminate racially designed divisions and begin healing. The only danger is that we become proud and take the credit for ourselves. Let God's power work and forget about power, control and influence and let's make the policy so that other ethnic groups do not get to wield their power unfairly either, because that will be human nature. Be brave!!!

166 19:18, Jun 21, Name not displayed, AL

I'm not going to demand the church do anything because I don't have that authority. Nevertheless, this is definitely the will of God in spite of all the arguments that anyone could use against it. We need to stop calling ourselves the "remnant church" if we are really not going to "keep the COMMANDMENTS of God and the testimony of Jesus Christ." This is God's command for this time "that ye may be one." The Holy Spirit will not be manifested as powerfully as He could be until we are one. The world will not recognize that we are truly Christians until we have "love one for another." Let's get real people, no prejudiced, bigoted, race-baiting fake Christians are going to make it to the kingdom of God. Furthermore, there will NOT be a segregated heaven with sections for Hispanic, Asian, Black, and White. We ALL will be living in the same place side-by-side so we might as well start down here because it is down here that we are being fitted for heaven.

152 13:43, Jun 18, Anna Maria Antonietta Riviello, Italy

149 21:14, Jun 17, Lois Gilliam, MO

I have been an Adventist for 56 years it's about time that we become one. There will not be separate heavens, so why should we as Christians have racial issues.

148 18:59, Jun 17, Cynthia Taylor, LA

Dear G.C Leaders: I have been a member of this church all of my life. But I have never understood why, when all other denominations around us (who do not have the truth) worship in mixed congregations and we who have the truth worship in segregated congregations (for the most part)?I was blessed to have been a member of the Racine SDA Church in WI because we were (are) a racially mixed congregation of worshippers and it worked for us. Are we so different from the rest of the Adventist brothers and sisters? One of the reasons heaven will be such a wonderful place is because ALL of GOD's children will be able to worship Him together..... My question to is why do we have to wait until heaven? Yours in Christ Our Lord, Cynthia Taylor

143 04:40, Jun 17, Donnie Stanley Jr., AL

I spoke on Racial Reconciliation about 3 weeks ago at 3 Angels Church, and to see this request sent out only strengthens my resolve to continue speaking out against Racial segregation here in the North American SDA Church. Please do pray that GC will faithfully represent the Master by doing this in Atlanta!

137 10:50, Jun 16, Carmen Hernandez, United Kingdom

138 14:02, Jun 16, Michael Michael, Ukraine

135 08:02, Jun 16, Alexis Yeap, Malaysia

130 17:30, Jun 15, Robert Jackson, NJ

My reason for my signature is confirmed in John 17. Also refer to a book by author; Pastor Kim Allan Johnson titled "The Team," which indicates that God's church should reflect the unity and harmony found in the Trinity.

122 17:05, Jun 14, Abraham F. Henry, NY

I'm a member of the Shalom SDA Church. I sincerely appreciate the initiative you are leading. I am in full support. I believe this should have been done a long time ago. If there is any way I could assist you, please be sure to let me know. I'll be keeping this initiative in my prayers. God Bless you!

#115 09:00, Jun 14, Cynthai Vincent, NC

God's blessings will see this issue through. What a mighty God we serve. What a movement this will become when we all come together with Christ as our Leader.

103 19:33, Jun 12, Michelle Riley Jones, MD

I believe the SDA organization should act, vote, organize, administrate, manage, and minister as Jesus prayed in John 17:20-22.

89 16:46, Jun 11, Candace Olusola, KY

This is a topic we discussed in Adventist Heritage with Dr. Lake. Pastor John Nixon preached about how this needs to be done. Sebastein Braxton voiced his concern about it Ky-Tn camp meeting last weekend.

It's the buzz of the world church right now. Please put this on the agenda. This cannot go on any longer.

78 14:02, Jun 10, Maximo Lunga, KY

This has been a thorn in the flesh for my whole life. I praise God for this Committee which has braved out. I have been and will continue to pray for this important matter. God bless you all.

73 02:39, Jun 10, Luyanda Mnyandu, South Africa

66 17:26, Jun 09, Stephen Proverbs, Barbados

How can a Christian organization so willingly hold onto a doctrine of the era of SLAVERY. Leaders of the Church lift your head up and right the wrong!!!

58 10:03, Jun 09, Kenneth E Caviness, TN

It's time for Christ's prayer for us to be realized: "That they all may be one…" John 17:21-23. God bless!

51 05:56, Jun 09, Brian Khumalo, South Africa

Let us be one Adventists as the Apostles, they were one in Christ and experienced the Pentecost. Unite above racial cultures, tradition, etc. so we can experience the Latter Rain of the Holy Ghost as we live in the End time. God Bless All Fellow Adventists in the World.

44 20:12, Jun 08, PATRICI WEBB-GOMEZ, Trinidad And Tobago

43 14:16, Jun 08, Dorothy Suggs, AL

I am 87 years of age and have been attending SDA churches since 4 years of age. I grew up in segregation of SDA's even though I was in the "North." I would really love to see a true desegregation before I fall asleep in the grave.

39 09:22, Jun 08, Edwin Reynolds, TN

We should have been the head and not the tail. Let's not delay another moment in bringing the church into the 21st century instead of staying in the 19th century. God's name is not honored by continuing to drag our feet on this. God's church should be one in all the earth. Why should even South Africa be ahead of us in this regard?

29 05:26, Jun 07, Khethiwe Bhebhe, Canada

We need to stop this foolishness of having White & Black conferences, yet we claim to be a remnant church. We SDA are delaying Jesus coming with all this madness

24 19:55, Jun 05, Anita Hughes, GA

Jesus is coming soon and He is not coming for separated conferences. We need to end the separate conferences now. If we cannot work together here, then how do we expect to evangelize the world? When we learn to love each other and work together then the world will want the gospel that we have.

16 17:28, Jun 04, Eleanor Wharton, Panama

I feel the plea for equality can be simplified by agreeing to live according to the letter and spirit of the Great Commandment; Love God, Love your neighbor. Who is your neighbor? Start looking within your own neighborhood of believers. As we learn to live in the way of "agape" we won't have to be concerned about growing more churches. They will grow themselves. Blessings on the movement I love.

9 10:47, Jun 04, Celia Jackson, GA

It's time to stop having Black & White conferences and Black and White churches. Heaven will not be segregated.

5 16:12, Jun 01, Michelle Sekulic, Australia

We have all been made in the image of God and are all equal in his eyes -Praise God (Birch et al, 2010)!

Extrapolation from the Theology of Reconciliation to the 21ˢᵗ Century Remnant

Paul encapsulates the essence of what Christ did to make Jews and Gentiles (all races/ethnicities) one in his personification--"He (Christ) is our peace" (Eph. 2:14ff). True, lasting peace can be realized only after reconciliation has taken place. Reconciliation must also be preceded by forgiveness. Forgiveness comes from a heart of love. Love is born of God. Charles L. Griswold suggests, "Interpersonal forgiveness is a necessary condition of reconciliation in the stronger sense of affirmation and friendship; but not of mere acceptance in the minimal sense of the term" (Griswold, 2007). Rev. Naim Ateek's suggestion in reference to the Israel-Palestinian conflict holds true for the remnant--

> "The possibility of reconciliation and forgiveness is enhanced when the process is based on justice and nonviolence, and when confession and admission of wrongdoing take place...As long as the injustice persists, the door to reconciliation and forgiveness is slammed shut...When the door is opened, we might be surprised to find that people who have suffered torture, humiliation, oppression, and the loss of loved ones are open to reconciliation. Indeed, many times those who have suffered most, on both sides, are the first to forgive. They are willing to give and receive forgiveness. When that happens, the process of justice, peace, and reconciliation has been completed and a sense of closure can finally be felt" (Ateek, 2009).

When SDAs in the US get serious about finishing the Lord's work here in preparation for the second coming of Christ, we will seek reconciliation between the races/ethnicities. At the spring meeting of the General Conference of SDA Executive Committee, on April 18, 2002, in a statement presented to the committee, the following was affirmed in an attempt to portray the Adventist Church as "the peacemaking remnant." It reads,

> Forgiveness is usually thought of as necessary to heal broken interpersonal relationships…If there is to be peace, it is vital to drop the burdens of the past, to move beyond well-worn battle grounds, and to work toward reconciliation. At a minimum, this requires overlooking past injustices and violence; and, at its best, it involves forgiveness which absorbs the pain without retaliating (Morgan, 2005).

In addition, members of the remnant should be advised that the best way to bring about reconciliation is for each of us to "become the change we want to see" (Ghandi).

Summary- There are some things in life that one must believe in and desire, in order for them to really happen. Reconciliation is one such thing. One has to desire reconciliation in order to reconcile. On the surface it would appear that reconciliation should not be very difficult to achieve since that is the essence of what our discipleship is about. We are the reconciled, called to go and reconcile others to God. But do we find this to be the case?

I have often heard adherents to our faith express their frustration that they do not think that reconciliation will ever happen, not until Jesus returns. Yet we cannot see Jesus in peace unless and until we have made peace with Him and each other. I submit that reconciliation is possible. Not only is it possible, it is imminent. Why would I make such a bold prediction?

Gerardo Marti recently noted the following:

> "Something is really changing in evangelicalism, and it's this social movement towards being diverse

congregations. The large churches are at the forefront; we're seeing that. But this is just going to grow over time. Churches have been the most segregated by far, so in one sense it's catching up to that. But I think it's way beyond that; because this has theological grounding, it will go way beyond society, and eventually the church will be the place that's the most integrated" (Emerson, 2010).

It is an established biblical and theological fact that Jesus is coming soon. Jesus cannot return until His people (the remnant) have reconciled with God. He cannot return until the remnant has finished the assigned task of calling all His own to be reconciled to Him. But he will come at the appointed time, whether or not any individual among us is reconciled to him or to fellow believers. Given the prominent role that the US will play in the end-time events (Rev. 13), and given its complex ethnic diversity, it appears that no one race or ethnic group will be able to complete the work. If the current socioeconomic trend in the US continues, we will have to harness and combine the evangelistic fervor and enthusiasm (and other gifts) of the Blacks, Hispanics, with the education and wealth of Asians, with the wealth, influence, knowledge and other gifts of the Whites in order to do this. My expectation is that as the events of the prophecies begin to unfold more rapidly, those among all the races and ethnicities who are truly converted will begin a movement toward reconciliation that the bureaucracy of the church cannot get in the way of. This will happen so rapidly. It will be incredible that something we have desired for so long could happen in such a short time. Undoubtedly, reconciliation is possible!

In reference to the work of reconciliation in the Evangelical movement, one reconciler recently wrote--

"It is in a pioneer stage. Ten years ago it was on the fringe; it's now becoming a topic of conversation. People are just beginning to understand this is more than a good idea, it is New Testament Christianity, and it's

about the gospel in the 21st century. They've embraced
the conversation but haven't committed to the idea as
a critical component of the Church" (DeYmaz, 2010).

As a remnant body the SDAC ought to take the lead in reconciling
its racial/ethnic members. Quite appropriately, other Protestant
Evangelical denominations have resolved to reconcile, others are still
engaged in discussions about it; the SDAC cannot keep on ignoring
this critical issue. This author joins the call for a resolution at the next
General Conference session in 2015.

"Old habits die hard," the old adage goes. The issue of racial/ethnic
segregation in the US Adventist Church and evangelicalism did not develop
overnight; neither will it disappear overnight. It will take methodical,
intentional, Spirit-led approaches to realize reconciliation among us.

Ignoring the problem will not cause it to go away; it will always
be here until we make deliberate efforts to rid ourselves of it. Among
the approaches we may use are practicing to love, forgive, make peace,
interact, appreciate, and fellowship with each other. These combined
with much praying could assist greatly in bridging the divide.

I showed above that the apostles Paul and John accentuate
the necessity to love (1 Cor. 13; 1 Jn. 5). Jesus collapses all Ten
Commandments of the Decalogue into two: you shall love the Lord
your God... and your neighbor as yourself (Mk. 12:30-31). Learning
to love each other without regard to race, gender, status, and so on is
the best place to start. Love is the key that will unlock all other aspects
of this problem. When one has decided to love, it becomes easier to
forgive. After forgiveness is achieved, peace becomes attainable. Peace
creates an environment to freely interact and get to know each other.
By getting to know each other, we can learn to understand one another,
even appreciate each other (culture, personality). This could lead to
greater trust, which could potentially eliminate the fear of each other.
With the fear gone, it may become doable to live like family.

Probably most Adventists, including church officials of all races and ethnicities, will agree that reconciliation is necessary and desirable, but is it achievable? In a recent telephone conversation with a vice-president of the NAD, the official admitted that it was necessary. They also informed me that many church officials do, but while they will acknowledge this in a one-on-one conversation, they will not lead the initiative to make it happen. This official also pointed out that a grassroots initiative could succeed in getting a resolution on racial and ethnic reconciliation passed at the GC session.

Numerous members of the SDAC are calling for reconciliation all around the world. We need to pass a resolution on racial and ethnic reconciliation at the GC level. Upon doing so and ascertaining that this filters down to the rest of the church through pastors, literature, media, workshops and other means, we could move the process of reconciliation ahead significantly.

The statement to the GC goes further--"We call upon Christian churches and leaders to exercise a ministry of reconciliation and act as ambassadors of goodwill, openness, and forgiveness" (Morgan, 2005). I reiterate the call for peace, for forgiveness, for reconciliation. Why does it appear, as has been expressed by others to me, that the rank and file of the church is ready for reconciliation, but the leaders of the church seem to be standing in its path? Was Dr. Rock correct that it is for reason of "political expediency" that there is a leadership vacuum in this matter? This has been expressed to me by several members.

The Church waits eagerly to hear local conference officials, union officials, division officials, and the General Conference officials call for reconciliation among us. Their constant call for unite is trite, given that these calls make no reference to racial/ethnic reconciliation. Instead they seem contented to sit quietly and watch the war between members of different races/ethnicities and conferences divided by race, jostle each other and wage race/ethnic warfare, often to their spiritual demise. Has the notion of reconciliation lost its missional appeal and has its pursuit become too apolitical? In other words: is it politically incorrect to call for reconciliation even in God's Church? Yet this is what Christianity is about—reconciliation. Then this begs the question--Has the remnant church lost its spiritual appeal in the US? Is this attitude a sign of the Laodicean Church?" Oh that the Lord would cause a prophetic voice to be lifted up among the remnant! E. E. Cleveland rightly affirms--"A strife-ridden world anxiously awaits the full manifestation of the love of God in His children. Heaven is waiting to bestow it. In whom will the love of God be perfected? In you" (Cleveland, 1969)?

9

A United Governance Structure: New Testament Exemplar

The worldwide SDAC is a culturally diverse body. Interestingly, American Adventists (predominantly Whites) must be credited with introducing the three angels' messages to the rest of the world outside of North America. The history of the work on every continent and in every country seems to point to an origin with an introduction usually by White American missionaries. The US and the Adventist Church in the US are arguably the most culturally diverse nation and Church in the postmodern world. Nevertheless something is lacking in both the nation and Church: this one thing: racial/ethnic reconciliation.

Anyone with even minimal familiarity with the regional conferences of the NAD of the SDA Church is aware of the tremendous growth that has taken place within their ranks since their organization. The state conferences have grown significantly also. In 1944 the regional conferences were organized with 17,000 members. By 1995 the membership had increased to 220,000 (Baker, 1996). In 2008 they were over 230,000 in combined membership. The membership of the Northeastern Conference (regional) stands at 45,000+ in 2010 (GC Statistical Report). Also, the diversity of the regional conferences is admirable. There are currently some eighty or more non-African American congregations in the nine regional conferences. As an example of growth in the state conferences, the Greater New York Conference (state) grew from a membership of just under 10,000 in 1992 to over 20,000 in 2005 and over 22,000 in 2010 (GC Statistical Report).

It is noteworthy that the population of the US has grown tremendously since 1944. From a population of over 76 million in 1900, it grew to over 131 million in 1940, 138 million plus in 1944 (Cox, 2001); the US population is now over 310,832,993 based on the most recent US Census Bureau statistics (U.S. Census Bureau, 2010). This growth is largely due to immigration. A significant percentage of the immigrants come from the Americas. A 1998 study by Richard Lawson, an Adventist professor at Queens College, New York, indicates that the Adventist Church in some of the metropolitan areas of the US is comprised predominantly of immigrants (Lawson, 1998). Most immigrants are from Latin and South America, the Caribbean and Africa; a small percentage is from Eastern Europe (Romania, Ukraine, Croatia) and still lesser from Asia (East and South).

These immigrant members have now joined the conversation that resulted in the 1944 second great disappointment of the remnant and which still presently persists. The issue of reconciliation in the Church, therefore, is not between Blacks (African Americans) and Whites (Anglo-Saxons) only anymore. It is a larger one. The conversation must include all of the above ethnic groups who, albeit, are interspersed in the state and regional local conferences. Immigrant members are conveniently identified as such, apparently for political reasons. And well qualified ordained pastors from among them are often overlooked for pastoral positions in these conferences. Some conference presidents have been quoted to say that they would not hire a Caribbean pastor in their conference. Their hiring records suggest that they were resolved in this declaration. Yet the membership of these ethnic groups is of significant percentages in their conferences. Churches have been known to withhold their tithe from conferences in order to force the hiring of their ethnic pastors. **This is wrong**. It begs the question, however, "How might we resolve these issues and create a level playing field for all ethnic groups and for each individual in the remnant?" In the preceding chapters I have shown that reconciliation is the answer and I continue to make that point in this final segment.

Adventist Immigrants

Immigrants have been contributing significantly to the work in the US since its earliest days. An early evangelist, referred to only as Durant, was an immigrant from Manchester, Jamaica. His Episcopalian birth did not deter him from accepting the Advent message in 1900, while living in the North East US. After entering the pastoral ministry in 1904, he was ordained in 1908. Thereafter he became an effective evangelist, conducting tent meetings and baptizing many into the SDA Church (Reynolds, 1984). Another Jamaican, a dynamic leader, J. K. Humphrey, came along later and was at the forefront of the charge to include Blacks in the leadership of the Church. As I mentioned earlier, his congregation in Harlem, New York, had about six hundred members when he withdrew from the denomination with them (Schwarz, 1979).

There are forty eight state conferences and nine regional conferences in the NAD. Although the Whites may see the state conferences as their territories and the Blacks may claim the regional conferences as theirs; the demographics show that it is not so. Greater New York, Southern California, and Florida Conferences, to name a few, are hardly White in membership. In fact, it has been over ten years now since the Greater New York Conference has become predominantly Hispanic and Black, with a mere sprinkling of Whites mainly from Eastern Europe. Northeastern Conference (a regional conference) is comprised primarily of Caribbean immigrants and Africans, many of whom have recently relocated to the South so that there is an influx in both the Georgia-Cumberland and South Atlantic Conferences. "Adventism in Metropolitan New York has become an immigrant church" (Lawson, 1998).

Research data show that over 95 percent of the membership in the New York area is immigrant. "Almost 90 percent of its membership is now 'new immigrant' and the two 'American' groups that were dominant in 1945 have diminished dramatically" (Lawson, 1998). By 1996, the percent of Caucasian members had dwindled to a mere 2.7 percent and African Americans to 8 percent (Lawson, 1998). State and regional conference officials will be hard-pressed to keep these ethnic groups out of the conversation pertaining to racial/ethnic reconciliation. And what advantage is there to doing that?

These immigrants are from integrated SDA territories where ethnic groups are organized without regard to ethnicity in whichever conference they happen to be geographically located. Many have expressed disappointment and frustration with the perceived unchristian arrangement in SDAC in the US, which, in light of recent social trends in the US, is also un-American. The disappointment and frustration is turning to impatience as they now see this governance structure as diabolical and political (see petition in chapter 9 above).

In a presentation to the Collegedale SDA Church in Tennessee on October 10, 2009, Monte Salin showed growth statistics for the SDAC worldwide, which indicated that growth in the church on the African continent between 1981-2000 was at 8.3%, Asia 6.7%, Latin America 6.2%, Australia 2.5%, Europe 2.3%, while in North America it was a mere 2.1% annually. Projections are that by 2020 the percentage of the SDAC in Europe will be 2%, NAD 4%, Asia 24%, Latin America 32%, Africa 38% (Salin, 2009).

	Asian & Pacific	Black	Hispanic	White	Multiethnic & other
Adventists	7%	27%	12%	50%	4%
US Census	4%	12%	15%	67%	2%

Based on this 2008 survey, the percentage of each race/ethnic group in the US population differs from what they are in the SDAC. While the US Census statistics show that Whites and Blacks make up the largest percentage of the population, the growth is slowest among them. The disparity between the percentages of the White and Black population and the percentages of their SDAC church membership is noteworthy. Blacks comprise 12 percent of the US population and 27 percent of the NAD membership; Whites comprise 67 percent of the US population, but 50 percent of the NAD. They are changing rapidly resulting in a declining percentage of the membership among Whites and African Americans in the US. The 2010 GC session in Atlanta seemed to provide a clear indication of who comprise the Adventist Church worldwide and in the US, despite the fact that the sessions were held in one of the most densely populous Adventist tri-state region.

Currently 31% of Adventists in the US were not born as American citizens. Since the 1980s the majority of accessions for most years have been among immigrants. The age group by percentage in the SDAC is twice as high among those over 63 years and about twice in the Millennial generation (ages 15-31 years old) in 2009 (Salin, 2008). This is due to the growth among Hispanic immigrants in particular, which have an average age in the US way below that of Whites and Blacks. Coupled with the massive annual attrition of members in the US, being second highest in the worldwide church, the NAD church is getting aging, except among Hispanic immigrants.

Hispanics- Hispanic Americans have immigrated to the US in droves over the better part of the last half century. They have come mainly from Mexico (59%), Puerto Rico, and Cuba; to a lesser degree, from the rest of Central and South America. Puerto Ricans reside mainly in New York; Cubans go to Florida, and Mexicans to Texas and California. California and Texas are the most populous with Hispanics, while New York and Florida respectively trail immediately behind. Notwithstanding, Hispanics numbered forty two percent (42%) of New Mexico's population in 2000 (U. S. Census Bureau, 2010).

According to the most recent US Census Bureau statistics, the Hispanic American population increased by 58% since 1990. It grew from 22.4 million in 1990 to 35.6 million in 2000. Hispanics have now (2010) overtaken African Americans (31.4 million in 1992) as the largest ethnic group in the US. Interestingly, nine out of ten Hispanics identified themselves as White alone with only 2 percent as Black.

In 2000 the Hispanic American population was 35.6 million but increased to 44.3 million in 2006. It is projected to get to 47.8 million in 2010 (15.5% of population) and 102.6 in 2050, that is, 24.4% of the population. The population of the US in 2009 was over 310 million; Hispanics were 15.8 percent, Blacks 12.9, Asians 4.6 percent, based on the US Census Bureau statistics. 2010 US Census estimated that Blacks were 13.5 percent (40.7 million) of the population (U. S. Census Bureau , 2010).

The SDAC in the NAD, particularly in these states above, have benefited greatly from this large scale immigration. With this nationwide spurt there has been a corresponding rapid increase in the Hispanic American church membership. Branson notes that the Hispanic membership constituted 40 percent of the Greater New York Conference and one-third of the Texico Conference by the 1970s. The Hispanic membership in the NAD also increased by 127 percent between the years 1980 to 1990. The prediction was for Hispanic membership to grow to 14.5 percent of the Adventists in the NAD by the year 1990 (Baker, 1995).

In *Telling the Story*, Baker averred--"Hispanics have not attempted to organize their own ethnically defined conferences" (Baker, 1996). On the contrary, however, while I was in New York in the 1990s, I was reliably informed by a Hispanic educator, who was involved in that ethnic pursuit, that Hispanics were seeking to organize under their own conferences, perhaps for reason of wanting to look out for themselves. They have been disallowed in that, although they have succeeded in obtaining vice-presidential positions in several union conferences. Hispanic churches have been organized in seven of the nine regional conferences in the NAD (Vasquez, 2000).

The first Hispanic Adventist church in the US was organized in Arizona on December 23, 1899 by Elders R. M. Kilgore and C. D. M. Williams. Not long after, on December 31, 1899 the second congregation was also orga+nized in Arizona (Baker, 1995; Vasquez,

2000). In 1900 Hispanics numbered 41 among the 111 members in the entire state of Arizona. Two of the 4 Adventist churches in the state were Spanish-speaking. Presently Hispanic members are scattered throughout all the state conferences in the mainland US. The Greater New York Conference, once a White conference, elected Dionisio Olivo as its first Hispanic president conference in 1997. Olivo went on to serve three terms (nine years) as president of that conference. The Hispanic membership and congregations now number more than a third of the Conference (Vasquez, 2000), which has a membership of over 22, 000(Adventist Archives, 2010).

Which ethnic group will be the next to request its own ethnic conference? What more will they demand while this governance structure obtains and the perception remains that each group must look out for themselves or else be left to survive on what is left whenever the "pie" is shared? Consequently, voices among these groups can be heard saying that they will not be occluded. Racial/ethnic reconciliation is the only Christian answer to our dilemma.

Afro-Caribbeans- The early twentieth century saw an influx of immigrants into the US from the Caribbean, particularly Barbados, Jamaica, Trinidad, and the British West Indies. The population of Harlem, New York was one-fourth West Indian (Afro-Caribbean) by the 1920s. While Afro-Caribbeans have been about one percent (1%) of the national Black population, they have been disproportionately overrepresented among Black businessmen, professionals, and public figures. They have also been earning considerably more than American Blacks, with second generation Afro-Caribbeans out-earning even the Whites. As of 1969 the incomes of this ethnic group was 28 percent higher than that of other Blacks in New York City and 52 percent higher nationally (Sowell, 1981).

The Adventist Church in New York is primarily immigrant. A study by Ronald Lawson, just over a decade ago, showed that the SDA Church in Metropolitan New York was comprised of over 95 percent immigrants. Changes to the US immigration law in 1965 (Hart-Cellar Immigration Act) resulted in a more ethnically diverse immigration. Immigrants from the Caribbean islands, Latin and South America came in droves, and among them were many Adventists (Lawson, 1998).

Africans- Blacks from the continent of Africa have been increasing since the 1990s. Between 1960 and 2007 it grew 40 fold (Terrazas, 2009). The majority of immigrant Africans is from Nigeria, Ghana, Ethiopia, Eritrea, Egypt, Somalia, and South Africa. They live mainly in Washington D. C., New York, and Atlanta. The Immigration Policy Institute estimated that 1.4 million foreign born Africans were living in the US in 2007 (Terrazas, 2009).

The SDAC has benefited from this growth among African immigrants, particularly in New York, Georgia, Maryland and Texas. African ethnic churches have been planted in these and other areas since the 1990s. The First Ghana S. D. A. Church in the Bronx, New York was among the first in the country. Since then the Ghanians have planted other churches in Toronto and Atlanta.

Asian Americans- Korean Americans are the largest group of Asian American Adventists. The largest percent of Asian Adventists live in the state of California. The first convert among them was T. H. Okahira in 1892. Their first congregation was organized in California also. A Japanese American was baptized four years later and became the first missionary to Japan. His son was credited with planting the first Japanese American church in Los Angeles in 1922. An interesting story of divine intervention surrounds the imprisonment of Japanese Americans in concentration camps in California during World War II. Among those imprisoned were 200 Adventists, but at the time of their release the Adventists numbered 350. From 1,000 members in 1965, by 1992 Asian American Adventists numbered over 20,000 in the NAD (Baker, 1995).

Adventists are obliged to seek reconciliation among all these races/ethnicities. It is a divine mandate. And when we have attained this, we can all then collaborate optimally under the aegis of the Holy Spirit as missionaries to America.

Missionaries to America- If the rest of the world church could be evangelized by White Adventist missionaries and a handful of African American missionaries, then immigrants (Hispanics, Asians, and Blacks) can be missionaries to American Whites and African Americans. Rather than assimilating, in this light, immigrant Adventists should constantly challenge the church to reconcile and exemplify reconciliation in their conduct with those believers who were born in the US. It may be that as some observe more of this genuinely Christian lifestyle, they may become changed. It appears that to advocate otherwise is to suggest that we serve an impartial, possibly impotent, and definitely wishy-washy God. But we do not. Our God is able to do far more than we can imagine or think. This is not to overlook the challenges posed by the socio-cultural dynamic cited in *Divided by Faith* (Emerson and Smith, 2000) among others. Yet how could we forget that it is "not by might, nor by power…" (Zech. 4:6, KJV)? Hitherto it often appears that unfortunately the church leadership panders to the prejudices of the members in an unsalvific manner and to the detriment of the cause of God.

A New Paradigm of Governance

The NAD local conferences were originally organized geographically until 1944 (Lawson, 1998). The current racially segregated structure of governance was not divinely designed and needs to be revisited with a view to restructuring it. We could either return to the former structure (which is not preferable) or develop a new structure based on a new geographic configuration. A new Paradigm of governance could be developed based on the new covenant of the Bible. The concepts of an old and a new covenant are first mentioned in the Jer. 31:31-33 and more elaborately referenced in the epistle to the Hebrews (Heb. 8, 9).

Old Governance Structure (old covenant)	New Governance Structure (new covenant)
Hatred	**Love**
Distrust	Trust
Cruelty	Mercy
Mean-spiritedness	Kindness
Greed	Generosity
Pride	Humility
Inferior/superior races	One New Humanity in Christ
Disgrace	Grace
Impatience	Patience
Grudge	Forgiveness

Figure 8 Old and new governance structures of the SDAC

In the Bible, the old covenant was inadequate (ratified by animals' blood) to accomplish the work of redemption. It was broken and obsolete. It was based on the promises of the people (Exod. 19:1-8). On the contrary, the new covenant was sufficient, ratified by the efficacious sacrifice of Christ, who is all that we need for salvation. The new covenant is better and is eternal. It is a covenant of love, better blood, and with the better promises of God (Heb. 8, 9).

Figure 9 illustrates that likewise, the old governance structure (White conferences/Black conferences currently being used) of the SDAC was developed based on hatred of each other, but the new flows out of love for one another. This hatred was a part of the racist ideology of the Anglo-Saxons (Whites are a superior race, Blacks are inferior race), which permeated the very fabric of the Evangelical movement (including the SDAC) and was the prevailing view in

Western society, the US in particular. This hatred resulted in centuries of systemic oppression, widespread lynching, economic deprivation, and the American *Apartheid*. The oppressed Blacks developed hatred for toward their oppressors and both parties are estranged. But in Christ we have this invitation in Scripture--"Dear friends, let us love one another, for love comes from God. Everyone who loves has been born of God and knows God" (1 Jn. 4:7, NIV). From the governance structure developed in hatred issues distrust, cruelty, mean-spiritedness, greed, pride, inferior/superior races, impatience, and disgrace. The governance structure developed in love produces trust, mercy, kindness, generosity, humility, One New Humanity in Christ, patience, grace, and forgiveness. This is the biblical approach to our dealings with each other and the governance of God's church.

In Gal. 5:22, 23 the Christian virtues of those possessing the fruit of the Spirit are evident in all believers. It follows also that under the aegis of the Holy Spirit, those who possess these virtues would agree to a governance structure developed in love rather than hatred. When this development is realized, the SDAC not only becomes a microcosm of the One New Humanity in Eph. 2, but she moves from disgrace to grace, from disunity to unity, from dysfunction to optimal function. Believers can then freely collaborate, utilizing their spiritual gifts cross-culturally and the kingdom of God is edified!

Biblical Antioch: The New Testament Model- Acts 13:1-3 provides a poignant picture of the New Testament view on racial/ethnic unity. The prototypical Christian church in Jerusalem was homogeneous and while God was still leading there, it did not become the first church to make the impression that its members were Christians. Rather, it was the church at Antioch (Acts 11:26b). Could it be because of its unity in diversity? For this reason the church at Antioch is the exemplar in focus with a leadership comprised of two Jews (Barnabas and Paul), two Africans (Simeon and Lucius), and a Greek (Manean). After evangelizing the Jews in Cyprus, moving on to Pisidian Antioch, Barnabas and Paul evangelized both Jews and Gentiles; God made them a "light for the

Gentiles" (vss. 16, 26, 46, 48, NIV). Orlando Costas cites the church of Antioch as an example that the early church "most effectively followed Jesus outside the gates of Jerusalem" (Conde-Frazier and Pazmino, 2000). Is it, therefore, any wonder that the racially/ethnically integrated SDAC outside of North America is more effective in its evangelism and growing at a much faster rate than the membership in the US with all its education and wealth?

Adventists should debunk the myth that we can only effectively labor among our own ethnic group or race. Besides its being disproved by cross-cultural ministries and churches already existing in the US, it is unchristian. History instructs that with the Holy Spirit imbuing us as Adventists, we can effectively labor for the Lord across racial/ethnic lines. Notwithstanding, we will sometimes be persecuted by those of our own race/ethnicity for doing so, as in the case of Barnabas and Paul (vss. 46a, 50). Yet the Lord will provide adequate encouragement from the sincere believers (vss. 42-43). And we must keep moving joyfully along with our mission, propelled by the Holy Spirit (vs. 52).

Adventist apologists strongly and correctly advocate the New Testament origin of our church. This (Antioch Church) is the New Testament model of the Christian Church, where the disciples were first called Christians, but we are hesitant to follow it in the US, the land of the SDAC's birth. The SDAC in the US could become the miniature model of the antitypical universal Christian church (the invisible remnant) when we reconcile and adapt a united governance structure.

The Southern Africa Union Conference: A Recent Model- The Southern Africa Union Conference (SAU) could serve as a paradigm for the NAD. In the early 1990s, while the spotlight was turned on the abolition of South Africa's apartheid, the GC exerted much pressure on its segregated local conferences to desegregate. That was requested in an effort to comply with the request of the Truth and Reconciliation Commission set up by the government of South Africa. The move has resulted in a painful yet necessary reconfiguration of the local conferences within the SAU Conference. When the agreement was reached, twelve White members of the Cape conference challenged the restructuring in the civil court with a lawsuit (Crocombe, 2006), which was later dismissed by a magistrate (Du Preez, 2010).

After much dragging of their feet nonetheless, with the Lord propelling them, after two years during the 1990s, they reached an agreement to integrate and issued the following statement:

> "We are constrained therefore by the love of God that has grown more keenly in our hearts to confess that we have misrepresented the gospel of Christ in our sins of omission and commission regarding apartheid. We realize that this has had a hurtful effect on our society, on our corporate church and its individual members. We are deeply sorry and plead for the forgiveness of God and our fellow citizens" (Crocombe, 2006).

This is a commendable admission of guilt and public repentance by the church in South Africa, even amid dissonance from those who have expressed that it was insincere and did not go far enough (Crocombe, 2006). In the case of the US, no nationwide scientific assessment of the impact of American apartheid on African Americans and Native Americans has been done to date. Some of the effects of this are obvious, however, in the economic and educational disparities between Blacks and Whites. Yet the thought of such a study elicits the questions: After over two, yea three centuries of deliberate debilitating, dehumanizing, and destructive oppression of coloreds, Blacks, and Indians by the Whites, what damage (psychological or otherwise) has been done to these peoples?

With over a century of discrimination and segregation of a similar nature as above, by the Adventist Whites in the remnant Church of North America, which was viewed with apathy by the GC leadership, is an apology not in order from the GC (Note Du Preez's recommendations for the South African Church; Du Preez, 2010)? Besides, when the GC offers an apology, if we are genuine about it, would it not be most fitting for the leaders to call for a resolution on racial reconciliation in the world Church? Further, ought the GC not engage in Christ-like fairness and show the righteous Christian character of the remnant by requesting of the NAD what it did of the SAU Conference? Could that which is spiritually good for the African Christians be similarly good also for the Americans? It is a tall order for any leader to seek such a reconfiguration in the US. Nevertheless God's leaders are called to carry out "tall orders" especially when the church is encountering tough challenges and faced with the reality of an imminent *Parousia*. A paraphrase of the words of the reconciler, Curtis DeYoung, is appropriate at this juncture: while reconciliation remains our greatest challenge, it is our only hope!

In a recent telephone conversation with an official of the NAD, I was informed that the fact that the SAU Conference was an attached field of the GC at the time (since 1983) made it possible for this restructuring to be done. When I last examined the chain of authority in the SDAC, it showed that the GC still has authority over the NAD. Or could it be that the Southern Africans are not as wealthy and sophisticated, hence more malleable and ductile than the Americans? And in this light, are the SDAC officials bartering the soul of the church for a wad of "greens"? It seems only right and Christ-like that the GC ought to exercise its authority to have the NAD reconfigure the governance structure of its local conferences.

Slavery, Reconstruction, and Jim Crow laws were all legal institutions in American. While they remained legal, the populace generally acted accordingly within the law, albeit often enforcing it on their own. When these heinous institutions were outlawed and replaced with just laws, the populace conformed also. I submit that the NAD needs to act boldly and reconfigure the present local conference arrangement and the membership will cooperate. It will be a painful process in the early years of its aftermath, but will get better over time. This should be done with much earnest praying and to seek the Holy Spirit's guidance. That being done, it will be done right and will produce the necessary result. Changes in the law tend to result ultimately in changes in people's behavior.

The current Southern Africa model is essentially the biblical model, which is being practiced in all the other divisions of the SDAC. Scripture is replete with portraits of reconciliation and unity. Acts 13:1-3 identifies this ecclesial unity in diversity in the Christian church of Antioch. Jews, Africans, and Greek labored together for the salvation of others. Not only did it result in an efficient operation but more notably, they became a united front, which made the group the first to become recognizable as Christians. Unity in reconciled diversity sends a strong and unmistakable message of the power of God. In addition, racial/ethnic unity energizes our witness.

Reconfiguration of Local Conferences- When the action to form regional conferences was adopted in 1944, all Unions in the NAD, with the exception of the Pacific and Pacific Northwest Union Conferences, quickly formed regional conferences shortly thereafter. One proposal which may be considered to resolve the issue of divided governance structure is for the NAD to dissolve all local conferences (state and regional) in the NAD and reconfigure their territories without regard for race/ethnicity. In this arrangement, some conferences may naturally retain a majority White or a majority Black membership and homogeneous leadership. But that would be fine since every local church should be allowed to fall naturally into its geographic region. Current conference officials of those conferences could be allowed to serve out their terms of office. At the end of their terms, new elections should be conducted with intentional efforts to have a diverse leadership throughout all of those conferences in the territories where there is a diverse membership.

Finances The matter of finances looms large in this proposal. The fixed and current assets of each local conference become matters of concern here and rightly so. It would be a long, painful process to do allocate the assets, but one nevertheless worth the effort. It seems, however, that each conference could retain its fixed and current assets. Meanwhile this could result in some conferences becoming slightly larger, others a little smaller (in terms of membership), some richer, others possibly poorer, but all being able to remain sustainable and autonomous. It may also become necessary to dissolve a few conferences where they overlap and where it could be proven to be more cost effective to eliminate one of those local conference headquarters. The assets could be sold or retained as necessary and the proceeds from such a sale could be distributed among the conferences in which those from the dissolved conference would be hired. If departmental directors and conference officials should be displaced, they could be assigned positions in churches, with the budget that they were already being paid from. The fact is, by eliminating some positions you reduce conference expenditure, but not overall remittances for the union or Division. Ultimately all our possessions amount to vanity. They were entrusted to our stewardship only for a time. To quote Jesus--we "cannot serve God and money" (Mt. 6:24, NIV). Why should we allow finances to become an obstacle to reconciling and collaborating to advance the cause of God?

Heterogeneous Leadership- The notion that we have to be led by someone of our own race/ethnic group to optimize our mission appeal is misguided, unbiblical, and unchristian. While research suggests that homogeneous churches are more cost effective than heterogeneous (Emerson and Smith, 2000), that could change if we did the right thing and trusted God to bring about the desired results. The economics could quickly change in favor of heterogeneous units. Besides, what value will we place on a soul? Many problem marriages that survived, ended up with more balanced children and healthier couples (after reconciliation), than they might have, if they had ended in divorce. The New Testament Church was led mainly by Jews who ministered to people of all ethnicities. Some of these ethnic converts joined the bishopry and ministered to Jews and ethnic people from various countries (Acts 2; 9; 13:1-3). The point here is that Christians are divinely endowed with the ability to rise above social norms and mores. Besides, God gifts his children according to the tasks he calls them to perform. But our lack of adequate trust in God is causing us to lack much of what God wants to gift us with, reconciliation being foremost among them. Let us pray for this faith among the remnant.

Paul, of the New Testament, was a Jew, who worked effectively among the Gentiles after he accepted God's call to do so. In fact, God called him specifically for the purpose and said to him--"depart for I will send you among the Gentiles" (Acts 26:16-18)… Timothy was the son of a Jewish woman and a Greek father and labored greatly with Paul until he went on his own among the Jews and Gentiles (Acts 16:1-4). This is not to say that cross-cultural evangelism will not be met with opposition in this society; rather it to remind us that this is the Lord's work and when he assigns us, he equips us to perform the tasks that he assigns (1 Cor. 12). It is currently being done in other Christian churches in the US and to a lesser degree in some congregations in the SDAC. Years ago I served as the pastor of a small congregation with Asians, Hispanics, Caucasians, and Blacks for over five years. And everyone got along just fine, across racial/ethnic lines.

An experience I had while serving a large (approximately 1000 member) Afro-Caribbean church in the Bronx, New York stands out. On a particular Sabbath a Caucasian woman visited our church with one of the Afro-Caribbean members, who introduced her to me. As I would normally do, I greeted her warmly and began to make small talk. While speaking with her I discovered that she was not a Christian and was not attending church regularly. I invited her back and offered to study the Bible with her. She accepted and we began Bible studies.

After studying for months, I asked her if she would invite Christ into her life. She accepted my invitation to accept Christ as her personal Savior and be baptized. But I noticed that she was tearful and I enquired why. Her response was, "Pastor Birch, I hope that after I get baptized you are not going to send me to another church (White) somewhere, for this is where I want to attend church." I assured her that we did not have such a practice and I would not be doing that. I proceeded to inquire of her as to some of her spiritual gifts and offered to have her join the choir and be a deaconess in the church. Instantly she became elated; smiles were just bursting from all corners of her face. She was now at ease and at home.

The members of the church welcomed her with joy and open arms and situated her nicely among themselves even though she was the only White person in this 99.9% Black congregation. It was my joy for years to come, to see her singing joyfully to the Lord on the choir and serving as a deaconess in her church. Guess what? She brought several others too, two of whom we baptized and situated in the fellowship of the church. Our God is able to assist us in ministering to each other regardless of race or ethnicity.

The issues pertaining to differences in worship styles and "White flight" from local churches can be overcome over time. Even with the present segregated arrangement, members still choose where they worship based on the worship styles of the local churches in their area, though most often they choose one of their racial/ethnic churches. That is far less of a problem than it may appear to be. The market place approach to worship poses a more serious challenge, because as long as members can choose, they will. And that is fine. The SDAC would be ill-advised to assume the approach of assigning members to local churches. When the change is made in the structure of governance, it will send a message to everyone that it is good to worship and fellowship with everyone without regard to race/ethnicity, especially in light of the changing national culture to embrace cultural diversity. With the change occurring in the governance structure, members will then begin to venture outside of their comfort zones. Leadership could also develop and create opportunities for meaningful interaction among members, which leads to better understanding and appreciation of each other among us.

Ethnic SDA Churches It probably would be disallowed for Blacks or Whites to choose as a name for a local church, a name which specified their races. There is no missional need or ecclesial benefit for Hispanic, Korean, Russian, Indian or any other congregation to specify their ethnicity in the name they choose for their local church. It is often done under the guise of language needs, but is totally unnecessary. The language needs may still be met without the sign. I suspect that even in this racialized society very rarely would anyone visit a church because it specifies the ethnic group worshiping there. And when that designation does attract someone, is that the reason for which we want to have them visit or become a member? I think not. This is off-putting and sectarian. Conferences should not permit this to happen. I submit that the SDAC ought to enact a policy against this practice. Nevertheless I am aware that the current governance structure pressures the average member and more so the politically inclined Adventists, to play the politics of survival. We ought to change it.

This ethnic-specific designation encourages sectarianism and segregation as is practiced by the advocates of HUD in the SBC and other Christian churches. Let us debunk the HUD and adopt a new paradigm for the NAD: a paradigm that is being used in the fastest-growing regions of our Church; a paradigm that is biblical, Christ-like, inclusive, and reconciling. Our racial/ethnic identity ought not to be allowed such prominence in our missional appeal or we may lack spiritual appeal. Our identity as Adventists is primarily and preeminently **CHRISTIAN** (Pollard, 2000); not Eurocentrism (Anglo-Saxonism), or Afrocentricism, or Asianism, or Hispanicism/Latinism, and so on. The Christian identity must be up front and center. All other identities should be of less prominence both in our missional façade and faith praxis.

As a remnant people we seek to promote unity in diversity. That which unites should gain prominence over that which could potentially divide. The concept is wholly New Testament and Christian. Paul embraced this concept and promoted it among all his churches; we should also. Yet unity in the Christian Church is never at the expense of our racial/ethnic identity. In all biblical literature we see clearly that unity in diversity ought to be a priority of the remnant. In our missionary endeavors and Christian lifestyles, we remain who we are racially and ethnically, yet we should leverage that identity to the advantage of our mission. We should celebrate out social identity, but not in a manner that potentially hurts our mission.

Pastors- Of much importance is the need for pastors to refrain from engaging in "politics by race." Pastors ought to lead the membership toward reconciliation instead of exploiting the prejudices they are striving to overcome. Ungodly leaders and more often managers, resort to the "divide-and-conquer" model of governance. The Rwandan example of a pastor who aided and abetted the murder of others is an example. I have seen the adverse effects of this practice on the local conferences. In order to have our way or for the reason of self- preservation, many members of our clergy often engage in this practice. My personal observation of this in our church has left a horrible distaste for it. I have personally pleaded on the floor of conference constituency meetings for us not to divide by race/ethnicity because it leads to further entrenchment of the races/ethnicities. Lay people have agitated against this also, but to no avail, probably because the rest of the clergy is silent. Pastors still lead in the twenty-first century remnant. When they speak, members still tend to listen and follow their lead. Whenever they are publicly silent on a matter, it sends another message. Pastors ought not to be silent on this matter, even when it seems politically incorrect.

Summary- The Afro-Caribbean members of the Seventh-day Adventist Church have shown similar earning trends in recent years to that cited above. These island people, who were first evangelized by American missionaries at the dawn of the twentieth century (Schwarz, 1979), are among the new missionaries to a secularized America and an aging Adventist Church. A Trinidadian, Clifford Jones, currently serves as associate dean of the Seventh-day Adventist Theological Seminary at Andrews. The first Caribbean person, a Jamaican-born and first Black person, Elder G. Earl Knight, was elected as president of the Greater New York Conference in September 2010. After serving two and a half terms (approximately seven years) as Executive Secretary of the conference, Knight now leads the predominantly Black and Hispanic (over 95%) conference (Lawson, 1998) whose membership is over

22,000. Another Jamaican, Elder Roy Brown also served as president of the Southeastern conference a few years ago. The Ontario Conference in Canada recently elected another Jamaican, Elder Mansfield Edwards, as conference president in 2010. In the 1990s the Church in Canada was led by a Union president of Caribbean origin (Lawson, 1998). There is a demographic shift in the membership of the NAD. This is rapidly becoming a division of immigrants and they are now unavoidably a part of the racial/ethnic reconciliation conversation.

How must the Church respond to this development? Will its officials at the GC and NAD continue to sit in apparent oblivion or obvious apathy? Or will they continue to point out the obstacles without making any meaningful if sincere attempts to seek reconciliation? Is the Office of Human Relations at the NAD proving to be a less than optimum use of the Lord's goods, since neither its function nor its impact is observable by the membership?

Despite its 1999 summit, this NAD office has no measurable result of the impact of that summit available for objective assessment. By its own account, there is no significant gain in the area of racial/ethnic reconciliation since then. In my recent conversation with an official there, the only substantive approach to reconciliation that they could currently recommend was to pray for a change of heart. I believe wholeheartedly in prayer and I am praying for reconciliation, but I have come to realize that the Lord wants to see His people adjust their mode of operation so that it indicates their willingness to be within His will even while they are praying. Notwithstanding, even with the platform that the Office of Human Relations has, they have not issued a call for prayer for racial/ethnic reconciliation across the NAD. Ought this Office to be taken seriously? It begs the question: "Are the Lord's goods being best used in maintaining this Office?"

Somehow I suspect that quite similar to how the present governance structure came into being in 1944 by the machinations of men, so it will in the twenty-first century. And if we refused to change the structure and the Lord came, would He hold us all accountable, in particular, those who now officiate and others who have officiated in offices where they could have led the remnant to reconciliation, but did virtually nothing? If some of us were held accountable for the sin of omission, could He also find still others among us guilty of the sins of commission? And does their culpability absolve the rest of us who do nothing to terminate racial/ethnic segregation in the remnant?

The Southern Baptist Convention has long been notorious for its racist shenanigans. They seceded from the Baptist Church in 1845 because of the refusal of their lay membership and clergy to end slavery among them (Emerson and Smith, 2000). Yet even without getting human rights, the doctrine of the sanctuary, the health message, and Sabbath doctrines right, in a resolution brought to the Convention at their 1995 session in Atlanta, their White and Black members, as well as their White and Black clergy voted to reconcile. Meanwhile, with all the right doctrines and a superb diet, the remnant remains reticent. The counsel offered by Ellen White should be heeded—

> "The day is coming when the kings and the lordly men of the earth would be glad to exchange places with the humblest African who has laid hold on the hope of the gospel…To him that overcometh will I give to eat of the tree of life, which is in the midst of the paradise of God… Many who claim to be children of God are children of the wicked one, and have all his passions, his prejudices, his evil spirit, his unlovely traits of character" (White, *Southern Work*, 19…).

From the Promise Keepers to the Presbyterians, Methodists, Southern Baptist Convention, numerous efforts are being made to achieve this. The Southern Baptist Convention issued a statement following the election of Barak Obama as president of the US. An article by Adele Banks in the June 24 *Christianity Today* records the statement—

"Southern Baptists on Wednesday overwhelmingly expressed their "pride" in President Obama's election as the nation's first African-American president while also criticizing his policies that they oppose. The resolution, adopted at the Southern Baptist Convention's annual meeting in Louisville, Ky., said Baptists "share our nation's pride in our continuing progress toward racial reconciliation signaled by the election of Barack Hussein Obama as the 44th president of the United States of America" (2009).

Now it is the Evangelical movement and the US society that are progressing toward racial/ethnic reconciliation. Where is the remnant in this pursuit? As a start we need to put in place a governance structure that discourages devilish vices and encourages Christian virtues. No more are we at war, when we are in Christ. We are all siblings and God's appointed servants (church officials) ought to call and lead us back together under one church in North America. Let us live by our creed.

The Adventist immigrants to the US, who came from integrated regions find themselves thrust into a hostile church environment when they come to the US. Yet they should not take sides and further deepen the divide, instead they should see themselves as missionaries to America. Maybe the immigrants can model love, collaboration, and unity to their American siblings in Christ. Pastors are called upon to take the lead in racial/ethnic reconciliation. Rather than exploiting the prejudices of members, they should assume the prophetic role to preach, teach, and lead against bigotry and sectarianism in the SDAC.

The words of this song appropriately express a most fitting counsel for the remnant in the twenty-first century—

1

"Rise up, O men of God!
His kingdom tarries long.
Bring in the day of brotherhood
and end the night of wrong.

2

Let women all rise up!
Have done with lesser things.
Give heart and mind and soul and strength
to serve the King of kings.

3

Rise up, O men of God!
The church for you doth wait,
her strength unequal to her task;
rise up, and make her great!

4

Lift high the cross of Christ!
Tread where his feet have trod.
Disciples of the Son of Man,
rise up, O church of God!

10

Conclusion

The history of the US is closely linked to the rise of the Evangelical movement, which began with the Great Awakenings of the eighteenth and nineteenth centuries. The Pilgrims came and purported to have fled the continent of Europe in search of religious freedom, but that was not all. They had another agenda. It was an agenda embedded in the racist ideology of advancing the interests of a "superior race." In so doing, and in order to justify their marginalization of Native Indians and enslavement of Blacks, Whites posited the construct of an anthropological pyramid, atop which was the Caucasians, with the Africans relegated to the very bottom as an inferior race. The first obvious signs of racism in the US began with the introduction of indentured African servants in 1619. That became the intellectual opinion of the day. Consequently, Evangelical ministers and members were slaveholders, and for centuries oppressed Blacks and marginalized Native Indians in order to survive at the top.

The Evangelical movement embraced and propagated this racist ideology by preaching it, teaching it, and ultimately indoctrinating their members with it. In addition, the Evangelical practice of "engaged orthodoxy" accorded the Evangelicals more power and influence in society to the extent that they have been able to shape the society and its government. Thus racism became the ideological foundation on which America was built and is largely being sustained. This intellectualized racism became so engrained in the society that even apparent well-meaning converts to other religious faiths accepted the ideology as biblical and "scientific", and accommodated *Apartheid* without any semblance of guilt or subsequent remorse. Meanwhile racism resulted in the dehumanizing, debilitating, and destructive treatment of Blacks and the marginalization of Native Indians and other ethnic groups. This attitude possesses the Evangelical movement and has permeated the SDAC to the extent that it goes unrecognized by many, in particular, its benefactors. Racialization comes as a consequence of racism and results in the further isolation of Whites (who moved to the suburbs) and Blacks (who are confined to urban areas). It results further in church attendees choosing to attend churches that provide more similarities than differences. All of this causes less interaction and greater ignorance of each race by the other and lack of understanding of the needs and challenges each face.

The Seventh-day Adventist Church, which is essentially Evangelical, became a victim of the society's racist ideology, at least to the extent that since the early years of the Adventist Church we have practiced racial segregation without any sense of moral culpability. Throughout its history, the SDAC in the US has never taken the position of racial segregation in writing, but has embraced it in practice since the late nineteenth to early twentieth century. Since then it has become embedded in the fabric of the society. Several pioneers of the SDAC made written public objections to slavery, but not once did the predominantly White SDAC issue an official statement decrying this evil system.

Segregation was the order of the day in the US during much of Ellen White's life and until her death. The segregation after slavery was enforceable by civil laws and by divisive elements within society that made it dangerous for Whites and Blacks to worship together. Ellen White acquiesced to the segregation of the time only as a temporary accommodation to a transient crisis. Her position has always been one of unity among all races/ethnicities and she made numerous statements emphasizing the common origin of humankind and the equality of all races before God.

On this basis, therefore, it becomes easier to understand why in 1944 when the Blacks requested participation in the leadership of the Church and the integration of the Church's health and educational institutions, it was flatly rejected and the White majority of the US Church voted instead to allow Blacks to organize under their own ethnic-led local conferences within union conferences where there was sufficient Black membership. Since that action was taken, the SDAC remains divided by race both in its governance structure and worship in the US at the local conference and local church levels.

The Evangelical movement holds to a philosophy of "engaged orthodoxy" by which it operates in its attempt to shape the culture of the society and the course of government. Democracy, with its freedom, individualism, and market principle, is entwined with the very fabric of the Evangelical movement and its premillennial teaching that holds to a post-church era in which God will reign on the earth. In their efforts to prepare for this, the Evangelicals' insistence on foisting their theological positions on the society is often perceived as an attempt to create a theocracy of the American republic. The congressional debate on the Terri Schiavo bill in 2005 serves as a classic case and borne out by the contribution of Republican congressman, Christopher Shays of Connecticut (Nagourney, 2005).

Christian unity is enjoined on all Christians in Scripture. Christ prayed for this and expects it of his church. Our ability to unite is one of the defining characteristics of the remnant that sets us apart from other organizations or Christian denominations. Yet this unity is not uniformity. Contrariwise, it is such that it embraces diversity within the doctrinal parameters of our faith and sets believers at ease in their social identity. The SDAC would do well emulating the first century church of Antioch referenced in Acts 13:1-3. This model could assist us in arriving at the unity in diversity that we urgently need.

The SDAC subscribes to a remnant theology that identifies her as the remnant church of God. This position was first taken by the pioneers and continues to be the position of the Church today. And rightly so, since the remnant of Rev. 14:12 is identified as those who keep the commandment of God and hold to the testimony of Jesus Christ. We Adventists do. Despite this, the SDAC is not an "exclusive club" (Folkenberg, 1994) of saints who will be the only recipients of the eschatological divine approbation. No! But the SDAC stands out among all Protestant churches as the one which embraces most of the biblical truths. Yet even with this "lofty" status, the Church remains divided along racial lines. "White flight' and "Black flight" are commonplace and there seems to be no substantive attempt on the part of the leadership to resolve the racial/ethnic dilemma. But remnant does not connote corporate salvation; it denotes individual accountability. I showed earlier in this study that remnantlessness is biblical. Hence while Adventists are a part of the remnant Church, in the same way that many Israelites were a part of Israel and were not in the remnant after a disaster, it could happen that many Adventists will be excluded from the remnant at the coming of Christ; condemned for lack of love.

The sordid history of race relations in the US and of the SDAC in the US has left some with countless painful memories, while the thought of the oppression and the current lopsided structure in society conjures up unpleasant emotions. It is a huge challenge to reconcile; yet reconciliation is a biblical mandate for estranged races/ethnic groups in Christianity. It will be costly, but should we work toward it? Most definitely! Reconciliation is at the heart of the biblical divine redemption. But true reconciliation occurs only we love each other. We must be reconciled in order to meet Jesus in peace. Hurts, wrongs, sins of the past must be forgiven. The Church needs to reconcile along racial and ethnic lines then we could leverage the power in the unity to make significant gains for Christ.

We need a new paradigm of governance without regard to race or ethnicity. A reconfiguration of the local conferences is in order. The Church must roll on militantly as one united body. With the vast immigration to the US in recent decades the demographics of the

SDAC has changed drastically. Non-whites now exceed Whites in the membership in the US and are projected to continue to grow at a much faster rate over the next few decades. Immigrants now form the majority of numerous state and regional conferences. They cannot be ignored any longer; they must be included in the conversation on this issue.

More importantly, we have a divine mandate to reconcile. Our ability to reconcile or remain unreconciled is reflective, not of the truth we possess but of the Truth which possesses us. Irrespective of the apparent gains that any race/ethnicity may have made since the divided governance structure was instituted, there is no justification for it. It is spiritually myopic to think that as a Church we could not have achieved more than the current accomplishments if we had reconciled. That research is showing that the religious people in the US society are more prone to practice racism is true. Yet that fact does not make it impossible to reconcile. The unity for which Christ prayed in Jn. 17 is not dependent on the research findings of social scientists or on any formula of humans; it is attainable only by the divine power of God. Christ would not have requested for us something which is unattainable by us. And to think that we cannot fix this problem and reconcile until Jesus returns suggests that we serve an impotent God. Finally, even amid the numerous existing and looming challenges, reconciliation is our only hope of escaping the final third Great Disappointment.

EPILOGUE

Growth in the SDAC is occurring most rapidly on the African continent. South America follows, with Asia next. Australia experiences a higher growth than both Europe and North America. Growth in Europe and North America is abysmal, except for growth by immigration. The countries where the SDAC currently has the largest or second largest Protestant denomination are Rwanda, New Guinea, Belize, Jamaica, and the Solomon Islands. Despite the genocide that took place in Rwanda in the 1990s Rwanda has been recovering and healing. Huge efforts have been undertaken to bring healing and reconciliation between the Tutsis and the Hutus. Since that time the church has grown to over 400,000 Adventists in Rwanda (ANN, 2010). All these regions have conferences that govern geographically, not racially.

None of these Divisions have unions or local conferences that are governed according to race/ethnicity, with the exception of North America Division (NAD) and one union in the Southern Africa Indian Ocean (SID) Division, that is, the SAU Conference. At the time of writing the decision to desegregate the local conferences in the SAU Conference is reached and the local conference restructuring is under way. That leaves the NAD as the only division in the SDAC with a segregate governance structure. *Is it any wonder then, that outside of the Trans-European Division, the NAD is experiencing the lowest rate of accession and the perhaps the highest rate of attrition?*

The above evidence of growth in these integrated areas of the Adventist mission field is a testament to the effectiveness of united governance and integrated congregations. While there may be other factors impacting growth, it is largely to be accounted for in the absence of segregation in governance and worship, which serve as obvious deterrents and turn-offs to prospective members.

In concluding this study, Christ's parable in Mt. 7:3-5 is instructive. In this parable Jesus depicted hypocrisy by telling the story of a man who had a log in his eye and was content with it, yet was overly concerned about his neighbor who had a mere speck in his eye. Obviously, Jesus chastised the former without exonerating the latter, because they both had a problem that needed their attention. This parable speaks to the situation at hand, as I juxtapose SAU Conference and the entire NAD, headquartered in the US. The SDAC in the US has the proverbial "log in its eye", but is ignoring it to this day, while for years now it has been reaching across the Ocean to extract the speck from Southern Africa's eye.

While it is necessary for the problem of racial/ethnic segregation to be fixed in Southern African, it is the more urgent for us to correct the behemoth in the NAD. The US and NAD are the places of the church's birth and the NAD has its headquarters in the same building as the GC. The GC exerted much pressure on the SAU and the SID to correct the problem of *apartheid* in the regional body of the church. And they did. Is the GC powerless in its relations to the NAD? Or are we interested in fixing the problem of racial/ethnic segregation in the church only in countries where the sovereign government has a Truth and Reconciliation Commission to which the SDAC is accountable?

One would expect the church to be more concerned about attaining righteousness than appeasing governments, albeit recognizing the need to be subject to the governing authorities of every country (Rom 13). This conduct on the part of the GC smacks of a double standard, however. When will this double standard if hypocrisy end? Who is holding the NAD accountable? We (membership) may be too powerful ("rich and increased with goods," [Rev. 3:17, KJV]) in the NAD to fall into the hands of men, but woe to us should we fall into the hand of God and it is too late to correct this sin. I submit that it will be bitterly disappointing. Should this ecclesial scourge persist, I am afraid that on the day of the Lord, many among the remnant, but not a part of the remnant (1 Jn. 2:18-19; Mt. 7:21-23), will awake on the day of resurrection to the Third Great Disappointment!

Excursus I

The Need for Race Reconciliation in the SDA Church in Rwanda, South Africa, and India

Rwanda:

The Rwandan genocide of 1994 left a horrible scar on the Christian church in Africa and the SDA was not left unscathed. These murders were committed for reason of hatred against another ethnic group, even though Christian. In a time of war, members of the SDAC abandoned their faith for their ethnicity. Over ten thousand Adventists were killed and several were apparently perpetrators of those murders. The Adventist News Network carried an article entitled—"Rwanda: Church Leader Talks Reconciliation, Unity." The article noted—

> "Twelve years ago the Seventh-day Adventist Church in Rwanda was thriving with some 285,000 members. But then came the spring of 1994 and more than 800,000 people were murdered during the first 100 days of the Rwanda genocide, including an estimated 10,000 Adventist church members. During the conflict, church affiliation became secondary to tribal designation." (*Philadelphia Enquirer, 1996; ANN, 2005*).

Among the perpetrators of these crimes were a SDA clergy, Pastor Elizaphan Ntakirutimana and his son, Gerard, a physician. After being extradited from Texas in the US, they were both convicted of aiding and abetting the genocide of thousands of Hutus and were sentenced to 10 and 25 years in prison respectively. The International Criminal Tribunal of Rwanda which convicted them, made a Press Release of the death of Elizaphan Ntakirutimana on January 23, 2007 at the age of 83, who was later released after serving the terms of his sentence (http://69.94.11.53/ENGLISH/PRESSREL/2007/512.htm). Since the genocide, the SDA Church has moved to bring reconciliation among the Tutsis and Hutus. Note this statement dated February 19, 2003 on the Adventist New network website—

> "Adventist world church leaders and the church in Rwanda have made reconciliation--both within the general community and among church membership-- one of their highest post-civil war priorities. In March 1998, a series of major "reconciliation conferences" were sponsored by the Adventist Church, and were aimed at promoting frank discussions and rebuilding trust between rival tribes. Adventist minister Esdras Mpyisi, once advisor to the former king of Rwanda, led out in the talks in which representatives from warring factions determined to work together toward mutual tolerance and understanding"
>
> (http://news.adventist.org/2003/02/rwaa-pastor-fou-guilty-by-u-tribual.html).

South Africa:

When the American missionaries first took the Advent message to South Africa they shared it only with the Whites. William Hunt, a disciple of John Loughborough, and a diamond-prospector entered the Southern Africa's Cape Colony in 1878 with the Advent faith. Two Dutch farmers, who had independently become convinced from their study of Scripture and a dream that Saturday was the Sabbath, came in contact with Hunt. Druten and his wife were the first, when on a Sabbath afternoon stroll they came upon Hunt studying the Bible instead of mining. Upon learning from Hunt that there was a Sabbath-keeping church organization in the U. S., they wrote and asked them to send a Dutch-speaking minister to teach more about the Bible. A party of seven missionaries was sent by the next July, but none could speak Dutch. They were concentrated in the Cape area among those of European descent and none worked among the African tribal people (Schwarz, 1979).

One among them, C. L. Boyd, by name, had an interest in reaching out to the Africans, but he received no support from his fellow missionaries because of his "'individualistic temperament'" (Schwarz, 1979). It would be many years before others would come along and take the Advent message to the African tribal people. The Church in South Africa moved back and forth between a united non-racialized structure and a racially divided one during the years 1902 to 1991. It was in 1925 that the first division into European, Colored, and Native occurred (Du Preez, 2010).

In 2006 Jeff Crocombe presented a paper at Oakwood University to the historical society of the Adventist Church on "The Seventh-day Adventist Church in Southern Africa—Race Relations and Apartheid." The study showed that the segregation in the Adventist Church there long preceded the legal system of apartheid. The segregation if oppression was not limited only to separate locales of worship and governance but also to ministerial function and compensation. Ordained Black pastors were disallowed from baptizing White members and had to stand back and allow White elders, even un-ordained White elders to do baptisms.

The Black members frequently contacted the leaders in the region and raised the awareness as to the goings on, but to no avail. Things remained unchanged for over forty years until the SAU Conference was placed under the direct jurisdiction of the GC in 1983. After the abolition of apartheid in 1990 the Truth and Reconciliation Commission (TRC) was formed to get faith communities to voluntarily come forward and desegregate their organizations. It was then that the GC exerted much pressure on the *Transvaal and Cape Conferences* to unite. Consequently, on December 10, 1991, 400 delegates from Lesotho, Namibia, and Swaziland came together at a joint constituency session at Helderberg College and voted to combine the two union conferences into a new united governance structure, the SAU Conference (Bediako, 1992). It took two years for them to formulate a statement to present to the TRC.

Even more exciting is the fact that by 1996 some local conferences had merged into one: the White and colored conference (Orange Natal Conference) joined with the Black Natal Field Conference to become the Natal Free State Conference (Adams, 1996). After uniting the Conferences in the Cape area in 2005, a 2006 combined constituency meeting to finalize the terms failed when the meeting was adjourned before the delegates could be seated. Twelve churches in the Transvaal Conference led by disgruntled members of the Cape Conference sued the SAU Conference for the 2005 action which enjoined on them a structure of governance led by the majority Black members. On September 8, 2009 the judged dismissed the case against the SAU's 2005 action and left the structure of the united governance intact (Du Preez, 2010).

The Statistics (1994) for the Southern Africa Union Conference: Conferences—*Cape Conference:* churches, 36; members, 3,757. Headquarters: Somerset West. *Good Hope Conference:* churches, 49; members, 7,359. Headquarters: Athlone. *Kwazulu-Natal Free State Conference:* churches, 72; members 4,457. Headquarters: Pinetown. *Southern Conference:* churches, 110; members, 13,940. Headquarters: Mdantsane. *Trans-Orange Conference:* churches, 146; members, 13,694. Headquarters: Johannesburg. Transvaal Conference: churches, 69; members, 8,158. Headquarters: Bedford Gardens (Neufeld, 2002).

The current conferences in 2010 are: Cape Conference, Kwazulu Free State Conference, Lesotho Conference, Namibia Field, Swaziland Conference, Trans-Oranje Conference, and Transvaal Conference.

India The first Adventist missionaries entered India in 1890. S. N. Haskell and P. T. Morgan crossed into India on a mission survey journey around the world. In 1893, two colporteurs, William Lenker and A. T. Stroup arrived in Madras and began canvassing for subscription books. By Lenker's account, a "faithful worker," an Adventist sister, Anna P. Gordon had been there nearly a year before they arrived. The work grew with remarkable success in the early years with the help of the colporteurs, missionaries, educational and health institutions (Neufeld, 1996).

A recent blog indicates that in India the SDA Church and other Evangelical denominations recently baptized thousands of Dalits ("the Untouchables"), who were excited about the message of a God who accepted everyone as equals. After they became members of the local churches, and realized that they were just as prejudiced as the Hindus, some 300 families of them returned to Hinduism. It has been reported that even the Christian cemeteries are segregated with the Dalits placed by themselves.

EXCURSUS II

(A document from the website of the Office of Regional Ministries)

THE FOLLOWING THREE INSERTS ARE COPIES OF DOCUMENTS REFLECTING THE ACTIONS TAKEN BY THE GENERAL CONFERENCE TO ENSURE RACIAL TOLERANCE AND FAIR REPRESENTATION IN ALL SEVENTH-DAY ADVENTIST CHURCHES AND ORGANIZATONS WITHIN THE UNITED STATES.

REGIONAL CONFERENCES AND HUMAN RELATIONS – 16 POINTS
16 POINTS: VOTED AT GENERAL CONFERENCE ANNUAL COUNCIL – APRIL 2, 1970
13 POINTS: (REVISED) AD HOC COMMITTEE – JULY 28, 1981
11 POINTS: (REVISED) PRE-COUNCIL OF UNION PRESIDENTS, NAD & GC OFFICERS – SEPTEMBER 28, 1981

1. Seventh-day Adventist churches open their doors to any would-be worshipper or prospective member regardless of race or color and welcome such with brotherly love and concern. Where it is felt that this principle is violated it is the duty of the next higher organization to investigate and recommend effective measures to correct.

2. The following additions to the baptismal vow and Church Manual are being recommended to the General Conference session: 6) All who enter the kingdom of heaven must have experienced conversion, or the new birth, through which man receives a new heart and becomes a new creature. Thus, regardless of ethnic or social background, he becomes a member of the 'whole family in Heaven and earth.'" (Matt. 13:3; John 3:3; 2 Cor. 5:17; Eze.

36:26, 27; Heb. 8:10-12; 1 Peter 1:23, 2:2; Eph. 3:15; Acts 17:26.) 13) Do you believe that the Seventh-day Adventist church is the remnant church of prophecy into which people of every nation, race and language are invited and accepted, and do you desire membership in its fellowship? At an appropriate time during this session a forthright statement should be made by the leadership of the Church dealing with and giving support to the position of the Church on race relations.

3. Conferences selecting qualified spiritual leaders as pastors shall not be limited by race or color. Should some black pastors be appointed to white churches and some white pastors appointed to black churches, a very desirable example of church fellowship and understanding would result; therefore, programs to this end should be undertaken with the support and guidance of unions

4. In order to make our public ministry more effective and to help members and potential members realize the importance of this brotherhood, conference administrators are urged to make clear to pastors and evangelists that it is their duty to teach these principles as a part of the gospel and our special message for the world. We further recommend that prospective members be so instructed either in the baptismal class or in personal Bible studies.

5. Special emphasis should be given to human relations workshops to implement resolutions which unless carried out, are useless. These workshops should include all workers-field, educational and institutional, and leading laymen from both black and white conferences and churches. It is recommended that and / or conference-wide human relations workshops be conducted in every union in North America before the 1971 Autumn Council.

6. Where normal entrance requirements are met, all Seventh-day Adventist schools from elementary to the university level shall admit Seventh-day Adventist youth to the school of their choice without regard to race or color. Where a church supported school fails to follow the counsel of the Church as stated to this

point, it is the duty of the next higher organization to investigate and recommend corrective measures.

7. A bi-racial commission of not more than 7 members shall be appointed in the North American Division to deal with complaints of discrimination or exclusion and other problems that arise in the area of race relations that may be appealed to it for help. This commission in cooperation and in counsel with the union conferences and/or local conference and/or the institution shall have authority to act immediately, making a thorough investigation and seeking solutions to these problems.

8. On the union conference level positive steps should be taken to open doors in the area of administrative and departmental leadership for those who have demonstrated their ability and qualifications to serve all segments of the Church. In unions where there are Regional Conferences or where there is an organized Regional Department, the administrative officer level should include black leadership.

9. Black personnel shall be selected to serve in our publishing houses, hospitals, academies, colleges, universities and other denominational institutions on the staff and/or administrative levels. Where it seems advisable institutions should institute training programs for the development of black personnel in technical and administrative skills.

10. There is a missionary magazine dedicated to the black community in North America. The circulation of this journal is primarily the responsibility of the Regional churches. The Autumn Council of 1967 voted to help finance a black circulation manager for Message Magazine. We reaffirm that recommendation on the basis of the 1967 agreement on union participation and ask that this be implemented in the immediate future.

11. At the time of the annual North American Union Conference Presidents' meetings one or more black administrators on the union level will be invited to participate as well as representation from the Regional Department of the General Conference.

12. In order to provide opportunity for the presidents of Regional Conferences (including the secretary of the Regional Department of the Pacific Union) to consult together regarding problems distinctive to their work, Autumn Councils will schedule two meetings of this group each year, under North American Division leadership, in conjunction with other regularly called meetings. When additional meetings are required such would be arranged by the North American Division administration.

13. The next edition of the Ministers' Manual should include as a part of the ministerial candidates examination before ordination questions regarding the candidate's attitude toward human relations.

14. We recommend that the General Conference lay plans to provide literature that would be useful in operating human relations workshops, setting forth standards, guidelines and procedures in this area.

15. We recommend that the General Conference officers develop some plan whereby reports of progress in human relations may be publicized throughout the constituency in North America on local as well as general levels.

16. We recommend the adoption in principle of the following plan of financial relationships involving Regional work.

AD HOC SIXTEEN POINTS REVISION COMMITTEE JULY 28, 1981
REGIONAL CONFERENCES AND HUMAN RELATIONS – 13 POINTS

After discussion, the following revisions of the Sixteen Points were recommended:

1. Seventh-day Adventist Churches open their doors to any would-be worshipper or prospective member regardless of race or color and welcome such with brotherly love and concern. Where it is felt that this principle is violated it is the duty of

the next higher organization to investigate and recommend effective measures to correct.

2. Conferences selecting qualified spiritual leaders as pastors should not be limited to race or color. A very desirable example of Christian brotherhood would be exhibited if pastors of black and other ethnic groups would be appointed to white churches and white pastors would be appointed to churches of black and other ethnic groups; therefore programs to this end should be undertaken with the support and guidance of unions.

3. In order to make our public ministry more effective and to help members and potential members realize the importance of this brotherhood, conference administrators are urged to make clear to pastors and evangelists that it is their duty to teach these principles as a part of the gospel and our special message for the world. We further recommend that prospective members be so instructed through personal Bible studies and in the baptismal class.

4. Special emphasis should be given to human relations workshops to implement resolutions which, unless carried out are useless. These workshops should include black, white and other minority educational, field, and institutional workers and leading laymen from all churches and conferences. This should be done on a continuing basis.

5. Where normal entrance requirements are met, all Seventh-day Adventist schools from elementary to the university level shall admit Seventh-day Adventist youth to the school of their choice without regard to race, color or ethnic background. Where church supported school fails to follow the counsel of the Church as stated on this point, it is the duty of the next higher organization to investigate and recommend corrective measures.

6. A multi-racial commission shall be appointed in the North American Division to deal with complaints of discrimination or exclusion and other problems that arise in the area of racial, cultural and ethnic relations. This commission, in cooperation and in counsel with the union conferences and/or local conferences and/or the institution shall have authority to act

immediately, making a thorough investigation and seeking solutions to these problems.

7. On the union conference level positive steps should be taken to open doors in the area of administrative and departmental leadership for those who have demonstrated their ability and qualifications to serve all segments of the church. The union administrative and departmental staffs should reflect the racial or ethnic composition of the union constituency. In unions where there are regional conferences or where there is a regional department, the administrative officer level should include black leadership. This principle should apply to other ethnic groups that have large constituencies.

8. Black and other minority personnel shall be selected to serve in our publishing houses, hospitals, academies, colleges, universities and other departmental institutions on the staff and/or administrative levels. Where is seems advisable, institutions should institute training programs for the development of black personnel and other minority personnel in technical and administrative skills.

9. There is a missionary magazine dedicated to the black community in North America. The circulation of this journal is primarily the responsibility of the Regional churches. This principle should apply to other ethnic missionary journals.

10. At the time of the annual North American Union Conference Presidents' Councils, one or more Black, as well as Hispanic leaders on the General Conference or union level should be invited to participate.

11. In order to provide opportunity for the presidents of Regional Conferences (including the secretary of the Regional Department of the Pacific Union and North Pacific Union) to consult together regarding problems distinctive to their work, Autumn Councils will schedule two meetings of this group each year, under North American Division leadership, in conjunction with other regularly called meetings. When additional meetings are required such would be arranged by the North American

Division administration. A similar arrangement should be developed for the Spanish Advisory.

12. We recommend that the General Conference lay plans to provide literature that would be useful in operating human relations workshops, setting forth standards, guidelines, and procedures in this area.

13. We recommend that the General Conference Officers develop some plan whereby reports of progress in human relations may be publicized throughout the constituency in North America on local as well as general levels.

REGIONAL CONFERENCES AND HUMAN RELATIONS – 11 POINTS

(Revised) Voted by the North American Division Annual Council October 6-14, 1981-Regional Conferences and Human Relations – Cross Cultural administrative Guidelines.

VOTED, To adopt human relations and cross-cultural administrative guidelines as follows:

1. Seventh-day Adventist churches to welcome to any would-be worshipper or prospective member with brotherly love and concern regardless of race or color. Where is felt that this principle is violated it is the duty of the next higher organization to investigate and recommend corrective measures.

2. Conferences considering qualified spiritual leaders as pastors are to select the best qualified individuals and not limit themselves to candidates of a particular race or color. A very desirable example of Christian brotherhood is exhibited when pastors of Black and other ethnic groups are appointed to Caucasian churches and Caucasian pastors are appointed to churches of Black and other ethnic groups. The Union Conferences are to give support and guidance to programs to achieve the above conditions.

3. In order to make public ministry more effective and to help members and potential members realize the importance of this

brotherhood, conference administrators are urged to make clear to pastors and evangelists that it is their duty to teach these principles as a part of the gospel and the special Adventist message for the world. Prospective members are to be so instructed through personal Bible studies and in the baptismal class.

4. Special emphasis is to be given to the conducting of human relations workshops that are to implement these guidelines which, unless carried out, are useless. These workshops are to include Blacks, Caucasians and various minorities, and are to consist of workers from the educational, ministerial, and institutional fields and leading laymen from all churches conferences. This is to be done on a continuing basis.

5. Where normal entrance requirements are met, all Seventh-day Adventist schools from elementary to the university level shall admit Seventh-day Adventist youth to the school of their choice without regard to race, color or ethnic background. Where church-supported school fails to follow the counsel of the Church as stated on this point, it is the duty of the next higher organization to investigate and recommend corrective measures.

6. On the union conference level, positive steps are to be taken to open the doors in the area of administrative and departmental leadership for those who have demonstrated their ability and qualifications to serve all segments of the Church. The union administrative and departmental staffs are to reflect the racial and ethnic composition of the union constituency. In unions where there are regional conferences or where there is a regional department, the administrative officer level should include black leadership. This principle should apply to other ethnic groups that have large constituencies.

7. Black and other minority personnel are to be selected to serve on the staff and administrative levels of Adventist publishing houses, hospitals, academies, colleges, universities and other institutions. Where there is a regional department, the administrative officer level should include black leadership.

This principle is to apply also to other ethnic groups that have large constituencies.

8. At the time of the North American Union Conference Presidents' meetings, one or more Black, as well as Hispanic leaders, on the General Conference or union levels are to be invited to participate.

9. In order to provide opportunity for the presidents of Regional Conferences (including Secretary of the Regional Departments of the Pacific Union and North Pacific Union) to consult together regarding problems distinctive to their work, Autumn Council is to schedule two meetings of this group each year, under North American Division leadership, in conjunction with other regularly called meetings. When additional meetings are required such are to be arranged by the North American Division administration. A similar arrangement should be developed for Asian and Spanish Advisories.

10. The General Conference is to lay plans to provide literature that would be useful in operating human relations workshops and setting forth standards, guidelines and procedures in this area.

11. The General Conference Officers are to develop plans whereby reports of progress in human relations may be publicized to the constituency in North America on local as well as general levels.

Throughout the world, the work of the Lord in the Seventh-day Adventist Church has grown significantly when leadership was put into the hands of the indigenous people. Putting leadership of the work for Black people in the United States under the direction of Regional Conferences sixty-three years ago has borne rich fruit. Since that time the membership has increased from 17,000 and is approaching the 330,000 mark.

These blessings have come as the respective Union Conferences and the North American Division leadership of the General Conference made accommodations for the successful growth and development of Regional Conferences. We praise God for the success we have enjoyed for it has only been by His might and power that these things have come to pass. Today we remain spiritually and organizationally joined together in unity with all entities of the Seventh-day Adventist Church. And together all of us remain determined that as one mighty army under God and with the power of the Holy Ghost, "this Gospel of the kingdom shall be preached in all the world for a witness unto all nations and then shall the end come." (Regional Conferences , 2020)

EXCURSUS III

Denominational Reconciliation in the
Evangelical Movement in the US

The Presbyterian Church

PCA Position Papers

30th General Assembly, 2002, 30-53, III,
Items 14 - 16, pp. 262 - 270.

RACIAL RECONCILIATION

14. That Overture 20 from Nashville Presbytery ("Racial Reconciliation") **be answered by the adoption of the following statement**. *Adopted.*

Whereas, the heinous sins attendant with unbiblical forms of servitude-including oppression, racism, exploitation, man-stealing, and chattel slavery-stand in opposition to the Gospel; and,

Whereas, the effects of these sins have created and continue to create barriers between brothers and sisters of different races and/or economic spheres; and

Whereas, the aftereffects of these sins continue to be felt in the economic, cultural, and social affairs of the communities in which we live and minister;

We therefore confess our involvement in these sins. As a people, both we and our fathers, have failed to keep the commandments, the statutes, and the laws God has commanded. We therefore publicly repent of our pride, our complacency, and our complicity. Furthermore, we seek the forgiveness of our brothers and sisters for the reticence of our hearts that have constrained us from acting swiftly in this matter.

We will strive, in a manner consistent with the Gospel imperatives, for the encouragement of racial reconciliation, the establishment of urban and minority congregations, and the enhancement of existing ministries of mercy in our cities, among the poor, and across all social, racial, and economic boundaries, to the glory of God. Amen.

Note:
The Presbyterian Church in America participated in addressing the question of racial reconciliation as early as 1977, through her delegation to the NAPARC conference on race relations, and the resulting statement adopted. That statement achieved a "consensus on a number of crucial issues" and it began by confessing serious inadequacies with respect to NAPARC member churches concerning race relations in the church:

We are convinced that we, as Reformed Christians, have failed to speak and act boldly in the area of race relations. Our denominational profiles reveal patterns of ethnic and racial homogeneity. We believe that this situation fails to give adequate expression to the saving purposes of our sovereign God, whose covenant extends to all peoples and races. We are convinced that our record in this crucial area is one of racial brokenness and disobedience. In such a situation the credibility of our Reformed witness, piety and doctrinal confession is at stake. We have not lived out the implications of that biblical and confessional heritage which we hold in common with each other, with its emphasis on the sovereignty and freedom of grace, on the absence of human merit in gaining salvation, and on the responsibility to subject all of life to the Lordship of Christ.

The statement continued with a summary of faithful biblical teaching adapted to address the defects confessed above:

Although there are marked distinctions and even divisions among men, including those of race, mankind, according to the teaching of the Bible, has a single origin. Later distinctions and divisions are indeed significant and may not simply be pushed aside; nevertheless, the Bible clearly teaches that the gospel is universal in its offer and its call. All men are created in the image of God and have fallen into sin, and are in need of redemption. All those who are in Christ are united together with Him as their Head in a new humanity, in which the distinctions and divisions that otherwise separate men are transcended in a new unity. True, the distinctions mentioned in the Bible as having been overcome in Christ are not primarily those of race, nor does the Bible think along lines that correspond with the distinctions of race as we understand them today; nevertheless, racial distinctions and divisions as we know and understand them today certainly fall under those things that have been transcended in Christ. How, then, is the new unity in Christ to be expressed in the communion of the church today as it bears on the question of race?

The description of God's people in I Peter 2:9, 10, as a chosen generation, a royal priesthood, a holy nation, reveals the church's visible oneness as the community of those separated into the Lord. It is a oneness on the order of the racial, cultic, and national unity of Israel (Exodus 19:6), and it has as its purpose the declaration of the wonderful works of God. Therefore, the church's identity transcends and makes of secondary importance the racial, national and cultic identities of the world.

We see in Revelation 7:9, 10, the chosen race worshiping the Lamb in heaven. They come from different backgrounds, yet worship with one voice. Is not the unity of our worship here on earth to be a copy of that which takes place within the heavenly sanctuary? Should not all those washed in the blood of the Lamb joyously worship together?

In the light of such scriptural teaching, the statement continued in the acknowledgement of sin on the part of the member churches:

In repentance we acknowledge and confess that we have failed effectively to recognize the full humanity of other races and the similarity of their needs, desires, and hopes to ours; and thus we have failed to love our neighbor as ourselves... Within the church, our members have exhibited such attitudes and actions as discourage membership or participation by minority groups... Our churches have not been free from such formal actions as discourage membership or participation by minority groups. They have been guilty of a lack of positive action concerning mission to ethnic groups in their own neighborhoods and to ethnic groups at large. They have practiced a kind of cultural exclusivism, thinking of the church as "our church" rather than Christ's. This involves the sins of pride and idolatry.

Yet the statement was able to acknowledge the work of grace evident in this matter, particularly in the seminaries that serve the PCA:

We commend ... Westminster Theological Seminary for its ministerial institute, which intends to assist inner-city pastors in their continued training in ministry and Covenant Theological. Seminary for its Urban Ministers' Institute.....

The statement concluded with a number of exhortations, among which are included:

We encourage congregations to reach out to the entire community around them.

We encourage congregations to rise to meet the challenge of racial diversity in changing neighborhoods.

We encourage members of our congregations to remain in those communities where there are racially changing patterns.

We acknowledge that in order to change our unbiblical profile, we should urge churches in NAPARC to give priority to a vigorous pursuit of evangelism and church planting in racially, economically, and ethnically diverse communities....

In reaffirming the great commission, we recommend ... that cross-cultural evangelism be encouraged in our churches through preaching, modeling, and discipling, through the elders and pastors, beginning with the use of our covenant families and homes, and house-to-house neighborhood outreach.

OVERTURE 20 from Nashville Presbytery (to B&O) "Racial Reconciliation"

Whereas, the Scriptures portray a covenantal pattern of both celebration of our rich heritage and repentance for the sins of our fathers; and,

Whereas, our nation has been blessed even as we have repeatedly addressed iniquity, redressed injustice, and assessed restitution for our inconsistent application of the ideals of truth and freedom; and,

Whereas, the heinous sins attendant with unbiblical forms of servitude-including oppression, racism, exploitation, man-stealing, and chattel slavery-remain among the defining features of our national history; and,

Whereas, the issues surrounding that part of our history continue to shape our national life, even creating barriers between brothers and sisters of different races and/or economic spheres from enjoying unencumbered Christian fellowship with one another; and,

Whereas, the aftereffects of that part of our history continue to be felt in the economic, cultural, and social affairs of the communities in which we live and minister;

We therefore confess our covenantal involvement in these national sins. As a people, both we and our fathers have failed to keep the commandments, the statutes, and the laws our God has commanded. We therefore publicly repent of our pride, our complacency, and our complicity. Furthermore, we seek the forgiveness of our brothers and sisters for the reticence of our hearts, which has constrained us from acting swiftly in this matter.

As a people, we pledge to work hard, in a manner consistent with the Gospel imperatives, for the encouragement of racial reconciliation, the establishment of urban and minority congregations, and the enhancement of existing ministries of mercy in our cities, among the poor, and across all social, racial, and economic boundaries, to the glory of God. Amen.

15. That Personal Resolution 6 be answered by reference to the Assembly's action with regard to Overture 20. [See 30-53, III, 14, p. 261.] *Adopted.*

Whereas, the Presbyterian Church in America was formed to preach and teach the truth of God's Word with the desire that its members would practice and live by the truth and as we are a young denomination meeting together for our 30`h Annual General Assembly, we want to thank God for the enabling grace to do this as well as we have done it and confess that when and where we have failed it is our fault and because of our sin; and

Whereas, we acknowledge that corporately as a denomination and individually as members of the Presbyterian Church in America we have sinned, (Romans 3:23), and

Whereas, we acknowledge that along with our many other sins, we may have corporately or individually sinned by slighting or offending a brother in Christ, and we as the people of God are called on in Scripture to repent of our sins as God reveals them to us by His Holy Spirit (Rev. 3:19, Acts 16:19-20, Luke 5:32, & II Cor. 7:10); and

Whereas, we recognize that each one of us must repent for our own sins as God holds each of us accountable for them (Ezekiel 18:20, Romans 14:12, Jeremiah 31:2930, Deuteronomy 24:16), and

Whereas, we also recognize that Scripture establishes precedents for the confession of the past sins of others without assessing personal responsibility for those past sins to the confessing party (Neh. 1:5-7, Neh. 9:13, Daniel 9:4-19), and

Whereas, we recognize the dangers of sins of omission as being grave as those of the sins of commission (James 4:17, Psalm 51:16-17, Proverbs 21:3, Luke 12:47), and

Whereas, God's Word warns strongly against mistreating or not loving a Christian brother (I Corinthians 6:8, I Thessalonians 4:6, James 4:11-12), and

Whereas, we recognize that some have in the past, by commission and/or by omission, offended and slighted their brothers and sisters in Christ (I John 1:8-10), and

Whereas, we desire that all members of the Presbyterian Church in America conduct themselves first as the people of God - without favoritism, prejudice or partiality (Leviticus 19:15 & I Timothy 5:21), and

Whereas, we desire that all members of the Presbyterian Church in America not only show love for their brothers but that they actually have love for their brothers in their hearts (I John 4:21, Hebrews 13:1, Psalm 133:1 & John 13:34-35), and

Whereas, we desire the blessings of God Almighty upon the work of our churches and of our denomination, and fear His withholding those blessings due to a lack of personal repentance for sins committed against our brothers in the Lord (Proverbs 10:22 & Proverbs 24:23-25), and

Whereas, we want as a denomination and as individuals the blessings of being used of God to see souls saved and the work of His kingdom furthered therefore we strive to be obedient to God; and

Whereas, we recognize the need for the work of the kingdom to progress wherever the descendants of Adam are to be found and desire the work of the kingdom to grow as the lost are saved (Matthew 28:18-20 & Acts 1:8),

Therefore, we--the undersigned do humbly ask this 30th General Assembly of the Presbyterian Church in America to resolve,

That, every member, Teaching Elder, and Ruling Elder in the Presbyterian Church in America be urged to examine themselves in the light of Scripture and by the leading of God's indwelling Holy Spirit to determine if there be any unrepented of and unconfessed sins of partiality, favoritism, or prejudice (Lam. 3:40 & II Cor. 13:5), and

That, if any such sins be discovered, either present or past, that these sins be admitted to and forgiveness sought from God and from those brothers so sinned against (Matt 5:23-24), and

That, the Presbyterian Church in America, at the denominational, local church, and personal levels, be encouraged to continue and/or begin to search out the lost wherever they are and lovingly and powerfully proclaim the gospel of Jesus Christ in culturally relevant and meaningful ways as God leads by His Holy Spirit and gives the wisdom to understand (II Tim 4:5 & I Peter 3:15-16), and

That, the Presbyterian Church in America seek to lead the way denominationally in racial reconciliation, regardless of color or ethnic background, for the sake of the Body of Christ and for the glory of God (Col. 3:23-24 & I Cor. 10:31-11:1).

16. That **Personal Resolution #2** be answered in the **affirmative**. *Adopted.*

Whereas, in the Great Commission of our Lord Jesus Christ commanded the church to "Go and make disciples of all the nations" (Matthew 28:18), and

Whereas, the theme of this 30th General Assembly is "Equipping the Saints - Evangelizing the Nations", and

Whereas, God's providence has now brought those from every nation to our very doorsteps, and

Whereas, amongst the responsibilities of the General Assembly are "carrying out the Great Commission" (BCO 14-1) "to devise measures for promoting the prosperity and enlargement of the church" (BCO 146.d.), and "to recommend measures for the promotion of charity, truth and holiness through all the churches under its care" (BCO 14-6.k.), and

Whereas, our mother church, the Presbyterian Church in the United Stated ("Southern church"), in 1865, in response to an inquiry concerning the appropriateness of the races worshipping together, expressed the hope that the rich fellowship such united worship in the past would continue, concluding "we see no reason why it should be otherwise" (from E. T. Thompson, Presbyterians in the South, Vol. II, p. 209),

Now Therefore, this 30th General Assembly of the Presbyterian Church in America calls up all those under its care to search their hearts before the Triune God, who is "no respecter of persons" (Acts 10:34), and to repent of and renounce any racism and/or class-consciousness, and

Further, this Assembly encourages its local churches to make known that the doors to its worship and the arms of its fellowship are open to warmly welcome all persons without regard to race, class or national origin, and that it welcomes into its membership all who, according to Book of Church Order Chapter 57 (and any general provisions including those regarding discipline) come with a credible profession of their faith in the Great King and Head of the Church and Savior of the body, the Lord Jesus Christ (http://www.pcahistory.org/pca/race.html).

The Southern Baptist Church

Resolution On Racial Reconciliation On The 150th Anniversary Of The Southern Baptist Convention
June 1995

WHEREAS, Since its founding in 1845, the Southern Baptist Convention has been an effective instrument of God in missions, evangelism, and social ministry; and

WHEREAS, The Scriptures teach that Eve is the mother of all living (Genesis 3:20), and that God shows no partiality, but in every nation whoever fears him and works righteousness is accepted by him (Acts 10:34-35), and that God has made from one blood every nation of men to dwell on the face of the earth (Acts 17:26); and

WHEREAS, Our relationship to African-Americans has been hindered from the beginning by the role that slavery played in the formation of the Southern Baptist Convention; and

WHEREAS, Many of our Southern Baptist forbears defended the right to own slaves, and either participated in, supported, or acquiesced in the particularly inhumane nature of American slavery; and

WHEREAS, In later years Southern Baptists failed, in many cases, to support, and in some cases opposed, legitimate initiatives to secure the civil rights of African-Americans; and

WHEREAS, Racism has led to discrimination, oppression, injustice, and violence, both in the Civil War and throughout the history of our nation; and WHEREAS, Racism has divided the body of Christ and Southern Baptists in particular, and separated us from our African-American brothers and sisters; and

WHEREAS, Many of our congregations have intentionally and/or unintentionally excluded African-Americans from worship, membership, and leadership; and

WHEREAS, Racism profoundly distorts our understanding of Christian morality, leading some Southern Baptists to believe that racial prejudice and discrimination are compatible with the Gospel; and WHEREAS, Jesus performed the ministry of reconciliation to restore sinners to a right relationship with the Heavenly Father, and to establish right relations among all human beings, especially within the family of faith.

Therefore, be it RESOLVED, That we, the messengers to the Sesquicentennial meeting of the Southern Baptist Convention, assembled in Atlanta, Georgia, June 20-22, 1995, unwaveringly denounce racism, in all its forms, as deplorable sin; and

Be it further RESOLVED, That we affirm the Bibles teaching that every human life is sacred, and is of equal and immeasurable worth, made in Gods image, regardless of race or ethnicity (Genesis 1:27), and that, with respect to salvation through Christ, there is neither Jew nor Greek, there is neither slave nor free, there is neither male nor female, for (we) are all one in Christ Jesus (Galatians 3:28); and Be it further RESOLVED, That we lament and repudiate historic acts of evil such as slavery from which we continue to reap a bitter harvest, and we recognize that the racism which yet plagues our culture today is inextricably tied to the past; and

Be it further RESOLVED, That we apologize to all African-Americans for condoning and/or perpetuating individual and systemic racism in our lifetime; and we genuinely repent of racism of which we have been guilty, whether consciously (Psalm 19:13) or unconsciously (Leviticus 4:27); and Be it further RESOLVED, That we ask forgiveness from our African-American brothers and sisters, acknowledging that our own healing is at stake; and

Be it further RESOLVED, That we hereby commit ourselves to eradicate racism in all its forms from Southern Baptist life and ministry; and

Be it further RESOLVED, That we commit ourselves to be doers of the Word (James 1:22) by pursuing racial reconciliation in all our relationships, especially with our brothers and sisters in Christ (1 John 2:6), to the end that our light would so shine before others, that they may see (our) good works and glorify (our) Father in heaven (Matthew 5:16); and

Be it finally RESOLVED, That we pledge our commitment to the Great Commission task of making disciples of all people (Matthew 28:19), confessing that in the church God is calling together one people from every tribe and nation (Revelation 5:9), and proclaiming that the Gospel of our Lord Jesus Christ is the only certain and sufficient ground upon which redeemed persons will stand together in restored family union as joint-heirs with Christ (Romans 8:17). [http://www.sbc.net/resolutions/amResolution.asp?ID=899]

Seventh-day Adventist Church Membership/Territory by Division

As of October 2010 the worldwide work was divided by territories according to the thirteen Divisions shown below and presided over by the following individuals:

> East-Central Africa Division, Blasious M. Ruguri.
> Euro-Africa Division, Bruno R. Vertallier.
> Euro-Asia Division, Guillermo E. Biaggi.
> Inter-American Division, Israel Leito.
> North American Division, Daniel R. Jackson.
> Northern Asia-Pacific Division, Jairyong Lee.
> South American Division, Erton Carlos Kohler.
> South Pacific Division, Barry D. Oliver.
> Southern Africa-Indian Ocean Division, Paul S. Ratsara.

Southern Asia Division, John Rathinaraj.
Southern Asia-Pacific Division, Alberto C. Gulfan Jr.
Trans-European Division, Bertil A. Wiklander.
West-Central Africa Division, Gilbert Wari.

East-Central Africa Division

Territory: Burundi, Democratic Republic of Congo, Eritrea, Ethiopia, Kenya, Republic of Djibouti, Rwanda, Somalia, Uganda, and the United Republic of Tanzania; comprising the East African, East Congo, Ethiopian, Rwanda, Tanzania, Uganda, and West Congo Union Missions; Eritrea Mission Field, Burundi Association, and the North East Congo Attached Territory.

With 10, 893 churches and a membership of 2,502,982, this is one of the largest memberships of any division. The church is growing rapidly in this division. For each of the last six years this division had baptisms of over 145,000 converts. None of these countries currently have union or local conferences that are divided according to race (Adventist Archives, 2010).

Euro-Africa Division

Territory: Afghanistan, Algeria, Andorra, Austria, Belgium, Bulgaria, Czech Republic, France, Germany, Gibraltar, Holy See, Iran, Italy, Libyan Arab Jamahiriya, Liechtenstein, Luxembourg, Malta, Monaco, Morocco, Portugal, Romania, San Marino, Slovakia, Spain, Switzerland, Tunisia, Turkey, and Western Sahara; comprising the Czecho-Slovakian, Franco-Belgian, North German, Romanian, South German, and Swiss Union Conferences, the Austrian, Bulgarian, Italian, Portuguese, and Spanish Union of Churches Conferences, and the Trans-Mediterranean Territories.

The Euro-Africa Division currently has 2530 with a membership of 176,247 in a population of 596,017,000.

East Asia Division

Territory: Armenia, Azerbaijan, Belarus, Georgia, Kazakhstan, Kyrgyzstan, Republic of Moldova, Russian Federation, Tajikistan, Turkmenistan, Ukraine, and Uzbekistan; comprising the Southern, Ukrainian, and West Russian Union Conferences; the Caucasus, East Russian, and Trans-Caucasus Union Missions; the Belarus, and Moldova Union of Churches Conferences; and the Far Eastern Union of Churches Mission.

The membership in this Division currently is 138,827 with 1,966 churches serving a population of 279,459,000.

Let us take an unscientific look at the effect of a united governance structure and worship setting in other parts of the world. The regions in which the remnant is growing by leaps and bounds are all integrated. Case in point, Inter-America, for decades the fasting growing division of the Church, is fully integrated at the local conference and local church levels.

Inter-America Division

Territory: Anguilla, Antigua and Barbuda, Aruba, Bahamas, Barbados, Belize, British Virgin Islands, Cayman Islands, Colombia, Costa Rica, Cuba, Dominica, Dominican Republic, El Salvador, French Guiana, Grenada, Guadeloupe, Guatemala, Guyana, Haiti, Honduras, Jamaica, Martinique, Mexico, Montserrat, Netherlands Antilles, Nicaragua, Panama, Puerto Rico, Saint Kitts and Nevis, Saint Lucia, Saint Vincent and the Grenadines, Suriname, Trinidad and Tobago, Turks and Caicos Islands, United States Virgin Islands, and Venezuela (Bolivarian Republic of); comprising the Caribbean, Colombian, Cuban, North Mexican, Puerto Rican, South Central American, South Mexican, and West Indies Union Conferences; the Central Mexican, Dominican, French Antilles-Guiana, Guatemala, Haitian, Inter-Oceanic Mexican, Mid-Central

American, and Venezuela-Antilles Union Missions; and the Belize Union of Churches Mission.

This Division currently has 10, 145 churches and a membership of 3,232,946, and serves a population of 268,528,000 collectively. The church in the Inter America Division is governed geographically in the various countries. None of the conferences in Central or South America currently have a racially divided governance structure. This Division has had the largest Adventist membership for decades and was for many years the fastest growing division in the SDAC.

Earlier in the development of the work, Ellen White called for a re-organization. Around 1901 she counseled the GC—"What we want now is reorganization. We want to begin at the foundation and to build upon a different principle" (Olson, 1986)… The leaders heeded her counsel and organized union conferences and union missions all over the world where it was advisable based on the staff workers. This has proven to be very advantageous to the work. She later admonished the Church that the decision to segregate was not the right one (**Southern Work, 1900?**)

North American Division

Territory: Bermuda, Canada, the French possession of Saint Pierre and Miquelon, the United States of America, Johnston Island, Midway Islands, and all other islands of the Pacific not attached to other divisions and bounded by the date line on the west, by the equator on the south, and by longitude 120 on the east; comprising the Atlantic, Seventh-day Adventist Church in Canada, Columbia, Lake, Mid-America, North Pacific, Pacific, Southern, and Southwestern Union Conferences.

The North American Division is the birthplace of the Adventist Church and currently hosts its headquarters in Silver Springs, Maryland. Presently this division has 5,243 churches and boasts a membership of 1.090,217 in a population of 340,583,000.

Northern Asia-Pacific Division

Territory: Democratic People's Republic of Korea, Japan, Mongolia, People's Republic of China including Hong Kong and Macao Special Administrative Regions, Republic of Korea, and Taiwan; comprising the Japan and Korean Union Conferences, the Chinese Union Mission, and the Mongolia Mission Field.

The Division has 1972 churches, 609,623 members, and a population of 1,563,757,000.

Southern Asia Division

Territory: Bhutan, India, the Maldives, and Nepal; comprising the East-Central India, Northeast India, Northern India, South-Central India, Southeast India, Southwest India, and Western India Union Sections; the Andaman and Nicobar Island Region, and the Nepal Field.

The Division has 3,798 churches, 1,461,894 members in a population of 1,199,531,000.

Southern Asia-Pacific Division

Territory: Bangladesh, Brunei Darussalam, Cambodia, Indonesia, Lao People's Democratic Republic, Malaysia, Myanmar, Philippines, Singapore, Sri Lanka, Thailand, Timor-Leste, Viet Nam, and islands of the Pacific, namely the United States territories of Guam and Wake Island, the Federated States of Micronesia, Marshall Islands, Northern Mariana Islands, and Palau; comprising the Central Philippine, East Indonesia, North Philippine, and South Philippine Union Conferences; the Bangladesh, Myanmar, Southeast Asia, and West Indonesia Union Missions; the Guam-Micronesia, and Sri Lanka Missions of Seventh-day Adventists; and the East Timor Attached Field.

This Division has 6399 churches, a membership of 996,198 serving a population of 779,784,000.

South American Division

Territory: Argentina, Bolivia, Brazil, Chile, Ecuador, Falkland Islands, Paraguay, Peru, and Uruguay, with adjacent islands in the Atlantic and Pacific Oceans; comprising the Argentina, Central Brazil, East Brazil, and South Brazil Union Conferences; the Bolivia, Chile, Ecuador, North Brazil, North Peru, Northeast Brazil, Northwest Brazil, South Peru, and West Central Brazil Union Missions; and the Paraguay, and Uruguay Union of Churches Missions.

The Division has 9711 churches, 2,080,539 members, and a population of 311,096,000.

South Pacific Division

Territory: Australia, New Zealand, Papua New Guinea, and the islands of the Pacific lying south of the Equator (including Nauru, Samoa, Solomon Islands, Tonga, Tuvalu, Vanuatu, and others) between Longitude 140 East and Longitude 120 West, and Kiribati north of the Equator; comprising the Australian, and New Zealand Pacific Union Conferences; and the Papua New Guinea, and Trans Pacific Union Missions.

This Division is home to 1,872 churches, 410,761 members, who serve a population of 35,415,000.

Southern Africa-Indian Ocean Division

Territory: Angola, Botswana, Comoros, Lesotho, Madagascar, Malawi, Mauritius, Mozambique, Namibia, Reunion, Sao Tome and Principe, Seychelles, South Africa, Swaziland, Zambia, Zimbabwe, and Ascension, St. Helena, and Tristan da Cunha Islands comprising the Southern Africa, Zambia, and Zimbabwe Union Conferences; and the Angola, Botswana, Indian Ocean, Malawi, and Mozambique Union Missions.

The Division now has 7,949 churches, 2,402,963 members, who serve a population of 159,164,000.

Trans-European Division

Territory: Aland Islands, Albania, Bahrain, Bosnia-Herzegovina, Channel Islands, Croatia, Cyprus, Denmark, Egypt, Estonia, Faeroe Islands, Finland, Greece, Greenland, Hungary, Iceland, Iraq, Ireland, Isle of Man, Israel, Jordan, Kuwait, Latvia, Lebanon, Lithuania, Montenegro, Netherlands, Norway, Oman, Pakistan, Poland, Qatar, Saudi Arabia, Serbia, Slovenia, Sudan, Sweden, Syrian Arab Republic, The former Yugoslav Republic of Macedonia, United Arab Emirates, United Kingdom, and Yemen; comprising the Adriatic, Baltic, British, Finland, Hungarian, Netherlands, Norwegian, Polish, and South-East European Union Conferences; the Middle East Union Mission; the Pakistan Union Section; the Danish, and Swedish Union of Churches Conferences; and the Iceland Conference, Greek Mission, and Israel Field.

This Division currently has 1,390 churches, 111,005 members, and a population of 638,155,000.

West-Central Africa Division

Territory: Benin, Burkina Faso, Cameroon, Cape Verde, Central African Republic, Chad, Cote d'Ivoire, Equatorial Guinea, Gabon, Gambia, Ghana, Guinea, Guinea-Bissau, Liberia, Mali, Mauritania, Niger, Nigeria, Republic of the Congo, Senegal, Sierra Leone, and Togo; comprising the Ghana Union Conference; and the Central African, Eastern Nigeria, North-Western Nigeria, Sahel, and West African Union Missions.

This Division is home to 3,187 churches, 834,899 members, who serve a population of 336,275,000.

WORKS CITED

Alexander, Danielle. "Forty Acres and a Mule: The Ruined Hope of Reconstruction." *Humanities*. January/February, 2004. *(25):1.* 19 October, 2010. http://www.neh.gov/news/humanities/2004-01/reconstruction.html.

Anderson, David A. *Multicultural Ministry.* Grand Rapids: Zondervan, 2004.

Andrews, Dale P. *Practical Theology for Blacks: Bridging* Black *Theology and African American Folk Religion.* Louisville: Westminster John Know Press, 2002.

Akite, Odhiambo. "Truth-telling on Trial," *Christianity Today*, July 12, 1999.

Alesina, Alberto; La Ferrara, Eliana. "Who Trusts Others?" *Journal of Public Economics.* 15 May 2000. citeseerx.ist.psu.edu/ viewdoc/download?doi=10.1.1.153.2060... 14 October, 2010.

Armstrong, Katrina et al. "Racial/Ethnic Differences in Physician Distrust in the United States." 30 May, 2007. *American Journal of Public Health http://www.medscape.com/viewarticle/561477.* 14 October, 2010.

Ateek, Naim Stifan. *A Palestinian Christian Cry for Reconciliation.* Maryknoll: Orbis Books, 2009.

Atkins, Debra. January 2006. http://www.kyria.com/topics/womensministry/ministryissues/2.31.html?start=4. 28 October 2010.

Baker, Benjamin. *A Place Called Oakwood*. Hagerstown: Review and Herald Publishing Association, 2007.

Baker, Delbert W. *The Unknown Prophet*. Hagerstown: Review and Herald Publishing Association, 1987.

_____,ed. *Make Us One: Celebrating Cultural Unity in the Midst of Diversity*. Boise: Pacific Press Publishing Association, 1995.

Baker, S. S. *Salt: "Ye are the Salt of the Earth."* New York: American Tract Society, 1891.

_____. *Telling the Story: An Anthology on the Development of the Black SDA Work*. Atlanta: Black Caucus of SDA Administrators, 1996.

Banks, Adele. "Southern Baptists Express "pride" in Obama's Election," *Christianity Today* Political Blog. June 24, 2009.

Banks, Robert. *Paul's Idea of Community: The Early House Churches in Their Historical Setting*. Grand Rapids: William B. Eerdmans Publishing House, 1980.

Bediako, Matthew. "Miracle in South Africa: Church Votes to Unite Across Ethnic Boundaries," *Adventist Review* 149: 12 (February 6, 1992).

Belden, Albert D. *George* White*field—the Awakener: A Modern Study of the Evangelical Revival*. London: Sampson Low, Marston & Co., Ltd., 1930.

Bennett, Jr., Lerone. *Before the Mayflower: A History of* Black *America*, 6th ed. Chicago: Johnson Publishing Company, 1987.

Berger, Naomi. Emotional Wellness Matters. http://www.thecouplesplace.net/files/berger_ewm-jf10_8-5x11.pdf. 19 October, 2010.

http://www.thepetitionsite.com/Birch, Canute et al. 26, May, 2010. http://www.thepetitionsite. com/ 1/race-reconciliation-in-the-seventh-day-adventist-church/19 October, 2010).

Bhutto, Benazir. *Reconciliation: Islam, Democracy and the West*. New York: Harper Collins Publishers.

Black, Barry C. "How We Can Help to Build God's Ideal Community," *Adventist Review*, 145: 9 (February 6, 1992).

Blanco, Jack J. *"A Critical Comparison of the Doctrine of Reconciliation in Evangelical Theology and the Teachings of the Seventh-day Adventist Church (As presented in the Dogmatik of Karl Barth),"* Ph. D. Diss. Pretoria: University of South Africa Dissertation. 1970.

Bliss, Sylvester. *Memoirs of William Miller*. Boston: Published by Joshua V. Himes, 1853.

Boers, Hendrickus. *The Justification of the Gentiles: Paul's Letter to the Galatians and Romans*. Peabody: Hendrickson Publishers, Inc., 1994.

Boles, John B. *The Irony of Southern Religion*. New York: Peter Lang Publishing, 1994.

Bonhoeffer, Dietrich. *The Cost of Discipleship*. 1937. Reprint, New York: Simon and Shuster, 1995.

Brand, Leonard. *The Prophet and Her Critics*. Nampa: Pacific Press Publishing Association, 2005.

Branson, Roy. "Ellen White—Racist or Champion of Equality," *Review and Herald*. April 9, 1970.

_____."Slavery and Prophecy." *Review and Herald*. April 16, 1970.

_____."The Crisis of the Nineties." *Review and Herald*. April 23, 1970.

Branson, William H. *Reply to Canright*. Takoma Park: Review and Herald Publishing Association, 1933.

Britto, Francis Maria. "Indian Christians Pressured to Abandon Faith for Gov't Benefits." 30 August, 2006. http://www.catholic.org / international/international_story.php?id=21069.

Bruce, F. F. *The Epistle of Paul to the Romans*. Grand Rapids: Eerdmans, 1963.

Burchfield, Lee Swafford. *Adventist Religious Experience, 1816-1868: A Comparison of William Miller and Ellen* White. Ann Harbor: UMI, 1996.

Butler, Christopher. "Ut Unum Sint-"That they may be one." http:// vatican2voice.org/6unity/ut_unum.htm," *Vatican II-Voice of the Church-The Church's English Voice*." 24 September 2010. http:// vatican2voice.org/6unity/ut_unum.htm. 12 December, 2010.

Canada, Mark. "History and Culture." 24 September, 2001. http:// www.holidays.net/thanksgiving/pilgrims.htmhttp://www.uncp.edu/ home/canada/work/allam/16071783/index.htm. 5 October, 2010.

Chilson, Adriel D. *They Had A World to Win*. Hagerstown: Review and Herald Publishing Association, 2001.

Church, Richard P. *First Be Reconciled*. Scottdale: Herald Press, 2008.

Conde-Frazier, Elizabeth and Pazmino, Robert W. "Antioch Revisited: Educational Implications." http://www.bostontheological.org/assets/files/11frazpazm.pdf. 3 December, 2010.

Cone, James P. *A Black Theology of Liberation*. Philadelphia: J. B. Lippincott Company, 1970.

Corbie-Smith, Giselle et al. "Distrust, Race, and Research." *Journal of the American Medical Association*. 25 November, 2002. **Error! Hyperlink reference not valid.**; 162/21/2458. 14 October, 2010.

Cordey, E. L. *History of the Great Second Advent Movement*. Dallas: Truth for Today, 1949.

Cottrell, Megan. "Should we fix the Black/White wealth gap?" *True Slant Web Site*. 11 Jun 2010. http//http://trueslant.com/megancottrell/2010/06/11/ should-we-fix-the-BlackWhite-wealth-gap/28 Sep 2010.

Cox, Wendell. "US Population From 1900. *Demographia*. 1 July, 2001. http://www.demographia.com/db-uspop1900.htm. 2 December, 2010.

Crocombe, Jeff. "The Seventh-day Adventist Church in Southern Africa—Race Relations and Apartheid." http://h0bbes.files.wordpress.com/2007/05/sdas-in-south-africa-j-crocombe.pdf

Dattel, Gene. *Cotton and Race in the Making of America: The Human Costs of Economic Power*. Chicago: Ivan R. Dee, 2009.

Davis, Burke. "The Price in Blood: Casualties in the Civil War" 1 Nov. 2004. http://www.civilwarhome.com/casualties.htm. 30 Sep, 2010.

DeYoung, Curtiss Paul, *Reconciliation: Our Greatest Challenge—Our Only Hope*. Valley Forge: Judson Press, 1997.

Dick, Everett N. *William Miller and the Advent Crisis*. Berrien Springs: Andrews University Press, 1994.

Domhoff, G. William. "Wealth, Income, and Power." *Who Rules America?* November 2010. http://sociology.ucsc.edu/whorules america/ power/wealth.html. 23 November, 2010.

DuBois, W. E. Burghardt. *The Souls of Black Folk*. New York: Penguin Books USA Inc., 1969.

Dudley, Charles Edward, Jr. *Thou Who Hath Brought Us*. Brushton: Teach Services, Inc., 1997.

_____. *The Genealogy of Ellen Gould Harmon*. Nashville: Dudley Publishing Services, 1999.

_____ *Thou Who Hast Brought Us Thus Far on Our Way-II*. Nashville: Dudley Publications, 2000.

Dunn, James D. G. *The Theology of Paul the Apostle*. Grand Rapids: William B. Eerd*mans* Publishing Company, 1998.

Du Preez, Gerald T. "The Organizational Development of the Seventh-day Adventist Church in South Africa amongst the Colored Community -- A Response to Racism?" 25-28 March, 2010. http://www.sdahistorians. org/uploads/DuPreez_Paper_2010.pdf. 24 October, 2010.

Du Preez, I. F. and Du Pre, Roy H. *A Century of Good Hope: A History of the Good Hope Conference, its Educational Institutions and Early Workers, 1893-1993*. East London: Western Research Group/ Southern History Association, 1994.

Dybdahl, Jon. "It's God's Call," *Adventist Review*. 9 May, 1996. http://www.adventistarchives.org/ docs/RH/RH19960509-V173-19__C/ index.djvu. 19 November, 1996.

Eckholm, Erik. "Recession Raises Poverty Rate to a 15-year High." 16 September, 2009. *The New York Times*. http://www.ny times. comhttp://www.nytimes.com/ 2010/09/17/us/17poverty.html. 15 October, 2010.

Elliott, Ralph H. *Church Growth that Counts*. Valley Forge: Judson Press, 1982.

Elphick, Richard and Davenport, Rodney, eds. *Christianity in South Africa*. Berkeley: University of California Press, 1997.

Edwards, Jr., Jefferson D. *Purging Racism from Christianity*. Grand Rapids: Zondervan Publishing House, 1996.

Folkenberg Robert S. "A People of Prophecy," *Adventist Review*. 6 October, 1994. http://www.adventistarchives.org/ docs/ ARAI/ARAI19941006-V171-40__C.pdf#search=%22south Africa%22&view=fit. 12 December, 2010.

Fowler, James A. "Evangelical Humanism," *Christ in You Ministries*. 1999. http://www.christinyou.net/pages/evanhuman. html. 13 December, 2010.

Fredrickson, George M. *The* Black *Image in the* White *Mind: The Debate on African American Character and Destiny, 1817-1914*. Hanover: Wesleyan University Press, 1971.

Galbreath, Edward. *Reconciliation Blues: A* Black *Evangelical's View of* White *Christianity*. Downers Grove: IVP Books, 2006.

Gallagher, Eric. *What the* Bible *Says about Reconciliation"* The Irish Council of Churches and the Irish Commission for Justice and Peace, 1988.

Gaustad, Edwin S. *The Rise of Adventism: Religion and Society in Mid-nineteenth-century America*. New York: Harper and Row publishers, 1974.

Gehring, Roger W. *House Church and Mission: The Importance of Household Structures in Early*. Peabody: Hendrickson Publishers Inc., 2004.

Ghandi, Mahatma. *Ghandi An Autobiography: The Story of My Experiments With Truth*. 1993.

Goldstein, Clifford. *The Remnant: Biblical Reality or Wishful Thinking*. Boise: Pacific Press Publishing Association, 1994.

Gordon, Paul A. *Herald of the Midnight Cry: William Miller & the 1844 Movement*. Boise: Pacific Press Publishing Association, 1990.

Graham, Roy E. *Ellen G.* White *Co-Founder of the Seventh-day Adventist Church*. New York: Peter Lang, 1985.

Graybill, Ronald D. *E. G.* White *and Church Race Relations*. Washington D. C.: Review and Herald Publishing Association, 1970.

Griswold, Charles L. *Forgiveness: A Philosophical Exploration*. Cambridge: Cambridge UNIVersity Press, 2007.

Haas, Werner. "Blacks and Religion in the United States," 31 October, 2006. http://www.associatedcontent.com/article/77411/Blacks_and_religion_in_the_united_states.html. 14 October, 2010.

Haloviak, Bert. "Impact of SDA Eschatological Assumptions on Certain Issues of Social Policy." 27 October, 1999. **Error! Hyperlink reference not valid.**. org/docs/AST/Race_Relations.pdf#view=fit. 19 October, 2010.

Hasel, Gerhard F. *The Remnant: The History and Theology of the Remnant Idea from Genesis to Isaiah*. Berrien Springs: Andrews University Press, 1972.

Hastings, Adrian. *The Church in Africa: 1450-1950*. Oxford: Clarendon Press, 1994.

_____ et al, eds. *The Oxford Companion to Christian Thought*. New York: Oxford University Press, 2000.

Hewitt, Clyde E. *Midnight and Morning*. Charlotte: Advent Christian General Conference of America, 1983.

Heyrman, Christine Leigh. "The First Great Awakening." January 2008. http://nationalhumanitiescenter.org/tserve/eighteen/ekeyinfo/grawaken.htm 8 October, 2010.

Holmes, Grace Bryan. *Time to Reconcile*. Athens: The UNIVersity of Georgia Press, 2000.

Horsman, Reginald R. *Race and Manifest Destiny: The Origins of American Racial Anglo-Saxonism*. Cambridge: Harvard University Press, 1981.

_____. *Expansion and American Indian Policy, 1783-1812*. London: University of Oklahoma Press, 1967.

Hough, Jr., Joseph C. Black *Power and* White *Protestants: A Christian Response to the New Negro Pluralism*. New York: Oxford UNIVersity Press, 1968.

Howell, Emma E. *The Great Advent Movement*. Tacoma Park: Review and Herald Publishing Association, 1935.

Horowitz, Mitch. *Occult America: The Secret History of How Mysticism Shaped our Nation*. New York: Bantam Books, 2009.

Isichei, Elizabeth. *A History of Christianity in Africa from Antiquity to the Present.* London: SPCK, 1995.

Jemison, T. Housel. *A Prophet Among You.* Mountain View: Pacific Press Publishing Association, 1955.

Johnson, Paul. *The Birth of the Modern World Society: 1815-1830.* New York: Harper Collins Publishers, 1999.

Johnson et al. "Mainline Churches: The Real Reason for Decline," March 1993. http://www.leaderu.com/ftissues/ ft9303/articles/ johnson.html. 7 December, 2010.

Jordan, Anne Devereaux. *The Seventh-day Adventists: A History.* New York: Hippocrene Books, 1988.

Kaiser, Jr., Walter C. *Toward an Exegetical Theology: Biblical Exegesis for Preaching and Teaching.* Grand Rapids: Baker Book House, 1981.

Kah, Gary H. *En Route to Global Occupation.* Lafayette: Huntington House Publishers, 1996.

Kellner, Mark A., ed. "Bryant: Adventist Church Growth Rate Trends Higher in USA, Canada, Bermuda," Adventist World Radio. November 11, 2009.

Kittel, Gerhard, ed. *"Koinonia." Theological Dictionary of the New Testament.* Grand Rapids: William B. Eerdmans Publishing Company, 1965.

Knight, George R. *Millennial Fever and the End of the World.* Boise: Pacific Press Publishing Association, 1993.

_____, ed. *1844 and the Rise of Sabbatarian Adventism.* Hagerstown: Review and Herald Publishing Association, 1994.

_____ed. *Earliest Seventh-day Adventist Periodicals.* Berrien Springs: Andrews University Press, 2005.

Knox, David and Zusman, Marty E. "Sexuality in Black And White: Data from 783 Undergraduates," *E Journal of Human Sexuality.* 26 June, 2009. http://www.ejhs.org/Volume12/Knox.htm. 30 November, 2010.

Koranteng-Pipim, Samuel. "The Power of the Gospel or the Gospel of Power?" *Adventists Affirm* (Spring 1997).

_____. *Must We Be Silent: Issues Dividing our Church.* Ypsilanti: Berean Books, 2001.

_____ ed. *Here We Stand: Evaluating New Trends in the Church.* Berrien Springs: Adventists Affirm, 2005.

Kosmin, Barry A. and Ariela Keysar. "American Religious Identification Survey (ARIS)," (2009). "American Religious Identification Survey" City University of New York; Graduate School and University Center. http://www.american religion survey-aris.org/reports/ARIS_Report_2008.pdf. 7 December, 2010.

Kyle, Richard. *Evangelicalism: An Americanized Christianity.* New Brunswick: Transaction Publishers, 2006.

Lake, Judson Shephard. *"An Evaluation of Haddon Robinson's Homiletical Method: An Evangelical Perspective."* Ph.D. Diss. Pretoria: University of South Africa, 2003.

_____. *Ellen* White *Under Fire: Identifying the Mistakes of Her Critics.* Nampo: Pacific Press Publishing Association, 2010.

Land, Gary, ed. *Adventism in America: A History* (Revised Edition). Berrien Springs: Andrews University Press, 1998.

Land, Gary, ed. *The World of Ellen G.* White: Hagerstown: Review and Herald Publishing Association, 1987.

LaRondelle, Hans K. *The Israel of God in Prophecy: Principles of Prophetic Interpretation.* Berrien Springs: Andrews University Press, 1983.

Lawson, Ronald. "From American Church to Immigrant Church: The Changing Face of Seventh-day Adventism in Metropolitan New York," *Sociology of Religion. 59:4 (*1998) http://socrel.oxfordjournals. org/content/59/4/329.full.pdf. 10 October, 2010.

London, Samuel G. Jr. *Seventh-day Adventists and the Civil Rights Movement.* Jackson: University Press of Mississippi, 2009.

Loughborough, J. N. *The Great Second Advent Movement Its Rise and Progress.* Nashville: Southern Publishing Association, 1905.

Lubetkin, Barry. "Why You Should Get Rid of a Grudge." 9 May, 1996. *Adventist Review.* http://www.adventistarchives.org/ docs/ RH/RH19960509-V173-19__C/index.djvu. 19 November, 2010.

Luo, Michael. "Evangelicals Debate the Meaning of 'Evangelical"Evangelicals Debate the Meaning of 'Evangelical,'"." *The New York Times.* April 16, 2006. http://www.ny times. com/2006/04/16/weekinreview/16luo.html. 10 October, 2010.

McGavran, Donald. *Understanding Church Growth.* Grand Rapids: William B. Eerdmans Publishing Company, 1970.

Marsden, George. *Jonathan Edwards: A Life.* New Haven: Yale University Press, 2003.

Marti, Gerardo. *A Mosaic of Believers: Diversity and Innovation in a Multi-ethnic Church.* Bloomington: Indiana University Press, 2005.

Matthews, Donald G. *Religion in the Old South*. Chicago: University of Chicago Press, 1977.

Matthews, Terry. "The Great Awakening." Fall 1995. http://www.wfu.edu/~matthetl/perspectives/four.html. 16 September, 2010.

Maxwell, C. Mervyn. *Magnificent Disappointment*. Boise: Pacific Press Publishing Association, 1994.

Mecom, Dorothy. Thesis, M.Sc. "Hispanics and Violent Crime in the United States: Examining the Effect of Segregation," Louisiana State University, 2002.

Michelson, Melissa R. Political Trust among Chicago Latinos." *Journal of Urban Affairs*. 16 April, 2003. http://www.onlinelibrary.wiley.

com/ doi/10.1111/0735-2166.00092/abstract. 14 October, 2010.

Moo, Douglas J. *The New International Dictionary of the New Testament*, "The Epistle to the Romans." Grand Rapids: Wm. B. Eerdmans Publishing Co., 1996.

Morgan, Douglas, ed. *The Peacemaking Remnant: Essays and Historical Documents*. Silver Springs: Adventist Peace Fellowship, 2005.

Moulton, Harold K, ed. *"Kattallage."* *The Analytical Greek Lexicon Revised*. Grand Rapids: Regency Reference Library, 1990.

Mulzac, Kenneth D. *"Ytr* as a Remnant Term in the Book of Jeremiah," *JATS* (2008) 19:1-2.

Nagourney, Adam. "G.O.P. Right is Splintered on Schiavo Intervention," *The New York Times*. 23 March, 2005. http://www. theocracywatch. org/terri_conservatives_times_mar23_05.htm. 3 December, 2010.

Neufeld, Don F., ed. *Seventh-day Adventist Encyclopedia, 2nd revised edition. Vol. 10.* "India." Hagerstown: Review and Herald Publishing Association, 1996.

Nichols, Francis D. *The Midnight Cry.* Tacoma Park: Review and Herald Publishing Association, 1944.

_____. *Ellen G.* White *and Her Critics.* Washington D. C.: Review and Herald Publishing Association, 1951.

_____. *Why I Believe in Mrs. E. G.* White. Washington D. C.: Review and Herald Publishing Association, 1964.

Noll, Mark A. *The Rise of Evangelicalism: The Age of Edwards, Whitefield and the Wesleys.* Downers Grove: InterVarsity Press, 2003.

Numbers, Ron L. and Butler, Jonathan M., eds. *The Disappointed: Millerism and Millenarianism in the Nineteenth Century.* Knoxville: The University of Tennessee Press, 1993.

Okholm, Dennis L., ed. *The Gospel in Black & White: Theological Resources for Racial Reconciliation.* Downers Grove: InterVarsity Press, 1997.

Olson, David T. "The American Church in Crisis," *Ministry Today.* http://www.ministrytodaymag.com/~ministry/index.php/ features/17090-the-american-church-in-crisis. 7 December, 2010.

Olson, Robert W. "God's True Church in 1986," Washington D. C.: Ellen G. White Estate, 1986.

Peters, G. E. *S.D.A. Accomplishments in Interracial Relations—1934.* 9 April, 1944. http://www.adventistarchives.org/docs/ RCO/RCO-01__B/index.djvu. 10 November, 2010.

Pierce, Ronald W. and Groothuis, Rebecca Merrill, eds. *Discovering Biblical Equality: Complementarity Without Hierarchy*. Downers Grove: IVP Academic, 2005.

Pollard, Leslie N., ed. *Embracing Diversity: How to Understand and Reach People of All Cultures*. Hagerstown: Review and Herald Publishing Association, 2000.

Promise Keepers. 2008. http://www.promisekeepers.org/ about/faqs/ whatwebelieve/eightprinciples. 19 September 2010.

Putnam, Carleton. *Race and Reason*. Washington D. C.: Public Affairs Press, 1962.

Rajshekar V. T. "Why Dalits Hate Hinduism?" February 2009 http:// therearenosunglasses.wordpress.com/.../why-**dalits**-hate-**hinduism**/. 17 October, 2010.

Raynor, Joyce. "Black on Black Crime Statistics." Sep 2010. http://www. hhscenter.org/bonbstat.html. 28 Sep 2010.

Reynolds, Louis B. *We Have Tomorrow: The Story of American Seventh-day Adventists with an African Heritage*. Hagerstown: Review and Herald Publishing Association, 1984.

Ridderbos, Herman. *Paul: An Outline of His Theology*. Grand Rapids: Wm. B. Eerdmans Publishing Company, 1975.

Rock, Calvin B. "A Better Way." *Spectrum*. Spring 1970. http://www. blacksdahistory.org/files/40119009.pdfhttp://www.blacksdahistory. org/files/40119009.pdf. 19 October, 2010.

_____. *Adventist Review*. 5 July, 2006. http:// adventistreviewarchives.com/2006/05/http://www.adventistreview. org/site/1/2006-1522/Calvin%20Rock%20rebuttal%20letter%20 Question%204[1].pdf. 19 October, 2010.

Rodriquez, Angel Manuel, ed. *Toward A Theology of the Remnant: An Adventist Ecclesiological Perspective*. Silver Springs: Biblical Research Institute, 2009.

Rosado, Caleb. *Broken Walls*. Boise: Pacific Press Publishing Association, 1990.

Rosenberg, Ellen M. *The Southern Baptists: A Subculture in Transition*. Knoxville: The University of Tennessee Press, 1989.

Rosenberg, Paula S. *Race, Class, and Gender in the United States*. New York: Worth Publishers, 2007.

Rowe, David L. *God's Strange Work: William Miller and the End of the World*. Grand Rapids: William B. Eerdmans Publishing Company, 2008.

Scholz, John Karl and Levine, Kara. "US Black-White Wealth Inequality: A Survey,"9 June 2003. University of Wisconsin. http://www.econ.wisc.edu/~scholz/Research/Wealth_survey_v5.pdf. 28 September, 2010.

Schwarz, R. W. *Light Bearers to the Remnant*. Boise: Pacific Press Publishing Association, 1979.

Schwarz, R. W.; Greenleaf, Floyd. *Lightbearers to the Remnant* Revised and updated edition, Nampo: Pacific Press Publishing Association, 2000.

Schuman, Duane. "Constant Struggle for Racial Harmony." Web Site: Indiana Conference of the United Methodist Church. . 5 October, 2010.

Shapiro, Thomas M. et al. "The Racial Wealth Gap Increases Fourfold." May 2010. *Institute on Assets and Social Policy*. 28 Sep 2010. http://iasp.brandeis.edu/pdfs/Racial-Wealth-Gap-Brief.pdf

Shuler, J. L. "Rediscovering the Faith of Scripture," *The Advent Review and Herald* 135:21 (May 8, 1958).

Sider, Ronald. *Rich Christians in an Age of Hunger: Moving from Affluence to Generosity.* Dallas: Word Publishing, 1997.

Skinner, C. *The Teaching Ministry of the Pulpit.* Grand Rapids, Michigan: Baker Book House, 1971.

_____. *The Scandal of Evangelical Politics.* Grand Rapids: Baker Books, 2008.

Snoke, David. "The Southern Presbyterian Church and Racism." http://www.cityreformed.org/snoke/racism.pdf.17 October, 2010.

Sowell, Thomas. *Ethnic America.* New York: Basic books, Inc. Publishers, 1981.

_____. "A Divine Plan for Unity," *The Advent Review and Herald* 135:20 (May 15, 1958).

Spalding, A. W. *Pioneer Stories of the Second Advent Message.* Nashville: Southern Publishing Association, 1922.

_____.*Origin and History of Seventh-day Adventists, Vol. 1.* Washington D.C.: Review and Herald Publishing Association, 1962.

_____. *Origin and History of Seventh-day Adventists, 3 Vols.* Washington D.C.: Review and Herald Publishing Association, 1962.

Steer, Tom. Needed: More Monocultural Ministries," *Christianity Today Magazine.* July 7, 2010.

Stout, Harry S. *The Divine Dramatist: George* Whitefield *and the Rise of Modern Evangelicalism.* Grand Rapids: William B. Eerdmans Publishing Company, 1991.

Swanson, David. "Down With The Homogenous Unit Principle," *Christianity Today,* August 2, 2010.

Taylor, John Wesley. "Politics—To Engage or Not to Engage? Seeking a Biblical Perspective," *JATS* (2008) 19: 1-2.

Terrazas, Aaron. "African Immigrants in the United States." February 2009. http://www.migrationinformation.org/USfocus/ display. cfm?id=719. 13 October, 2010.

Thayer, Joseph H, ed. *"Apokatallasso." Thayer's Greek-English Lexicon of the New Testament.* Peabody: Hendrickson Publishers, 1996.

Thernstrom, Stephan and Thernstrom, Abigail. *America in* Black *and* White*: One Nation, Indivisible.* New York: Simon & Schuster, 1997.

Thomas, Pierre; Ryan, Jason. "Stinging Remarks on Race from Attorney General." *ABC News.* 18 February, 2009. **Error! Hyperlink reference not valid.** Law/story?id=6905255&page=1. 2 November, 2010.

Thompson, G. Ralph. "God's Rainbow," *Adventist Review.* 6 October, 1994. http://www.adventistarchives.org/docs/ ARAI/ ARAI19941006-V171-40__C.pdf#search=%22south Africa%22&view= fit. 12 December, 2010.

Tocqueville, Alexis de. *Democracy in America.* Translated by Elizabeth Trapnell Rawlings. Boston: Bedford/St. Martin's, 2009.

Van Sertima, Ivan, ed. *African Presence in Early America.* New Brunswick: Transaction Publishers, 1993.

Vasquez, Manuel. *100 Years of Hispanic Work.* Hagerstown: Review and Herald Publishing Association, 2000.

Watkins, Boyce. "CNN's Black in America Gets it Wrong on Black White Wealth Gap," *Black Voices Web Site.* 20 Sep, 2010. http://

www.bvonmoney.com/bass/writing/sources/kinds/ citeinternet/
organization.html. 28 Sep, 2010.

Wellcome, I. C. *A Brief History of William Miller the Great Pioneer in Adventual Faith*. Boston: Advent Christian Publication Society, 1915.

West, Cornel. *Race Matters*. New York: Vintage Books, 1993.

West, Cornell and Claude, Jr. Eddie S., eds. *African American Religious Thought: An Anthology*. Louisville: Westminster John Knox Press, 2003.

White, Arthur L. *Ellen* White: *Woman of Vision*. Hagerstown: Review and Herald Publishing Association, 2000.

White, Ellen G. *Early Writings of Ellen G*. White. Washington D. C.: Review and Herald Publishing Association, 1882.

_____. *The Desire of Ages*. Mountain View: Pacific Press Publishing Association, 1898.

_____.*Christian Service*. Takoma Park: General Conference of Seventh-day Adventists, 1947.

_____. *Testimonies for the Church, Vol. 1*. Boise: Pacific Press Publishing Association, 1948.

_____. *Testimonies for the Church, Vol. 8*. Mountain View: Pacific Press Publishing Association, 1948.

_____. *Testimonies for the Church, Vol. 9*. Mountain View: Pacific Press Publishing Association, 1948.

_____. *Patriarchs and Prophets*. Mountain View: Pacific Press Publishing Association, 1958.

_____. *The Southern Work*. Washington D. C.: Review and Herald Publishing Association, 1966.

_____. *The Great Controversy*. Mountain View: Pacific Press Publishing Association, 1971.

White, James. *Sketches of the Christian Life and Public Labors of William Miller*. Battle Creek: Steam Press of the SDA Publishing Association, 1875.

White, Jim, ed. "Pastors' challenges differ by region, speakers say," *Religious Herald*. 7 August, 2008. **Error! Hyperlink reference not valid.**. 7 December, 2010.

Wilcox, Francis McLellan. *Seventh-day Adventists in Time of War*. Takoma Park: Review and Herald Publishing Association, 1936.

Wilcox, John, ed. *Symposium on Mission and Social Action: The Role of Social Ministry in the Seventh-day Adventist Church*. Silver Springs: ADRA International, 1997.

Williams, David R. and Collins, Chiquita. 7 March, 2004. "Reparations : A Viable Strategy to Address the Enigma of African American Health," American Behavioral Scientist. http://abs.sagepub. com/. 6 December, 2010.

Williams, David R. "The Racial Divides, Part 1-6." 1 January, 2010. http://www.campus-press.org/thinktank/?p=248. 23 November, 2010.

Wilson, Ted N. C. "A People Who Look Forward in Anticipation," *Adventist Review*. September 23, 2010.

Wojcikowski, Jennifer J. "American Baptist Home Missionary Society." 2 October, 2005. http://www.bookrags.com/tandf/ american-baptist-home-missionary-tf/. 1 October, 2010.

Yancey, George. "Color Blindness, Political Correctness, or Racial Reconciliation - Christian Ethics and Race," *Journal of Christian Ethics*. 35:15 (2001): 4

Younis, Mohammed. "Muslim Americans Exemplify Diversity, Potential." 2 March, 2009. GALLUP. http://www.gallup.com/poll/116260/Muslim-Americans-Exemplify-Diversity-Potential.aspx. 11 October, 2010.

The Daily Argus, October 22, 1844.

"apartheid." Mirriam-Webster's Online Dictionary, 2008. William Webster online.

"Diakonos." Kittel, Gerhard, ed. *Theological Dictionary of the New Testament, Vol. II.* Grand Rapids: Wm. B. Eerdmans Publishing Company, 1993.

"Leitourgia." Kittel, Gerhard, ed. *Theological Dictionary of the New Testament, Vol. IV.* Grand Rapids: Wm. B. Eerdmans Publishing Company, 1993.

14 October 2010. http://www.merriam-webster.com/dictionary/hacker

The Annie E. Casey Foundation. 2009. http://datacenter.kidscount.org/data/acrossstates/Rankings.aspx?ind=107. 1 December, 2010.

"This book offers a fresh analysis of historical gems from early Adventism as they relate to the development of race relations in the church. Congratulations on a timely and honest treatise of a complex issue that today's church leaders and members can ill afford to ignore."—*Dr. Greg Rumsey, Dean, School of Journalism and Communication, Southern Adventist University, Collegedale, Tennessee.*

INDEX OF AUTHORS
AND NAMES

INDEX OF SUBJECTS

C

California 117, 198, 200, 203, 267
Cambodia 258
Cameroon 260
Canada 36, 189, 216, 257, 264, 270
Caribbean 101–103, 115, 197–198,
        202–203, 212, 215–216, 256
Carolina 48, 61–62
Castes 57, 163
Catholic 25, 58, 67, 184, 264
Caucasian 184, 198, 212, 239
Caucasians 6, 69, 212, 220, 240
Caucasus 256
Cayman islands 256
Census 71, 197, 199–201
Central states 84
Challenge xvii, 61, 101, 104, 119, 129,
        182, 204, 209, 213, 223, 246, 265
Challenges xii, xiv, 38, 40, 92, 99, 104,
        119–120, 125, 151, 181–182,
        204, 209, 221, 224, 280
Character 6, 47–48, 76, 138, 177, 209,
        217, 267
Charity 251
Chicago 154, 262, 265, 273
Chinese 103, 258
Chippewa 19
Christ xiv–xvi, xviii, 3, 12–15, 22,
        27–32, 35, 37, 40–41, 43, 45, 47,
        54, 56–57, 63, 77, 79, 96–97,
        104–105, 107, 112, 118, 126,
        129–133, 135–136, 138–140,
        143–146, 148–153, 155–156,
        161–164, 167–169, 173–175,
        177, 181–182, 185–188, 190,
        205–206, 208–209, 212,
        214, 218–219, 222–224, 226,
        244–246, 248–254, 267, 282
Christian vii, xiii, xv–xvi, 8, 25–28,
        32–35, 43–44, 47, 50–51,
        55, 57–58, 66–67, 69, 72, 77,
        94, 112, 118, 128, 136, 140,
        142–143, 145, 147, 151–152,
        155, 163, 166, 172, 179, 181–

182, 184, 188, 194, 202, 204,
        206–207, 209–210, 212, 214,
        222, 228, 232, 237, 239, 247,
        249, 253, 261, 269, 279–281
Christians ix, xi, xiii–xiv, 8, 10, 24,
        29, 32, 43–44, 47, 50, 55,
        60, 65, 81, 105–106, 109,
        112, 117, 134–135, 138, 140,
        146, 150–151, 153, 156–158,
        162–163, 166–172, 180–181,
        186, 206–207, 209–211, 222,
        244, 264, 277
Churches ix, xi–xii, xiv, xvii–xviii,
        8–9, 14–15, 17–19, 25, 46, 51,
        53–55, 57, 60–61, 67–70, 73,
        76–77, 81–82, 84, 88–90, 93–94,
        99, 101–106, 114–115, 120, 126,
        128, 157–159, 184, 188–189,
        192, 194, 197, 201–203, 207,
        211–214, 221, 223, 231–240,
        244–247, 249, 251, 255–260,
        262, 267, 270
Cincinnati 12
Clergy xvi, 10, 17, 54, 59–60, 183, 215,
        217
Cleveland 179, 181–182, 195, 283
College 47, 56, 72, 79, 111, 115–116,
        122, 197, 231
Colombia 256
Colombian 256
Colored 17–18, 41, 78, 81–82, 90–91,
        119, 135, 138, 230–231, 266
Colossians 146, 174
Columbia union college 128
Columbus 16
Comprise xii, 43, 47, 66, 102–104,
        199–200
Comprised 43, 51, 117, 197–198, 202,
        206, 282
Conference xi, xvi, 22, 31, 33, 69, 77,
        79–80, 82–85, 88, 90–91, 93,
        97, 102–104, 119–120, 129, 183,
        194, 196–199, 201–202, 207–
        211, 215–216, 222, 225–226,
        230–231, 233–241, 244, 256,

289

Y

Z

About the Author

Canute Birch, Ph.D., holds degrees in biblical archaeology and history as well as in theology. He is an ordained minister of the Seventh-day Adventist Church. Dr. Birch discerned the call to write on this subject during his morning devotion as he reflected on the obvious divides of his beloved Adventist Church, to which he was introduced at birth by his parents. He grew up in the church with an apparently naive sense of its sacredness, even while realizing that it is comprised of broken people, who, like him, are being transformed into the likeness of Jesus, the Christ. This brokenness seemed more pronounced as he observed race relations among its membership, both as a student at its flagship institution, Andrews University, as a pastor in the Greater New York Conference, and especially after he relocated with his family to the state of Tennessee, there serving briefly as an adjunct faculty at Southern Adventist University and being a member of the University Church, which was (in 2005) and remains today over eighty percent White.

www.ingramcontent.com/pod-product-compliance
Lightning Source LLC
Chambersburg PA
CBHW070907120626
46546CB00001B/164